Report from Berlin

Report from Berlin

BY JÖRN DONNER

translated by Albin T. Anderson
with a Foreword by *STEPHEN SPENDER*
and photographs by the author

INDIANA UNIVERSITY PRESS · BLOOMINGTON

PUBLISHER'S NOTE

The publishers wish to express their gratitude to Professor C. Leonard Lundin of the Department of History at Indiana University for bringing the Swedish version of this book to their attention, and for his invaluable assistance on editorial problems.

Contents

Illustrations

Sometimes I regret that when I was young I spent those two or three years, after I had left Oxford University, in 1930, in Berlin. Why did I not live somewhere beautiful and study the Renaissance?—the thought of Italy ravished my mind. Why did I not go to France and cultivate the friendship of the most talented and intelligent of my contemporaries in the world?

For Berlin is a center, but a very centrifugal kind of center. To an old Berliner like myself, some of the amusement in Mr. Jörn Donner's instructive and serious book is his attitude toward his own being in Berlin. One has—more than ever today—to be in Berlin for some reason. The reader starts off then knowing Mr. Donner's reason for being there: he is writing a book about Berlin. Gradually, however, one begins to suspect that there are other reasons as well. After he has put into our hands an immense amount of information, casually but sharply sketched in, about politics, personalities, cabarets, and so on, there is, toward the end, a mood of strangeness in his book. He describes the bareness and desolation of the city near the Potsdamer Platz where he watches an "old woman pick some flowers near the burned-out Columbiahaus." And a few pages further on, after telling us of the impassioned discussion by the mayor, Willy Brandt, and Senator Lipschitz over the question of whether or not the West Berlin politicians should have any sort of discussion with those of the East, he writes: "When I leave Britz it is late in the evening. The parks are empty. The violent antagonisms and the heated debates seem to recede like an empty shadow. . . . I wander along empty streets until I see finally a beam of light and movement somewhere in the distance. I head that way, since where I go is of little consequence."

Quite apart from the attractiveness, and, in general, the accessibility, of some of its inhabitants, there is something about Berlin which makes it different from other cities, and which one falls a bit in love with.

To begin with, even before the bombings, Berlin was, if not the Cinderella, one of the Ugly Sisters among cities, and one could, in the old days, feel protective about its architecture, full of false starts toward the German Imperial Style, and its lapses into something much more resembling that of a lady of pleasure turned landlady, and surrounded by trophies of her ornate, but somewhat tasteless and pretentious youth. Then, although Berlin has—or had—no beautiful architecture (even today the modernized post-World-War-II style seems, in relation to our century, as bogus as did *Unter den Linden* to the nineteenth), the city is spacious, agreeable to sit or walk out in, and always very much itself.

Christopher Isherwood, in *Goodbye to Berlin*, wrote about the city in a way which made it as familiar as the back of the reader's hand. He showed genius in doing this, but he also owed something to the peculiar quality of Berlin: take any section, dissect and analyze, and it will contain the same elements as any other section, one feels. This could not be said of any other large capital, unless, perhaps, of postrevolutionary Russia. It might be objected that the Kurfürstendamm was different from the slum district of the Hallesches Tor. The difference simply was, however, that the Hallesches Tor area was poor and vulgar, the Kurfürstendamm rich and vulgar. The considerable vulgarity has to be faced but Berliner vulgarity, being allied to coarseness and frankness, is of the most forgivable kind.

A lot of this comes out in Mr. Donner's book, its implicit point being that the difference between East and West is purely circumstantial. They are the same Berliners. And if it is true that the West is genuinely freer than the East, it is also true that the vices of prosperity flourish like the green bay tree in the Western Zone, while the Eastern has some of the virtues of its strait jacket.

The homogeneity of Berlin comes, of course, from the people. Berliners wear their hearts on their sleeves—though a good many of them would smile skeptically if you told them this, and suggest that you implied some other organ. But in fact heart is their outstanding quality, and it is what, to anyone who knows Berlin well, makes one passionately defend them against the charge that they are "Prussians." In the old days, there used to be a Berlin rhyme—*Berlin bleib Rot, Sonst Straf und Tot*—and what this expressed was not so much the Red Berlin of Social Democracy, which would remain Red, despite battery and murder, as the self-conscious warm proletarian assertiveness of the Berliner.

Mr. Donner publishes many conversations and interviews. This method is more rewarding in Berlin than elsewhere, on account of the Berliner's extreme consciousness of all his circumstances and feelings, and his complete lack of reticence. You stop anyone in the street and ask him or her questions—it is like taking up a thread of a ball of wool at any point, which will always unwind the whole ball and lead to the same center. More than ever today the Berliner of course knows about the pincers of East and West. He is the man caught between them. But he has, to a lesser degree, always felt the pinch of being between Europe and Russia.

Berliners have, historically, the attitude of those who live in an arbitrarily fixed center, which, however justified it may be by geography, remains artificial to the whole country, to Hamburg, Munich or Frankfurt, let us say. The Prussian Kaisers decided that Berlin must be the center of their empire. The result was, beyond the façade of architectural pomposities, a complete lack of anything that might be called style. A few high-sounding names—von Humboldt and von Moltke, Hindenburg even—echo through Berlin—but their quality is derived from estates and campaigns, and their spiritual home is Potsdam. So Berlin remains simply a place where Berliners live. Whatever group happens to be outstanding at a particular moment of history takes over Berlin as though it inherited it. At one time after the first World War there were the cosmopolitan writers, artists, and actors who thronged the Romanisches Café, and attended performances of *Dreigroschenoper* and *Mahoganny*. Then in the early 1930's Berlin became the kingdom of jour-nalists, writing their foreboding prophecies of the fall of Europe, and describing Berlin, with its night clubs and cabarets, as the Decline of the West incarnate. Today it is the city of Americans and Russians, and German mayors in the West (Reuter and Brandt), Communist officials in the East.

Reading Mr. Donner's pages, I know why I chose to live in Berlin, and, until Hitler came to power, never got away from it. Berlin was living history, and I belonged to a generation whose fatality was that we had to experience and understand the time in which we lived—even if we forgot everything else, and even if we were left stranded when history, which seemed, for a moment, prepared to turn its head at the call of the intellectuals, went back to its real masters, the dictators and the revolutionaries.

Berlin was history in the 1930's, when the Communists and the Nazis improvised battles in its streets. Today it still is his-tory, but of a far more passive kind. If the Berliners still seem independent, it is because their independence derives from their utter dependence on allies who allow them their freedom. If they show a peculiar fearlessness which excites the almost unbelieving wonderment of the world, that is because they have reached that place on the far side of fear, where, being utterly at the mercy of the conflict of the great powers, they feel there is no use being afraid, and therefore they have nothing to be afraid of.

The people of Berlin live today a kind of hypothetical existence in which they carry on "as if" the present situation—which seems the most temporary in the world—were going to last for ever, because no other attitude is possible. But in doing this, are they not living out, from threat to threat, and rumor to rumor, what is in fact true of the rest of us, who are protected from realizing terror, by a shield made up of distance, day-to-day living, trivialities? Just as in 1930, Berlin was the true-life drama of the struggle between Nazis and Communists, today it is the vacuum of the struggle between the power-paralyzed giants. In the Western Zone, Berliners live out a life which is a kind of parody of Western freedom; while in the East they lead one which is equally a parody of Communism. Reading this book, one wonders whether excess of mechanical power and the strength of impersonal forces have not made a parody of all our lives.

STEPHEN SPENDER

Translator's Note

THE responsibilities of a translator seem simple enough. He has an obligation to the creative author to render faithfully in another language the facts, ideas, and if possible the nuances and overtones which have been sealed into the original text. His obligation to the reader is not very different. The reader must be assured that he is communicating with the true author. How well this responsibility has been acquitted here, for both the Swedish text and the frequent German quotations, is for others to judge.

In the translation of such a book one develops very quickly a mental image of the author. My own image is that of a sensitive young Finnish intellectual, who is not trying to solve the problems of Berlin, or of Germany, or of the world, but is trying to understand them. The vignettes which he has drawn are both symbols and realities. They are landmarks in his Berlin experience—physical, intellectual, and emotional. They are high points in his progress toward understanding.

The book is autobiographical in the sense that it deals primarily with one man's experiences. It is biographical in the sense that it seeks to describe, analyze, and understand a people, a city, perhaps a country, perhaps our world. Although the author disclaims any efforts at profound research, and denies that this is a scholarly book in the normally accepted sense of the word, there is no denying its merits as both biography and autobiography. If it is not history it could well be the stuff out of which history is made.

American readers particularly are well advised to remember that this is not a book by a national of one of the Great Powers.

In terms of the power struggle which has been going on, Jörn
Donner does not speak as a protagonist of either East or West.
But neither does he resort to any "plague upon both your
houses" attitude. On the basis of his observations and experiences for more than a decade he has come to certain conclusions, and these are abundantly clear. He is one of those
who Norman Cousins would undoubtedly concede "speaks for
man." Such voices, in our age or any other, rarely influence the
course of events, but frequently they achieve eventual historical
vindication. Not everything said in his book may be wise, but
there is much wisdom in this book.

ALBIN T. ANDERSON

University of Nebraska

When an ordinary traveler comes to a big city with which he is not familiar, he asks himself and others: Can I have a good time in this city? The virtuoso, actor, speaker, or writer asks: Can I conquer this city? A scholar or a psychologist says to himself: Can I understand this city? And in the measure that the traveler enjoys, the virtuoso conquers, and the scholar understands the city they get pleasure from their stay there.

It is even a pleasure to discover how a large city, which at first is strange, little by little becomes one's home. A street in which one has access to no home, in which one knows no individual or family, soon becomes a dead street. It becomes a living thing only when it becomes familiar, when one knows where it contains people who have an affection for you. Such houses then become points of light which illuminate the street, or perhaps an entire block.

GEORG BRANDES, 1885

What is most striking for one who returns after three years is Berlin's good humor, a kind of cheerfulness which comes from its reserves of strength.

HEINRICH MANN, 1921

"Let's agree then, the Germans are all of the highest type of beauty and they have preposterously fine manners. Look at all the heel-clicking and bowing from the waist and elegant high-toned voices. And how polite and smiling a seven-foot policeman can be when he is getting ready to crack your skull open. I have seen it. No, Hans, you have a great culture here, no doubt, but I think no civilization. You will be the last race on earth to be civilized, but does it matter?"

KATHERINE ANNE PORTER, 1934

A tourist to a taxi driver (on the way from the Zoo Station): I hardly recognize the place. I haven't been in Berlin for twenty years.

The taxi driver (indifferently): Well, you haven't missed anything.

A BERLIN JOKE OF 1955

1 *Dedication*

I love the loneliness of the big city—when bathed in warmth as in Rome, or in the tradition of freedom as in Paris. But above all I love the dangerous, menacing loneliness which is Berlin. The landing or arrival may vary, but the encounter is the same.

One time: the plane taxis under the cover at Tempelhof. I have seen the masses of houses and the thin, dirty snow covering. I can feel the whistling wind, the dampness which is about to encompass me. It is a winter which casts its homeless chill over places and the fields of ruins. I proceed slowly through customs with my baggage.

Outside stands the monument to the airlift, the three broken bars thrust out into space. A monument to American, French, and British flyers who risked their lives for a population of several millions. A love token to those who offered themselves for a city which was not only a city, but an idea.

The dampness, which will soon become ice, envelops me in the subway. The faces around me are serious, and not overly curious.

Another time (an early summer morning) I am approaching Berlin by car. The city does not emerge in front of me like trees or mountains. We halt at the checkpoint manned by Russian soldiers.

The gray uniformity of the suburbs recurs with growing frequency. The road runs along a railroad embankment; we are in Berlin without having noticed it. On the way into the city we pass a Stadtbahn (City Railroad) train.

The heat beats upon me in waves from which there is no cool or peaceful refuge. On such days I sense, or at least imagine

1

that I sense, the odor of ruins, the taste of burned brick, and the fragrance of young birches growing in the abandoned courtyards.

But now, as often before, I pass through the suburbs in thickening darkness, in weather of mixed snow and rain. Rows of lights which say nothing, suburbs which are merely oblivion, places I know and faces without names. This is a return trip for me but I feel no burning desire, only a menacing loneliness that grows, grows. A foreboding of the demoniacal which can hide behind this German face, this fat, perhaps slightly apathetic look which I have encountered frequently.

I practice indifference and passive repose.

The metallic glitter of rails is all around me. I change to the S-Bahn at Ostbahnhof. This is the route of memories, the way to the West, to Bahnhof Zoo. It is Saturday evening and people are rushing into the dark shafts of the U-Bahnhof Alexanderplatz. The sparse illuminated signs in the Eastern portion of the city leave the impression of phantoms, of fright.

The clock on the red city hall points to eight. At Friedrichstrasse the synthetic female voice in the loud-speaker imparts the information that this is the last station in the *democratic* sector.

Only now do I fully comprehend that I am in Berlin, not in any other big city, in any other local train, with any other language in my ears.

And I am swallowed in the darkness and light of the city prepared to hear stories of their fate; that is, of the inhabitants of Berlin. In this mirror I understand again the fate of our world, its division and its fear. This is my report from Berlin. It is dedicated to a city but deals also with a continent: Europe.

2   *The Remnants of Weimar*

Dull blows echo from the ruins. Hammers are at work on the remains of a building over whose entrance I read: *Dem Deutschen Volke* (To the German People). The ruins are encircled by a fence so high that I have no desire to climb over it. But the fence could never be so high as to conceal completely that it is the Reichstag building, that ruined monument of German parliamentarism.

It seems like a capricious and useless decision on the part of the rulers in Bonn to begin restoration work in the tart-like ruins of the Reichstag. But such thinking is typical of Bonn's relationship to Berlin. The Reichstag building lies near the sector boundary. There is nothing to hinder Walter Ulbricht* from taking a promenade on Ebert Street right next to the building, even though the Parliament might meet there some day. Bonn, which has refused to recognize the existence of two German states, would—in the Reichstag building—be painfully reminded of the proximity and the collision of these two states.

* Walter Ulbricht, born in Leipzig in 1893, became a member of the German Social Democratic Party before the first World War. At the conclusion of that struggle he joined the Spartakusbund, which attempted a revolution against the German Provisional Government in December, 1918, and January, 1919. Like other Spartacists, he went over to the new German Communist Party, in which he remained active. During the Hitler period he lived abroad, in Prague, Paris, and Moscow. He helped found the Socialist Unity Party (SED) after the second World War, and eventually became First Secretary of the Central Committee of the SED and First Vice-Chairman of the Council of Ministers of the German Democratic Republic. In 1960 he became Chairman of the State Council (see note on p. 190). He is regarded as the most powerful figure in East German politics.—ED.

But the repairs will take some years. The frame, the outer shell, will be put into condition first. The pillars are to be sand-blasted and white, one corner is covered with an emplacement of steel rods. The reconstruction has been primarily on that side which faces West Berlin and Platz der Republik. On Ebert Street, facing East Berlin, there is deep shadow, the People's Police, and a long wooden chute that empties the rubbish from the inside on to trucks which haul it away. The sun peeps through the empty windows, but despite all the building exudes "the same hard, dreary coldness which characterizes the entire city. It has the same gloomy, impersonal beauty as all other beautiful buildings here—beautiful, but without warmth and charm, imposing, but frightening and cold." So wrote a Swedish author in 1913.

For those who have decided to reconstruct the building in all its former splendor the ruins are a symbolic acknowledgment of parliamentary democracy and of the work done—in vain, unfortunately—by the Weimar Republic to create a German state which was both stable and democratic.

On Platz der Republik I am reminded of what Friedrich Stampfer, a former member of the German Weimar Reichstag, has written:

The Reichstag Building of the noble Herr Wallot was only the expression of an altogether too transitory grandeur, more that of the new riches than of the new Reich. . . . This whole building was the embodiment in stone of a delusion of grandeur, for which the German people have paid too dearly. This pomp and splendor, which was profaned by loathsome scenes of violence, burned by the Nazis, and shot to pieces by the Russians, must not rise again. In its place let there emerge a new building, which will embody with simple dignity the nature and the will of a reunited, free nation.

Could it be that the hammer blows in the building are just a reminder that the reunion of Germany and Berlin is still

old Parliament being repaired. It stands almost on the border between East and West Berlin.

Congress Hall, a great contrast to older German architecture

thought of as desirable, a kind of theme slowly being hammered out in brick and granite? If that is the case, the expectations are too great. There can be no question of fidelity to the unrestrained, sick anarchism of the Weimar period. Weimar was a temporary setback in the German search for *Ordnung* (order); it was a free, cosmopolitan breath of air, and the last breath, before darkness set in over Germany. It was not only barricade fighters of German democracy who spoke in the Reichstag building, not only Ernst Thälmann and Theodor Heuss, but also Doctor Goebbels and Hermann Göring.

I am on a stroll near Unter den Linden. It is the first warm Sunday in spring. On the previous evening I had seen a pair of ducks peacefully ambling along beneath the linden trees. No car, no person, frightened them. Now I walk past the People's Police, who are peering into the automobiles on their way to the East or to the West. And I decide suddenly to take a look at the piles of stone and the artistically shaped structures which are next to the Reichstag building. In order to see them at close range I need only take a short walk of some fifteen minutes.

The Brandenburg Gate* sparkles from newly-cut stone. A

* The Brandenburg Gate was in the early centuries of Berlin an exit toward the west (and toward the town of Brandenburg) from the city, through the old city wall. In the years 1788-1791 the present monumental structure, designed by Carl Gotthard Langhans in the classical style fashionable at the time, was erected. It was surmounted by the "Quadriga," a copper statuary group created by Gottfried Schadow. This represented a goddess of victory driving a chariot drawn by four horses. As the city grew and spread out, particularly to the west, the Brandenburg Gate came to be a central focal point of the city. Since it towered over one end of Unter den Linden, the great monumental boulevard, it served as the background for many stirring parades in the history of the city, and was regarded as something of a symbol of the capital. During the second World War it was badly damaged—the Quadriga so badly that it could not be repaired, and was taken down, to be replaced by the Soviet flag. A replacement of the sculpture group was eventually made in West Berlin;

firm which is "owned by the people" (*Volkseigener Betrieb*)
has done the work; out in Wilmersdorf in West Berlin they cast
the great four-spanned sculpture of Schadow in the old moulds,
just as important a symbol for old Berlin as the red flag which
dominated the gate alone until 1958. Now the flag has been
replaced by the statuary. Only the boundary between East and
West was not changed.

Millions of people have seen the horses—before. Millions
have seen the red flag. The difficulty was to choose a suitable
day for the change of guard in the summer of 1958. Someone
proposed the 20th of July, since on that day Germany celebrated the memory of the brave men who attempted to remove
Hitler from the scene, but it was pointed out that East Germany
does not in the least consider the men of July 20 worthy of
honor since they were clearly bourgeois, in fact, positively conservative.

So it didn't come off on the 20th of July, although the statuary
was delivered punctually by the foundry in Wilmersdorf. It
was placed on the east side of the Brandenburg Gate while they
were waiting to raise it. The news that Schadow's figures were
there spread like wildfire throughout Berlin, and the people
began a pilgrimage by the hundreds of thousands to the spot
near Brandenburg Gate. The People's Police of East Berlin
were helpless in the face of this flood of people, which was
a spontaneous demonstration of local Berlin patriotism.

---

but, as the author indicates, there were difficulties in reaching an agreement with the authorities of East Berlin, in whose territory the Gate lies.
With the division of Berlin into sectors after the second World War, the
Brandenburg Gate fell just within the Soviet sector. A favorite camera
subject for Western tourists was the monument, topped by its red flag,
serving as a background for a sign warning passers-by that they were about
to leave West Berlin. In the East Berlin rising of June 17, 1953, one of
the symbolic acts of the rioters was the hauling down of the red flag
atop the monument.—ED.

Brandenburger Tor, seen from the West

Kurfürstendamm at night

But the following night the horses disappeared and no one knew where they might be found. The mayor of East Berlin, Friedrich Ebert, issued a reassuring statement that the horses would no doubt be placed where they belonged. But the newspapers of East Berlin suddenly were filled with "spontaneous" letters from readers who insisted that "the iron cross, symbol of German militarism" ought to be filed off the oak-leaved wreath over the statuary. Furthermore, a doubt was raised as to which direction the horses should face. Originally they were galloping in the direction of Siegessäule, that is to say in the direction of present-day West Berlin. They decided finally to face the thing toward Unter den Linden and East Berlin, and after a strange interval of quiet, it was finally lifted to its resting-place. The red flag now waves on both sides. Berlin's old trade mark has been resurrected—but the iron cross is gone.

When I get to the west side of Brandenburg Gate I ask the policemen what they say to the automobile drivers and their passengers.

"We ask: Are you entering of your own free will?" answers one policeman. "We do not want any more kidnappings."

The square in front of Brandenburg Gate is one of the most popular excursion spots for West Berliners. Busses filled with soldiers in civvies drive up, and the passengers proceed slowly to the huge Soviet monument with its menacing cannon and the two tanks which it is said were the first to reach Berlin. This monument exudes the coldness and uncommunicativeness of Russian neo-classicism. A feeling of menacing power sweeps over me.

The guides spiel off their clever lines: "The Russians built this monument right after the war. Russian soldiers stand watch day and night. But it is located in the British sector."

The guards stand there in their fur caps. Their faces are immobile. The Canadian woman in gray who is standing next to me tries to read the inscription. Then she takes out her camera, stands right next to one of the guards, and snaps a picture. He does not move. The civilian-clad soldiers are strangely quiet. Perhaps they sense the memory of blood and death. I hear the song of a bird, an automobile starting up.

The Platz der Republik is directly behind the monument. It is here that the large Western demonstrations take place. Loud-speakers carry the sound across the line. The stage effects are excellent. In the same spirit Charlottenburger Chaussee, which runs to the Brandenburg Gate, has been renamed Street of the 17th of June. It was on this short stretch of asphalt that the last airplanes of Hitler's Reich landed and took off. It was from here that the last contacts were maintained with Dönitz' isolated government. And it was here that Hitler accepted the homage of the faithful masses. The latest name change dates from the summer of 1959. Zeltenallee, which begins at Brandenburg Gate and ends at Congress Hall, was renamed John-Foster-Dulles-Allee. I am not certain if this was the first street to adopt his name after his death, but the speed with which the change was made says a good deal about the political attitude of West Berlin.

I proceed further toward Siegessäule. This monument to the German victory of 1871 is no longer inconvenienced by trees or collections of statues in the Tiergarten. The big park is gradually taking shape again after its destruction. During the war the freezing Berliners cut down the trees and used the wood for fuel. The huge assemblage of statues and busts of Germans,* the great as well as the less great, is reduced now to three:

° The Siegesallee, in the Tiergarten, was formerly a road and promenade flanked on each side by a row of white statues of Germans, mostly rulers of Prussia. These were executed in the worst of nineteenth-century taste, with photographic "realism," even in details of clothing, and were for years the subject of satirical comments.—Ed.

Roon, Moltke, and Bismarck. The artists and writers have disappeared, the military heroes are dead, and Tiergarten has lost its horror attractions. There is a persistent rumor that there are plans afoot to repair the broken statues and restore them to their original setting.

For the time being Siegessäule alone must symbolize ugliness. It costs 30 *pfennigs* to enter, and residents of the East Sector are permitted to pay in their own currency at par. The iron staircase is bracketed fast to the inner walls of the column. It is damp and cold inside. American, German, Russian, and French inscriptions on the walls give fraternal evidence that even victory monuments can be used for the same literary ends as toilet walls.

A father, bespectacled and sharp-nosed, out with his two children, gets angry when I try to hurry up to the balustrade beneath the Goddess of Victory: "I paid to get in, and I can look as long as I please. Everybody should go in proper order."

Up here the huge gilded goddess of victory seems more repulsive than ever. One can understand why the French raised the tricolor over this German idol when they came to Berlin in 1945: "Berlin's heaviest female," say even the local inhabitants. The statue weighs seven tons.

A slight mist veils the horizon and the pointed church steeples. I can see the city hall in Schöneberg and the red-brick tower of East Berlin, symbols of two opposing city sectors. And from this height Berlin looks like an ordered city—the Spree, the broad avenues, and the dark S-Bahn lines form a web of arteries among the gray buildings.

But I have gone up to take a look at the Congress Hall, which, with its daring architectonic shape, breaks with the Berlin tradition of uniform cubes and plaster ornamentation. The vaulted gigantic roof structure, which narrows down toward two supporting pillars, gives the impression of a giant leaf that has come to rest over the building. I think of lightness and space, flight and elegance: free breathing. This is a new style and a new way of life which has broken through in Berlin. The Americans could not have created a better monument to compete with the pile of stone which is Siegessäule, the Russian tanks, or the coldness of the Reichstag building.

But the real beauty of the Congress Hall is best evident at night, when the roof is illuminated from below and floats on the landscape, and rests in a state of harmony and beauty in sharp contrast to the dreariness and uniformity in the contours of the land. Berlin has many magnificent façades, many "copies of copies," but the Congress Hall is simplicity itself, light and air instead of darkness, free form instead of pseudo-classicism.

I climb down from the Siegessäule and walk to the restaurant of the Congress Hall to buy a beer. The Spree flows just outside, and water is everywhere. Inside the restaurant, with its elegant play of colors, I discover that this architecture too has its inhuman aspect. For fear of disturbing the pure form and the play of lines I hardly dare to sit down in the salon. I am human and I feel superfluous, a victim of the threatening beauty of the architecture.

3   Sperlingsgasse

Every day I make discoveries in the old Berlin—I mean in the very oldest, the indestructible, and yet destroyed Berlin near Friedrichsgracht (East). One day I meet Karl, a bargeman,

who has been in all of the Northern countries, in some of them
as a soldier. At another time I converse with Heinz, wood
dealer, who has a little shop near the Spree.

Quietness prevails in Friedrichsgracht, despite the river
traffic and the proximity to the busiest sections of East Berlin.
So I enjoy myself there, sitting on the edge of the wharf, listening to the water, and to nothing.

One evening I discover Sperlingsgasse. It is a narrow lane
winding down to the river; it is blocked in the middle, and I
must make a detour through some ruins. I come to the narrow
arm of the river right next to Jungfernbrücke, Berlin's oldest
preserved bridge, reproduced thousands of times by artists and
photographers.

Before me on Sperlingsgasse glows the inviting sign "Raabe-
Diele." Above the low entrance is the name Else Konarske. A
shepherd dog, which is lying on the sidewalk, growls softly and
raises himself as I enter. The hour is 10:30 at night.

Raabe-Diele is a small place, with three tables, a counter,
benches along the walls, simple and shabby chairs. The walls
are covered with photographs, sketches, and verses. Most of
the pictures suggest much drinking and great hilarity. In a
corner, between the exit and the door to the toilet, hangs the
bearded patriarchal portrait of Wilhelm Raabe, serious as befits
the face of a classical German author.

First I must tell the story of Raabe and Sperlingsgasse.

In early times the narrow alley served as a quick connecting
route between the Spree and the very distinguished quarters
near Breite Strasse and Brüderstrasse. Until 1862 it was called
Spreegasse, but its name was changed to Spreestrasse by order
of the highest government authorities. The expanding Berlin,
soon to become the capital of the holy German Reich, was not
to have any alleys, only streets.

In the years 1854-56 the young student Wilhelm Raabe lived

in a house on Spreegasse, which today has been leveled to the
ground. For the most part it seems that Raabe was primarily
engaged in the writing of his first book, *Die Chronik der Sperlingsgasse* (1856), a careful but lively account in informal
diary form of the alley in which he lived. Raabe's chronicle is
a confession of love for the Spreestrasse of his day:

In the big cities I love the older sections with their narrow,
crooked, dark alleys in which the sunshine hardly dares to peep. I
love their gabled houses and wondrous eaves, and the old cannon
and field pieces which have been placed like curbstones on the
corners. I love these centers of a past day, around which has sprouted
a new life with streets and squares regularly laid out with military
precision.

During the one hundred years which have passed since Raabe
wrote his account over half a million copies have been published
in German. On the hundredth anniversary of Raabe's birth
(that is, 1931) the magistrates of Berlin decided to change the
name of Spreestrasse to Sperlingsgasse. At the same time the
owner of the pub in the building next to Raabe's, Herr Friedrich
Konarske, decided to change the name of his place. It became
Raabe-Diele. The portrait was then hung up between the entrance and the toilet door. There it still hangs.

The name remains, but Raabe and Herr Konarske have been
dead many years. Sperlingsgasse, as well as the old, medieval
Berlin, is largely gone. In the middle of this destruction, like a
fossil from prehistoric times, I find the remains. Raabe-Diele,
located in a house built in 1621, is one of the oldest pubs in the
whole of Berlin. In the West they have been replaced by es-
presso bars and cafés, in the East by a network of ale houses
established by Handels-Organisation.

I sit down on the long bench near the counter and order the
usual combination, beer and schnapps. A fat old woman, with a

fresh reddish complexion, is sitting on a stool near the counter.
She gets up with a sigh and takes the schnapps bottle from the
cupboard. She pushes the beer and the schnapps toward me
and sits down again. I show my identification papers but she
waves her hand without interest.

This is Frau Konarske, eighty-two years of age, the widow
of Friedrich Konarske, and now sole proprietor of Raabe-Diele.
She has worked behind the same counter for fifty-seven years,
since 1901. This is more than twice the span of my life.

She seems still full of strength, living but tired of work. She
drives the dog into the kitchen and starts talking. Not with me,
however, but with a little humpbacked man who has already
drunk three schnapps but only one beer.

"They have promised to restore the old," she says with a sigh.
"But when will that happen? I will be long dead."

The only woman in the bar other than Frau Konarske is a
tipsy forty-year-old, who has probably seen better days. She
drinks lustily and declares proudly that she has recently under-
gone a severe stomach operation. She orders one more drink.
Frau Konarske does not stir, but now she begins to talk to me,
with a raised voice that everyone can hear:

"I tell you that ten drunk men are better than one half-sober
female. That one over there can't get home on her own when
she is drunk. And she talks about stomach operations. She
oughtn't to drink, then. Men are sensible enough to sleep when
they have been drinking. Women? Never! Drunken women are
the worst."

Two middle-aged men are sitting at the table by the window,
each with a guitar, a glass of beer, and a pipe. They strum their
instruments and strike a few chords. They have already played
their entire repertoire and now seem uncertain as to what they
should do, drink or go home.

"Play 'Lili Marlene,' " shouts the hunchback at my table in a small squeaky voice. "Play 'Lili Marlene,' that's what I want to hear. And then I'll buy you a round."

"That's war propaganda," says the best-dressed man in Raabe-Diele. He is deadly earnest, and dressed in a dark suit. His face is hard and immobile.

"What's that!" complains the hunchback. " 'Lili Marlene' was played during the war to voice, yes voice, the longing of the soldiers for peace. That song was written decades ago. It has nothing to do with Nazism or war. Americans and Englishmen played and sang it."

"Germans also," says his comrade, a young man with a boxer's nose, cauliflower ears, a gaudy necktie, and dark yellow finger tips.

"It's an international, a universal, melody."

The atmosphere begins to grow threatening. The musicians are hesitant, the dark-clad one is still firm in his stand. No one else shares his point of view. He would not be any friendlier if I were to tell him that Hans Leip, the author of the song, was treated in a friendly way by the Americans when he was captured at the end of the war. He would undoubtedly answer that one couldn't expect anything else of imperialists.

"If you don't want to listen you can leave," suggests the boxer-type. He begins to sing the first verse. Then the two musicians come to life, their hands begin to move. With such dripping sentimentality that a tremor rises in us all we join in singing "Lili Marlene."

> Vor der Kaserne
> Vor dem grossen Tor
> stand eine Laterne,
> und steht sie noch davor,
> so woll'n wir uns da wiederseh'n
> bei der Laterne woll'n wir steh'n
> wie einst, Lili Marlene.

The man in the dark suit says nothing, continues only to sip his beer. We fumble quickly through the song and then gather ourselves for the grand climax of the last verse:

> Aus dem stillen Raume,
> aus der Erde Grund
> hebt mich wie im Traume
> dein verliebter Mund.
> Wenn sich die späten Nebel dreh'n,
> werd' ich bei der Laterne steh'n,
> wie einst, Lili Marlene
> wie einst, Lili Marlene.

Everyone except the dark-clad one has been warmed by this historic experience. The mood lifts, Frau Konarske serves schnapps and beer to the house. Even I am included in the invitation, with the result that I am forced to return the hospitality. This proves rather expensive, despite the fact that Raabe-Diele is one of the cheapest places.

On the wall there is a small framed text dating from the days of the war: "We shall go to our death just as naked as we came into the world." The text is a memento from the night raids of the recent war. Presumably the hunchback sat in a dark bomb shelter then and sang "Lili Marlene."

The man in the dark suit has really no reason for his annoyance. Has not the East German poet Jan Koplowitz written an emotional song reminiscent of "Lili Marlene"? In it, among others, occur the lines:

> Die Taube muss gepanzert sein,
> darum bin ich Soldat.
> Halt' ich mein Mädel fest umspannt
> ihr Mund wie goldner Wein.
> Mein Herz schlägt sturm bis an den Rand.
> Wir werden glücklich sein.

Frau Konarske begins to open up:—Do you think that anyone will take over my place after I am gone?" she asks rhetorically and sits down. "All of my relatives and friends are in West Germany. Do you think they want tó come over to East Berlin and work in a little hole from ten in the morning until two at night? No."

I, too, have difficulty in believing that. Frau Konarske is much too old to dare think about a future. Raabe-Diele will be closed, no dog will lie on the sidewalk. No useless persons will stagger across the Jungfernbrücke and open the door of Raabe-Diele, a part of Berlin's past, its forever lost past.

The sketches and pictures on Frau Konarske's walls bear many signatures and carefree dedications. Some are inscribed: "To Friedrich Konarske from Heinrich Zille." This does not surprise me. Frau Konarske and her guests can be associated with Zille's drawings on the walls, his world of coarse, open, and living faces.

Here is the same "Fifth Estate" which was Zille's own. It has now shrunk to a little group of disappearing types in one of the last pubs. Zille's leftist friends complained that he portrayed almost exclusively the ragged proletariat, without due attention to the positive, constructive elements. Frau Konarske and her friends, I am sure, are not of that kind either.

Quite the contrary. With a destructive endurance and thirst we tarry at her place long after the hour of closing. The guitar players taper off, the man in the dark suit assumes more human qualities, and we are all one big family by the time Frau Konarske resolutely casts us out into the cold night air.

This description of entertainment at one of the last outposts of private enterprise is already history and legend. As she suspected, Frau Konarske's relatives did not want to take over the pub when she could no longer work there. She rented the place and retired to her apartment above the pub. She took with her the dog (who had growled outside), the portrait of Raabe, and the philosophical texts on the walls and the sketches with Heinrich Zille's dedications. The woman who has charge of the place now is about fifty, and she stares at me coldly when I go in. She sits in Frau Konarske's old corner stool, she has a younger girl as an assistant. I don't enjoy myself there any more.

4   Zille's City

Heinrich Zille was urged by his teacher to seek his motifs in the street, in the open. He followed this advice literally. His milieu became the street, the alley, the bar, a bathing beach, and places of popular amusement. He became an artist of Balzac's breadth and social sensitivity. I have often wondered how these now classical portrayers of Berlin have affected my view of the Berlin that once was. They have created a world which can easily be identified with Berlin, despite the fact that each one has rendered only one part of the city, a certain nuance, or a class.

This applies to Zille, but also to Kollwitz and Arnold, Liebermann and Nagel, and above all to the keen satirist, George Grosz, who died in Berlin in the summer of 1959 after his return from the United States. Where Zille was broad and folkish, with a forgiving sense of humor, Grosz constructed terrifying visions which even today have a fearful sharpness despite the fact that Grosz, in his autobiography, converts his past into a nothingness: "But we were pure, unadulterated nihilism, a

vacuum, a hole." More sharply and mercilessly than others Grosz
has drawn a picture of the German vices, the German oppression, all experienced in a Berlin where chaos was struggling
against construction.

Zille was often less blunt than Grosz, he was softer, but he
had basically the same goal. Through his realism, the carefully
studied details, and his keen understanding · of the life and
speech of the people, Zille constructed in the simplest of his
drawings a social indictment of the period when Germany and
Berlin were experiencing the great changes from handicrafts
to big industry, from Empire to Republic, from monarchy to
revolution and counterrevolution. There is throughout a dark
thread of misery.

The collapse of handicrafts occurs at the time that social dis-
tress is at its height. In Raabe's day there were eighteen houses
on Sperlingsgasse and most of them were owned by artisans
who lived in their own houses. Twenty years later a large part
of the houses had passed into other hands; the alley degenerated. Twenty women were living under police inspection in one
of these houses. One day a porcelain painter by the name of
Franz Füssel threw all of his tools and equipment into the river.
This deed had more than symbolic significance.

This period and these persons are physically captured in
Zille's drawings. His knowledge seems inexhaustible; he varies
the simplest of his motifs without showing repetition or routine.

When he was elected to the Prussian Academy of Arts in 1924
he delivered an initiation speech in which, among other things,
he depicted his youthful experiences. The famous dance hall,
Orpheum, was in the same building in which he began his study
of lithography in 1872:

I had to fetch the beer for breakfast. We could get this at the
Orpheum from the waiters, who had their own canteen and who
were there scrubbing floors and polishing mirrors. Drunken men and

women were still lying around in alcoves and loges. These were the
happy heirs of Unification, who were reaping the harvest from the
victories of 1870-71. Once I saw how the waiters had placed a fat,
heavily-intoxicated whore over a chair and then sat and played cards
on her bare bottom. The lithographers at that time made dozens of
sketches, in all sizes, of German military leaders and princes; sometimes they copied photographs of mutilated and healed soldiers and
reproduced them on stone for medical books; pictures of saints, of
Madonnas with bleeding hearts, the Crucifixion, etc. [were pro-
duced] which were hung to the left and right of the wall clock in
the homes of the poor people.

Zille quickly became popular. He was known throughout
Berlin from east to west and from left to right. Zille Clubs and
Zille Bars were established, Zille Festivals were arranged and
his books were printed in even larger editions. Films were shot,
using the motifs of his *Milljöh*. Clever businessmen did their
best to dupe the credulous artist, who at the same time was conducting a private assistance project. Like most artists Zille had
nothing but contempt for the practices connected with popu-
larization and publicity, their thoughtlessness and their deceit.
But he was not strong enough to renounce and reject them completely. To renounce is always more difficult than to follow the
tide of popularity.

Zille's fame in Berlin is evidence of how folkish, proletarian,
and critically sensitive the metropolis was despite its pomp and
worldliness.

With steely determination the Nazi regime undertook to
uproot the anarchical, "estranged-from-the-people," Jewish,
revolutionary elements in the capital city, Berlin. Luckily for
the Nazis, Zille had been dead since 1929; it was possible to
hold his memory in respect. Zille could be found not only in
books and drawings. The sculptor August Kraus borrowed his
friend's features, potato-nose and all, for the bust of Knight

Weddigo von Plothow, which was placed on the Siegesallee in the Tiergarten.

Behind the worship of Zille lies the sentimental feeling of Berliners for their own city. It is just as strong now as ever, in both East and West. Zille is the lost Berlin, the never rediscovered. His is the kind of humor for which present conditions provide no outlet. Daydreams about Zille are not unlike a longing for paradise .

It just happens that paradise, too, has not been found.

5   *The False Pearl*

Political regimes are peculiarly shortsighted in their passion to change the names of streets in their capitals. At least some effort should be made to insure permanence for such changes.

That Berlin's exterior pomp is traceable in part at least to the Age of Empire is clearly evident from the names that date from those years. There is Kaiserdamm (the stretch up to Reichskanzlerplatz); there is Wilhelmstrasse. But nowhere can one find traces of Hitler and his henchmen.

The difference between the rulers of West Berlin and of East Berlin could be easily determined, it seems to me, by a list of deserving persons who have left their imprint in the form of place names. In West Berlin you have Lucius D. Clay, the American general and one of the authors of the airlift; Otto Suhr

and Ernst Reuter, both former mayors. But also Marx: Karl
Marx Strasse in Neukölln is one of the busiest business streets
in one of the liveliest workers' sections of the city. Historical
events which have been turning-points have also left their
mementos: Platz der Luftbrücke (Square of the Airlift) in
Tempelhof, Street of 17th June (named in honor of the East
Berlin demonstrations in 1953), which radiates from Brandenburg Gate.

In East Berlin the first Russian commandant, Bersarin, has
his own street, also Stalin and Lenin. German socialists are
represented by Liebknecht, Zetkin, Luxemburg, Marx, Engels,
Ulbricht, Pieck, and several others, all of whom have either
streets, squares, or sporting palaces named after them. But in
the distribution of names, that of the questionable Lassalle and
those of the hated revisionists are missing.

Special status is given naturally to Ernst Thälmann, who will
be honored by a giant monument on the spot where Hitler's
Reich Chancellory stood. But I think it is worth noting that Paris
and several other western European cities have their Stalin-
grad squares, but not Berlin, either in East or West.

These new names concern me because visiting foreigners and
news correspondents have developed a sleepwalker's almost
automatic mania for describing only the obvious contrasts between Kurfürstendamm and Stalinallee.

This comparison is made not only by Western journalists who
want to demonstrate the humane and political attraction of
West Berlin to the population of "the [Eastern] Zone." Writers
from Moscow and Shanghai have pointed out the same contrast,
but they see it as a contrast between socialist labor and the neon-
lit false coinage of capitalism.

Unfortunately, both streets are only in the slightest degree
representative of the respective sectors of Berlin. *I* cannot complain about that. If the alleged contrasting conditions were in

fact that clear, and correctly interpreted, it would not be worth my time to spend a single day in Berlin.

But one cannot avoid speaking of the two streets. When one of the editors of *Süddeutsche Zeitung* was describing the Elector's old riding path to Grunewald—that is to say, Kurfürstendamm—he wrote, among other things, the following:

> On Kurfürstendamm one can find the most expensive jewelers right next to second-hand automobile dealers, and in front of exclusive restaurants with shiny marquees one can see old ladies silently standing with outstretched hands. Kurfürstendamm, once the most feudal of avenues in the German Reich, has today, especially in the clamoring promiscuity of its night signs, a quite fatal similarity to the Reeperbahn.

Kurfürstendamm—retorted a West Berlin newspaper immediately—is four kilometers long, but has only seventeen jewelers and ten second-hand automobile dealers. A police check of beggars shows that their number is less than ever before! "Kudamm" is not Reeperbahn. But there is something that corresponds to Hamburg's entertainment district. This is Neue Welt in Hasenheide.

The protest in the Berlin newspapers smacks of provincial vanity. Even if the details in the *Süddeutsche* report are correct, I believe that the tone is contrived.

Kurfürstendamm is really not West Berlin's façade. But it is made to seem such in the tourist propaganda:

"We are now on Berlin's Champs Elysées, Berlin's chief artery. To the left we have the Volkswagen salesrooms of the Eduard Winter Company. In this place alone Winter sells thirty cars per day. He is one of Berlin's richest men; in addition to automobiles he sells Coca-Cola." The guide gives forth with a self-satisfied laugh, wipes her mouth, adjusts her beret, and continues:

"Several of the leading hotels in Berlin are on Kurfürsten-damm. To the left is Hotel Kempinski, and on the same side the new skyscraper of the Hamburg-Mannheimer Insurance Company, and to the right—yes, back of those cars on display—the Theater am Kurfürstendamm. And there over yonder the symbol of free Berlin, the tower of Kaiser-Wilhelm-Gedächt-niskirche, and the new center for textiles, then the Zoo garage, and further off Hotel Hilton, the Hilton Berlin, pride of the city."

The Hilton Berlin is on Budapester Street, and it had its formal opening in the autumn of 1958 with a gigantic festival where champagne flowed freely and all the finest clothes of Berlin were on display. Among those present were Conrad Hilton and a plane-load of Hollywood stars, a number of Jesuit fathers from California, and Willy Brandt and wife. From the elegant roof bar one has a view over the Tiergarten all the way to East Berlin.

But this is not Kurfürstendamm. On Kurfürstendamm, from Tauentzien as far as Wittenbergplatz, are the finest and most elegant stores and shops. Kurfürstendamm is an international, worldly street, with gaudy window displays. Kurfürstendamm is full of color, at least some of it, but becomes dreary and poor as one proceeds from the Zoo on the way to Halensee, where the street ends. In the sidewalk restaurants on Kurfürstendamm or (on cold days) in the enclosed terraces heated by infra-red rays one can enjoy the experience of being one among thousands of anonymous spectators. For example, at the Café Kranzler, which was established originally in 1825 at the corner of Unter den Linden and Friedrichstrasse (in present-day East Berlin) but which is now situated at the corner of Kurfürstendamm and Joachimsthaler Strasse, where a branch café had been opened in 1932. Or in any of the other classical cafés, which are really no longer classical but have classical names.

Yes, this is Berlin (West).

There are Berliners who have never been on Kurfürstendamm.

There are foreigners who have been only on Kurfürstendamm.

When I go into the Café Schloss Marquardt, which is on the lower floor of the Hotel Kempinski, a number of elderly gentlemen with Van Dyke beards and urbane manners are standing near the entrance. They are wearing black overcoats and are speaking Russian, but they are not Soviet citizens.

There is a little notice on the wine list of the café in which the management expresses the hope that they will soon get back the spot on the edge of town where the Café Schloss Marquardt first got its reputation. There is just one small difficulty: the place is in East Germany. Reunification will not be hastened by any such pious hope.

6   *Tour with a Guidebook*

I have a number of older Berlin guidebooks. One is Grieben's *Reiseführer,* published in 1917 during the war and bought by my father in Berlin, and another one printed in 1928. Both speak of Kurfürstendamm as one of several centers of interest in Berlin. The book dating from 1928 describes the street as a leading business avenue, with an "urbane, international character, containing a diversity of accommodations, some of them luxurious, in the way of lodging and entertainment." It is pointed out, however, that this applies only to the short stretch between Gedächtniskirche (Memorial Church) and Uhland-strasse, some 500 yards in length. In *Good-Bye to Berlin* Christopher Isherwood speaks of "the cluster of expensive hotels, bars, cinemas, shops around the Memorial Church, a sparkling nucleus of light, like a sham diamond, in the shabby twilight of the town." This feeling of shabbiness possesses me even now, even though Kurfürstendamm has now extended its sophistication further in the direction of Halensee.

For example, it extends even to the bar Old Fashioned, one of the night clubs for people who are seen in public; that is to say, around whom there is an aura of money. I knock on the little door, and a huge doorman—most of them seem to be huge —asks if I have my key with me. One need only answer affirmatively. The key is the password to happiness.

Red lighting and two attractive bar girls, one dark and the other blonde. They will accept whiskey to a moderate extent (it's helpful to stifle yawns, confesses one of them). I sit down in one of the comfortable bar stools (they have arm rests) and give my order. The blonde is occupied for the moment. A man in his fifties, sitting in a corner to the right, has got hold of her arm. He is licking and kissing it, further and further up toward the armpit, until she wearily draws it back. After she has served me, and has been presented with another highball by the man, the act is repeated. He kisses her palm and then proceeds again up the length of the arm.

When she leaves to wait on some other people he takes off his glasses and polishes them carefully. He is a business executive from Düsseldorf on a short visit to Berlin. No, he would never think of going to any other place than Old Fashioned on Kur-fürstendamm. For him Berlin is a foreign country and a local province all wrapped into one, and profitable because his enter-prise in Berlin receives a lower tax assessment. Many industries send semimanufactured articles to Berlin, finish them there, and then ship the finished products out again. The tax advantages are greater than the costs of transportation.

Even liquor, for that reason, is somewhat cheaper in Berlin. When I leave there is a couple on the dance floor, an old man and a young woman in a dark red dress with black, narrow shoulder bands. She is holding him tenderly, and the hour is late. I have a warm stickiness like the taste of vomit in my mouth.

Since West Berlin has not yet had the opportunity to rebuild any of the other sophisticated centers—they are just inside the sector boundary or in its immediate proximity—an effort has been made to create a substitute in the cultured pearl, Kurfürstendamm.

Other centers in West Berlin have a more neutral countenance of human labor and ordinary necessities. I am thinking of Schlosstrasse in Steglitz (which, even at that, is somewhat sophisticated), of Karl-Marx-Strasse in Neukölln, of Müllerstrasse, Badstrasse, and Bornholmer Strasse in Wedding. In these sections the life of the people is Berlinish, without pretensions.

My guidebook of 1928 gives the following as one of the chief objects of a tour in Berlin: "Through Berlin's Monuments and Art Collections." This is the stretch, Unter den Linden-Lustgarten-Museuminsel-Schlossplatz-Gendarmenmarkt. Even today one can follow this route, but with some important alterations. The dominating building on Unter den Linden is the Soviet Embassy, with its 600-foot façade. Of the castle there is nothing left except the memory; that is to say, a square with a speakers' platform and flagpoles, the present Marx-Engels-Platz. The museums are only in part preserved, although they are being rebuilt as quickly as possible despite the fact that some of the art treasures and collections have been lost. Some are in

West Germany, and will under no circumstances be returned to East Berlin.

Another tour has a heavier concentration upon the contemporary. It is entitled: "To the Chief Sites of Community and Business Life, and through Old Berlin." The route goes from Potsdamer Platz to Leipziger Strasse and Königstrasse. At Potsdamer Platz the three sectors meet, and Leipziger Strasse is a quiet, dead street. Without some previous knowledge of the district one would not be able to identify the ruins of Wertheim and Tietz, the two large department stores. The walk continues to Alexanderplatz, both then and now the traffic hub of proletarian Berlin.

The big police headquarters is gone. Everything is bare and cold. In the distance one can see the shiny tiles on the houses at Strausberger Platz, where the socialist structures on Stalinallee begin.

The third and shortest tour goes through "the street of entertainment," by which is meant Friedrichstrasse.

I decide to take the stroll, keeping in mind the notations in the guidebook. I begin in the south, where two U-Bahn lines cross at Hallesches Square. Friedrichstrasse itself begins at Mehringplatz (formerly Belle-Alliance-Platz) in the West Berlin district of Kreuzberg. It is just as provincial and dead here now as it was when the guidebook was published. The only café on Friedrichstrasse in West Berlin is called Krebs, and in the afternoons is patronized by a few sleeply elderly ladies who drink coffee and munch on cakes. I drain my own cup in a hurry to escape the pressing silence.

Behind Hallesches Square a large library has been built with American money. Its façade faces toward Friedrichstrasse and the Eastern sector. This, too, becomes a symbol of freedom!

The magistrates of East Berlin plan to widen Friedrichstrasse right on that side where the West has constructed a huge

building, Landesarbeitsamt Berlin—a sort of ministry of labor.
A West Berlin insurance firm also has a new building on Friedrichstrasse.

Then comes the sector boundary.

Every time I go through customs—and this means the border
police—I am afraid, and feel like a lawbreaker. Even now I
blush as I slip across the border to the East. The only com-
promising thing I have with me is the newspaper *Die Welt*.
Women wander over the border loaded down with full shopping bags. The check made by the guards seem perfunctory:
"After all, we are all Berliners." The young police officers of
East Berlin are not anxious to start any trouble. But on the other
hand, neither do they want to lose their jobs.

The vice center, according to the guidebook, begins at the
corner of Leipziger Strasse. It would be an exaggeration to say
that there are traces of the cabarets and night clubs, the homo-
sexual pubs, and the traditional beer halls. Quiet prevails on
Jägerstrasse (rechristened Otto-Nuschke Strasse). One can
catch a glimpse of Hotel Adlon at the end of Behrenstrasse.

The "bright cafés and restaurants, almost all of them with
musical entertainment," as the guidebook says, are now limited
(before one reaches Bahnhof Friedrichstrasse) to the two dance
halls, Alt-Bayern and Rhein-Terrassen, one shabbier than the
other, but both of them packed on Saturday nights.

The ladies, "powdered and painted appropriately for their
age and appearance," who are mentioned in the guidebook,
seem to have migrated to some unknown destination.

The big-city personality of F. is maintained as far as the Spree.
Near its terminus it becomes again provincial and similar to the
Reeperbahn, and in the late hours of the evening the earlier mentioned female beauty is found not only here but in the area around
the Stettiner Bahnhof, where it is particularly noticeable.

At Bahnhof Friedrichstrasse one can easily imagine that one
is in a large Western city. The lines of the U-Bahn and the S-
Bahn intersect here, above the tracks the illuminated newspaper
of *Neues Deutschland* blazes at night with East German football scores, the speeches of Ulbricht, Russian statements, and
news items concerning Western imperialism. In the evening
the automobile traffic is lively, but most of the license plates
indicate that they belong in West Berlin.

The only place where the above-mentioned female beauty
can be seen, although it is hardly striking, is right at the entrance to the so-called Pressecafé. Women can often be seen
sitting there, one or two together, sometimes three. But, as an
all-German popular song puts it: *Das kann man mit Geld nicht
bezahlen* (one can't buy that with money).

We (and by this *we* I am adopting the insufferable, collective
expression of the guidebook)—we arrive at Weidendamm Bridge
with its cast-iron eagles and nineteenth-century ornamentation.
I would sometimes stand here a while at night, watch the reflection of lights in the Spree, and listen to the trains going by. It
is near the theaters and cinemas, near the West trains and East
trains, and the water. I remember the view in the winter when
the ground has a light cover of snow, while the dark waters flow
slowly on their way. Suspended above the water is an electric
sign advertising watches: *Ruhlaer Uhren—begehrt, bewährt*.

The section usually identified as most nearly like the Reeperbahn is not without interest. I cross Max-Reinhardtstrasse and
walk by some ruins whose proud past has not been enough to
sustain the fallen walls and the rusty girders. This place was
called Haus der Technik. There are a few small shops on the
ground floor.

It was in this area that *die Stundenhotels* (one-hour hotels)
stood tightly built against each other at the intersections. Here

were pubs, a cheap night life. Here Berlin was erotic. In this paradise of vice the Haus der Technik was a reminder of German technical capacity for self-destruction. It is empty here now. Empty houses are signs that people have moved. But George Grosz is one who has recalled this world of 1912:

> In our search for excitement we would walk along the whore infested streets of Friedrichstadt. The ladies of pleasure would stand in the doorways like sentinels dangling their handbags, the sign of their guild.
> The most famous hangout for prostitutes was the Café National on Friedrich Street.

West Berliners try to buy cheap liquor here at the dance bar, Kleine Melodie. But they are out of luck now. They are politely and firmly refused.

Why? Let me quote from an article in the London *Times* of February 16, 1959:

"West Berlin shops sell a curious kind of purse, which has two coin pouches and two note compartments. It is not seen in other cities in West Germany, but for practical-minded West Berliners it is a great convenience." After the currency reform of 1948 West Berlin had West German marks and East Berlin East German marks. Both are called Deutsche Mark (DM) but in Berlin they are referred to as "Ostmark" (East mark) and "Westmark." In the period after 1948 is was simple for West Berliners to exchange their Westmarks for Ostmarks. For the most part the exchange rate was 1:5 although the real value of the two currencies was not necessarily identical with the unofficial exchange rate. For several years a number of West Berliners did their daily shopping in East Berlin, went to bars there, etc. Gradually the authorities in the East delimited this freedom. One could not buy anything, except books and papers, without an *Ausweis* which proved that you were an East Berliner. For a while, however, it was permitted and possible to spend a happy and cheap evening in a pub in East Berlin. Even this is now no longer possible without an *Ausweis,* which, for all practical purposes, means that West Berliners are barred from pubs in East Berlin. It is, of course, theoretically possible if one goes to a bank in East Berlin and exchanges currency at the 1:1 rate, but few do that. On the other hand one can still attend the theater or the cinema without an identity check.

But it is obvious that the man on the street has a need for the currency of the other part of the city—hence the purses with "two coin pouches and two note compartments." From a strictly legal point of view the import or export of Ostmarks is forbidden. People who go by the S-Bahn to East Berlin and have Ostmarks in their pockets are currency smugglers. If, then, it is impossible for a West Berliner to visit a pub in the East it is almost as difficult for an East Berliner to go to a pub in the West, since he must exchange his Ostmarks at a rate which is not only disadvantageous but incorrect. This long explanation, alas, seems necessary if one is to understand why West Berliners are turned down at Kleine Melodie—and why only an intoxicated West Berliner would make the effort. When sober, they would not dare; it is hopeless without the magical *Ausweis.* Says the *Times:* "Violators, i.e., those who exchange money in west Berlin and who are found with it, are punished with fines (usually 10 times the amount, in west marks, involved in the transaction). Often, if the violator is an east German, he is punished by a jail sentence as well."

I have become sick and am living in Hotel Hanke, a private hotel on Friedrichstrasse, in the same building as Kleine Melodie. An old couple owns the hotel. They take turns resting on a broad sofa which is in what was once the dining room. An unpolished samovar stands on the counter. The old woman comes toddling in and notes that I have on all the lights in my room.

"You will run us out of electricity," she says angrily as she switches off the ceiling light.

I lie on the bed and try to read. It is dark and I feel dizzy. I can neither swallow nor talk. It is evening, and I decide to go to the bar for refreshments.

The bartender is a striking copy of Folco Lulli, the Italian actor. He has a wide face, a drooping mustache, friendly, but somewhat tired, eyes. He has worked in pubs for forty years and knows Friedrichstrasse inside out. But he has no illusions about its past or future glory. Eroticism flowered here, both the cheap and the expensive. But what Berlin bitch would have any desire to sell herself for Ostmarks?

Two diligent musicians take care of the dance music in Kleine Melodie. The bar is situated near the entrance and the dance floor is at the other end of the long barroom.

Several People's Police come in. They take off their heavy tunics and sit down at two of the round tables. They are young, well fed, well cared for and content. They enjoy security, at least until they make a mistake. Many young men apply to join the People's Police because of the pay and the social advantages.

I watch a young couple. She is tall and slender, he is thin and wears glasses. They drink wine and nod to each other. They don't talk, neither do they dance. They seem as though they had been brought together by chance. And yet I sense something deeply strained between them. What I cannot perceive is whether it is great love or great hate. They are exercising themselves in the difficult art of seeming indifferent.

My hoarseness and fever begin to abate—I think. I am no longer dizzy and so can read, with a clear head, what is inscribed on the wall behind the bartender: "Thirst is worse than homesickness."

This, then, is Friedrichstrasse, which begins at Mehringplatz

(West) and ends at Oranienburger Tor (East). The people at Kleine Melodie are more simply dressed than those on Kurfürstendamm, they drink cheaper liquor and they smoke poorer cigarettes. Are they unhappy?

7   *Whatever Will Be, Will Be*

The prostitutes of Berlin have been disturbed in one of their favorite corners. This is at the intersection of Augsburger Strasse and Joachimsthaler Strasse. Here it is that they are digging the new underground, Steglitz-Moabit-Wedding.

With supreme assurance the whores whisk their clients to the Pension Joachim or some other *Studenhotel* in the neighborhood. They are fast and cheap, hardly more expensive than a couple of highballs at a nightclub.

Many young girls come to West Berlin from East Germany. Their faces can suddenly overflow with tears. They do not have permission to travel further; they are prisoners in Berlin. Their tears are false tears, professional tears for money. But they have real justification. These can be girls without a work permit or a passport, whose lives are stamped by the political dividing line, East-West.

Others work in bars or night clubs. Take for example the especially Reeperbahn-like Remde's St. Pauli near Kurfürstendamm, where the patrons for the most part are middle-aged men dutifully accompanying their wives.

At Remde's the guests sit in front of a stage with light red drapes. A magician entertains the audience by plucking 20-mark bills from the clients' pockets and then returning them after a little while. It is a tremendous hit. I notice that the man next to me seems to enjoy having his money snitched. But he seems doubly happy to get it back. The magician concludes his performance by pulling two long pickles out of a man's pockets.

In one corner a shabby man of some sixty years is sitting with his wife. He holds his arm tightly around her shoulders as the waiter pours the white wine. The master of ceremonies goes to the stage and introduces the feature number, "Nights in Capri." The spotlights are thrown on an effectively banal stage scene. Against a background composed of a blue landscape, an over-ripe crescent moon, and the play of moonbeams on the cardboard wall, the *Hausballet* (ballet corps) performs in hideously prim nakedness, while the star of the show croons one of the over-worked songs of Capri.

The largest and blondest of the girls draws most attention to herself. She sways slowly toward the audience, pale flesh jiggling in time to the music. Fathers, with their wives and daughters at the table, applaud.

After this nudeness comes a dressing number. Four solid citizens from the audience clothe the girls with *"Perlon"* (German artificial textile)—a boost for German industry! The creation "Longing" wins the contest, and the man receives a small bottle of brandy as a prize.

A serious young man with glasses is sitting at my table. He is Heinz, a clerk from Düsseldorf. This is his first visit to Berlin. He is living with friends out in Spandau.

Every ten minutes he asks me: "Do you know when the last train leaves?"

He is twenty years old, has thin lips, and drinks champagne: Henkell Trocken. He wants to know where one can dance and have fun. When the program is over he empties his bottle, gets up stiffly, bows, and departs. It is 2 A.M. and the last train for Spandau has undoubtedly left.

The Berlin night spots imitate imitations, which in turn have imitated something. I have wandered into jazz bars which, despite the soft lights and the nude art on the walls—in the older Haymarket style—are quite sinless. The customers drink either König-Pilsener or Coca-Cola, if they drink anything at all. Remde's copies the Reeperbahn, Badewanne copies the jazz halls of other European cities, whether they are called Taverna Mexico in Milan or Fatty's Saloon in Vienna. Badewanne (the bathtub) has been visited by an unusual number of celebrities, who either have been sketched or have themselves written their names on the walls. But when I have a beer with the orchestra leader, Johannes Rediske, he tells me of other visitors to Badewanne:

"East Germans and East Berliners are here frequently, and if a jazz band from Poland or Czechoslovakia performs in East Berlin, you can be sure that the musicians will come over here right after they have finished playing for the evening in the East sector. Otherwise my public comes from all classes of society, from models and speculators to musicians and students. That's why I like to play here; it keeps me in touch with people."

Then he goes to the little platform where his quintet is playing, fingers the electric guitar, and the dance floor becomes packed again. At the tables there are German girls who are sitting and trying to look like anything but German girls. There are American soldiers anxiously eyeing the clock. Fritz, who is a student at the Free University, also watches the clock. He does not dance, does not smoke, just listens. And the words go: "Whatever will be, will be."

This is an international hit, and its fatalistic outlook is as appropriate here as in any other Western jazz hall. Everything is as it used to be—if we can only get rid of the raw air of late winter and snow outside.

I flee from Badewanne, and discover other songs at Kelch on Prager Strasse, songs which have become ritualized.

"I am going to sing some Russian folk songs," says a young man in a woolen sweater as he gets up from his table. He has thick lips and a languishing look. He has been sitting with his friends while awaiting a chance to perform. The stout Frau N. is sitting behind the counter reading a horoscope, which seems particularly appropriate for her, for this day, for other people, and for the world generally. Her bosom quivers as she laughs out loud.

The audience grows quiet. The young man sings *Seh't, dort kommen die Kosacken* (See, Here Come the Cossacks).

I hear nothing except the guitar and his song, which fills the place with Russian longing, Russian folksiness, and a drop of Western Gorbatshov-vodka. A man whispers in my ear: "We love Russia and the Russians—the real Russia and the real Russians."

He is the only one, except for the young man, who dares to open his mouth.

No other songs, not even the newest ones from Paris, can attract such a devoted public. For the people at Kelch the songs of this young man about the Russian steppes and the Cossacks are the real Russia, while the Red Soviet Union, the power on the other side of the Brandenburg Gate, is a sham, a crime, a fraud.

In this climate of narcosis they empty their glasses and sink into a meditative mood, which must not be confused with empty-mindedness.

8   City in Gray

"Concierges are the most important persons around here," says an acquaintance in East Berlin as he meets me at the entrance. I have been announced ahead of time but the concierge has refused to allow me past his sacred cubicle.

"Why are the eastern sections of large cities often the poorest?" asks a sociologist in West Berlin, who himself lives on the extreme western fringe. "Why do people of property move to the west?"

A general rule applicable to Berlin is that the city's eastern sections have been proletarian, poor, gray, while the fashionable people have built their houses in the west. It was to impoverished Eastern Berlin that the Russians came, and they retained eight of the city's twenty districts. Most of these eight districts have a proletarian tradition.

Into this world the autocratic concierges have thrust themselves. These are men and women who are empowered to issue passes, who watch over all visitors, and inscribe them in an endless register. I have never quite learned just who it is that reads these long lists of visitors.

There is a dictatorial concierge also in this building on Stalin-allee, where I am visiting party functionary P. He lives on the sixth floor, but since the elevator is out of order we puff our way up to his apartment. The staircase is narrow and high. On occasional landings there are optimistic reliefs showing the life of the people.

"This is where I live," says P. as he opens the door to his three-room apartment. The hall is only a cluster of doors leading in various directions, which open against each other, and are brownish and much the worse for wear. P. has TV and radio, a few shelves of books (Zola and Marx, Gorki and Maupassant) and broad, clumsy furniture. The separating walls are solid, like those of an impregnable fortress; the bathroom is suspiciously similar to the décor in a surrealistic comedy.

"Good and cheap," says P., as he throws himself into a chair and offers me Chinese cigarettes.

I smoke. We have a view over the Moscow-like Stalinallee, where most of the apartments are just as poorly planned and built as P.'s. Socialist city planning has failed badly here. Seldom have I seen such bleak buildings, such cheerless and stupidly planned living quarters.

I convey this idea in milder terms to P.

"Certain mistakes were made, but they are being corrected."

But the buildings cannot be torn down. The East German word for stupidity is mistake. In this big mistake which is named Stalinallee lives part of the East German elite, party functionaries, intellectuals, heroes of labor, national prize-winners and other prominent persons. I get the impression of camouflaged petty bourgeoisism. There is an undertone of fatness and apathy. P. is that kind of person. He is not without intellectual interests. We can carry on a relatively free conversation, but as soon as the question of principles is raised he is transformed into a steely Hundred Percenter.

The inhabitants of Stalinallee have cars, proper dark clothes, and an unlimited opinion of their own dignity. The shops on Stalinallee are the best in East Berlin, the rents unbelievably low.

Previously it was called Frankfurter Strasse and Frankfurter Allee. Despite the width of the street, and the landscaping effort to create a garden-like city sector between the tiled barracks, the street still bears the invisible marks of its past, the proletarian Frankfurter Allee, with its darkness and tragedies. After the war it was one of Berlin's worst-destroyed streets.

The trees do not do well on Frankfurter Allee. Trees are sensitive beings, sensitive even to noise and confusion. They stand there with their sparse crowns between two lines of constantly whining trams and two rows of constantly rattling trucks and look like youths who have aged prematurely. They turn yellow in the middle of the summer and their leaves fly crazily in the whizzing draft of the street cars. They swirl downward like the fateful descent of a human being in the struggle of the big city. On hot summer afternoons women and children seek melancholy refuge in their thin shadows; from the depths of sunless courtyards, from desolate cellars and basement workshops they crawl out into a storm of noise, heat, dust, and smoke. The gray, embittered faces of women, the angry shrieks of children—young ones who seem as though they had come into being against their own wishes and those of their parents. Bitter expressions of lifelong, deep-frozen contempt, hard glances from under gray eyebrows. Their faces are like battlefields—battlefields of lifelong quarrels, lifelong hates, hungers, and humiliations. The look of an infuriated tiger in a menagerie, the look of people who, with bleeding fingernails, cling to the sharp precipices of life's abyss, holding to life with grim tenacity even though to endure has no meaning.

In this same piece Vilhelm Ekelund describes the uses to which nature can be put in the big city. One night a sixty-year-old landlord in the building where Ekelund lived hanged himself in a tree on Frankfurter Allee. When he was discovered in the morning he was stiff and straight like a soldier. Only in death did he attract attention and annoyance.

I see no dead hanging from the balconies on Stalinallee today unless one wishes to consider the name of the street and the large statue of Stalin as ghosts and reminders of an unhappy past.

But in the final battles for Berlin in the early spring of 1945 there were Nazis who murdered people, hung them on a tree, and fastened to the corpses pieces of paper with the inscription: "Here N. N. hangs because he refused to defend wife and child."

In these parts of Berlin Dr. Alfred Döblin worked as a neurologist for twenty years and then wrote at the close of the twenties the novel, *Berlin Alexanderplatz*, which more than any other writing conveys the dismal grayness of poverty.

It is the story of Franz Biberkopf, newly released from a rather long prison sentence. He comes out into a Berlin that has grown unfamiliar to him, and he now wants to be honest and live a clean life. Gradually he is again pushed down.

Döblin's description of the poor of Berlin reveals unsparingly the frightening connection between poverty and hunger, crime and unemployment. The streets and pubs of Berlin, the night fog and the raw cold near the newspaper stand in Alexanderplatz come to life in Döblin's frightening book. Franz Biberkopf cannot live honorably because he lacks support and hope. During a trip in a car he is tossed into the street by his former companions and he loses an arm. His girl is brutally strangled.

It was this world which Hitler "sanitized" in his own effective way. It was this world which the bombs tore asunder. It is this world which the magistrates of East Berlin are seeking to uproot. New streets are built, an effort is made to create another kind of world. Despite mistakes, false ornamentation, and unfortunate buildings the last mementos of Biberkopf's milieu will disappear.

When I have finished smoking P.'s Chinese cigarettes and grown weary of his self-praise I take my leave and turn off on one of Stalinallee's cross streets, where the white turns to gray and black, where there are old structures, old people, the old way of speaking and the proletarian talkativeness, far from Stalinallee's party pomp and Muscovite tile-covered structures.

At Alexanderplatz, where Döblin's hero froze and starved while selling pornographic magazines, I encounter Uwe in a restaurant. Uwe is one of the lowest civil servants in the East German hierarchy. He is eating *Bratwurst*, like me, and like me he is smoking cigarette after cigarette. I offer him a Western smoke and he stamps out his mossy, pungent Salem, a travesty on cigarettes. He speaks in short sentences:

"I do not live on Stalinallee." Coughing. "That you can be sure of. But I have heard that damned word so many times that. . . . Yes, it gets on my nerves. It's enough to drive you crazy."

"From what?"

"We are caught inside a training institution." He glances around with that furtive look that I know so well from Prague and Budapest: is anyone listening?

Fear is in him, a fear of the same type as that of Franz Biberkopf. But Döblin's hero feared the police, the law, while Uwe is afraid of the Party, Power. Perhaps it is the same fear of making a mistake, the same fear of punishment. Neither Biberkopf nor Uwe can expect reconciliation, for none is to be found.

Biberkopf's consolation stemmed only from some singularly happy hours with women.

9 *Flight and Freedom*

The only Communist regime which is in open (and uneven) competition with Western Democracy for the loyalty of citizens is that of East Germany. Because Berlin provides the possibility of a choice between two Germanies the city is, in a moral sense, a trump card for the West, a burden for the East: over half the refugees find their way out through Berlin.

It is not alone "deeply humanitarian" motives which have made the Americans so generous to Berlin. No help, however, can be so generous that the refugee camps in West Berlin can be made to look much better than prisons or concentration camps. The huge number of people who find their way to West Germany will retain a permanent mental picture of Berlin as the desolate factories and office buildings where they had to wait for their clearance before flying from Tempelhof to freedom.

In this stream of exiles East Germany loses not only its best elements, but also its worst. Most of the refugees with whom I have talked seem sunken in their shoes, crouching, smoothed down, flattened, and full of anxiety. They have sworn to become loyal citizens of the Federal Republic, they have been investigated and examined. There has been a good deal of sharp and justified criticism of tendency toward mental conformity (*Gleichschaltung*) produced by the procedure in the reception centers. But in West Berlin one frequently hears the reply: "Those who come to us are not always the best." This is sharply contradicted by statistics which show that academic and professional people are a constantly increasing element in the flood of refugees.

From the window in the Red Cross refugee home, Henri Dunant, at Askanischer Platz I can see out over East Berlin. It is 200 yards to the border. Here I sit in a little room together with K., a man in his mid-thirties, already a little stout, who has come from a medium-sized town south of Berlin. He was a salesman for television and radio sets in the city's HO-Store.

He seems timid. What he says he has already told many others.

"I had a good job and I was never exactly persecuted." (What he says seems familiar and routine to him.) "But it was painful to see how the bureaucracy stifled all initiative and how badly the business was run. But, I could have endured that.

"Then one day I tuned in the TV in the shop to a football match between England and France. I was warned for that: it was a Western game over a Western TV station. But what does a football game have to do with politics? *Das ist doch Blödsinn!* [That's idiotic!]

"Another time I tuned in the radio on some music. When the number was over I found that I had picked up NWDR in Hamburg. I got a warning for this, too, this time by the state security police. Once I was ordered to destroy 500 phonograph records because the music was offensive.

"The biggest farce was the allocation of TV receivers. Our quota was fifty per year. I assembled in good time orders from those who thought they could afford it. But when the fifty receivers arrived I had a visit from the manager of the store. He explained that certain specially deserving persons had a priority claim on TV sets. These were functionaries in the SSD, a few party bigwigs, etc. When the manager's list was finished I had only two machines left for the customers on *my* list. My two customers were happy and surprised over their good luck. They assured me that nothing like that had ever happened to them before."

"And then?"

"Now I am here with my wife. We came together. I'll get a job as a radio mechanic."

Originally it was not necessary for all the members of the family to flee together. But the new East German Law on Flight from the Republic, of December, 1957, applies certain new principles. Members of a family can be punished if it is proved that they have had knowledge of the flight plans of any relative. There are also new and more stringent rules in regard to passports. On the other hand one gets, paradoxically, the impression that the People's Police look the other way when they think that someone is planning to flee. The official East German policy is thus somewhat in contrast to actual practice, and the avenues of escape have not been closed off so effectively as was perhaps intended. In the most recent years the stream of refugees has abated somewhat, but usually it is a matter of seasonal fluctuations.

Henri Dunant at Askanischer Platz is one of the twenty-three refugee homes maintained by the Red Cross in West Berlin. The participation of other organizations in the care of refugees is insignificant. When the refugees have passed through the first check point at Marienfelde they are assigned temporarily to a refugee home. "Temporarily" can mean anything from one week to a year. They cannot go elsewhere until they have been accepted as West German citizens and been assigned housing in West Germany or Berlin. There are some refugees who have been in the homes for years without being accepted. These exceptions are outside the provisions of the West German *Notaufnahmegesetz* (Emergency Reception Law) and are not recognized as genuine political resistance fighters. They have no work permits but often find some kind of surreptitious employment in Berlin. In addition to food and shelter they receive thirty-five pfennigs per day.

The assistant manager of the Dunant home is himself a refugee. He had a private business in East Berlin but came over a year ago.

"It's not exactly cozy," I say.

"What shall we do?" he says helplessly. "Our state support is 2.85 DM per day. From that we must first deduct the refugees' daily money allowance. Then we must buy food, cooking utensils, bed clothes, clothing, beds, and then pay wages to the forty people who work in this home. To be sure, we can handle 2,000 refugees at one time, but it isn't easy to provide for them.

"We try to arrange it so that families can live together," he continues. "That is possible now because only one-fourth of the home is occupied. In an emergency situation this is impossible. We try, however, to provide some little comfort."

He opens a door to the particular attraction in the home, a wedding chamber with flower designs on the walls. From the window there is a view of ruins, and of silence.

"We have had many weddings here," he says encouragingly.

This was once the office building of the Siemens Company. It is in such buildings that the refugees sit and yearn to get away from Berlin, as far away as possible, and to experience a freedom that they do not know. And finally the day arrives when they leave Berlin and the dirty office building, and head for the waiting economic miracle, with guaranteed happiness for all.

Despite the hope and the wait suicide is not uncommon in the camp. People throw themselves down elevator shafts. Some-one meets an informer among his fellow refugees, an SED (Socialist Unity Party of Germany) man who has smuggled his way into their midst. Fights are common, sometimes murder. Refugees do not hesitate when they feel themselves threatened. Many of them have been influenced by the propaganda of the extreme Right. The paradoxical consequence of East German Communism could conceivably be that neo-Nazi tendencies would win support.

10 Marienfelde

Marienfelde lies far to the south, beyond Tempelhof and the brick tower of Ullstein's publishing house. I ride there in the S-Bahn and en route I read an East Berlin newspaper in which there is an article on the refugee problem, which summarizes a discussion out in Weissensee.

A hairdresser, Krause, from Weissensee has fled; he is a man who "together with his wife had a prosperous business at Schönstrasse 21 at Weissensee, a man who had his living and an income, and further, who owned his own automobile, television set, and motorboat; all in all: a respected, well-situated citizen of our Republic."

"Why did Krause flee?" asked the participants in the discussion. It must be a mystery to many that a man could, without a second thought, leave TV, a car, and a motor boat behind him.

Kurt Knöfler, a soldier in the People's Army, was rightfully indignant: "No matter what the motives may be, whoever supports the Bonn ruling circles in the present situation, while they are openly arming for war, betrays not only the German Democratic Republic but the entire German working class, which is engaged in a bitter struggle to preserve the peace."

As the train speeds toward Marienfelde I ask myself if Hairdresser Krause had any reason to be loyal to the working class. Perhaps he had no sympathy for it? Perhaps he had had his fill of the workers' and peasants' state? And as for the soldier,

Knöfler, was he perhaps girding himself against an inner urge to flee? After all, more than 600 soldiers of the People's Army and 3,000 People's Police fled from the East in 1957.

When I get out of the train at Marienfelde I notice some large signs which warn the passengers to awaken any sleepers on the train and point out that West Berlin ends here. The S-Bahn has the disadvantage that its lines terminate in the Zone, that is, in East Germany, rather than in East Berlin. The violation of the border by an innocent Berliner (even in his sleep) might result in long inquiries and arrest for one day.

A tree-shaded avenue leads to the low buildings where 500 persons are employed to register and interview the refugees. I can see people walking along the avenue with suitcases and bundles. At the entrance they file into a narrow corridor where I can see them sitting with listless and immobile faces. They are awaiting a doctor's examination, an interrogation, and then more interrogations. The route to West German freedom goes through American, British, French, Federal German, and other "information bureaus," where the autobiographies of the refugees are patiently heard.

It is said that every refugee must repeat his life history at least fifty times before he is finally cleared.

The camp area is filled with simple four-story buildings, which will be occupied by ordinary Berliners later, when Germany is reunited. No one tells me just when they expect this to happen.

"What do you do with all of these buildings?" I ask my guide.

"The Federal Republic's central offices of investigation and inspection operate here. Then we have temporary quarters for those who are about to leave; they gather here and are taken in busses to Tempelhof. And then some refugees live here who are not yet placed in a home in Berlin. Over there"—he points with a shoulder to one of the buildings—"we have quarters for women 18-25 years of age. There are some doubtful characters among them."

No one tells me what the Western Allies do with this mass of interrogation material. More than a half million refugees have been funneled through Berlin since 1949, and 13 per cent have been allowed to stay in West Berlin. But what does one do with half a million unreliable autobiographies? It is understandable that the refugees put as political a complexion as possible on their motives. Only a hypocrite could doubt that crasser motives play a part in most cases—a longing to get to a richer country, dreams about getting an automobile quickly, followed next year by a trip to Italy in a tourist bus, or simply the desperate urge to stop giving a damn about society. Until the next war breaks out.

The reception center is encircled by a high steel fence. Just outside ordinary Berliners live in ordinary German villas. These are sleepy-looking houses in the afternoon sun, but inside the steel fence there is plenty of life and movement.

Now in the spring some 150 to 200 refugees are received per day, but in the summer the figure rises sharply. Even 200 per day means that in a year there is a population equivalent to a medium-sized city. The population of East Germany is declining year after year. If Germany is still divided in the year 2000 there won't be many inhabitants in the eastern part.

This is a calculation which rests upon the undoubtedly false premise that both the population and the regime in East Germany are unchangeable. As a matter of fact there are, even now, people who have returned to the East, fled back again; refugees who for years have been in doubt as to which is their Germany. The movement of refugees to the East, moreover, is certainly not composed exclusively of Communists who are suffering from their illegal status in West Germany, but also unemployed mine workers, and even academic people. However, East Germany continues to show an enormous population decline, which justifies one part of the East's propaganda: "There is no unemployment here!"

Yes, there are lots of positions open, or positions that will be open!

I mentioned that the refugees seem depersonalized, gray. In the East they have been exposed to political pressure which has tried to impose upon them *one* party, *one* will, *one* concept of the social order. Instead of freedom they have had to listen to slogans such as "future and well being," "socialism," etc. They are now trying to free themselves from this totalitarian demand upon the individual.

Presumably the refugee will become a conformist in West Germany. But he has freely chosen the norms to which he will be subordinated and loyal. That is why he prefers the West, even though he is faced there in the same way with an illusion of freedom.

The Red Cross has its biggest refugee home in the factory of the Lorenz firm, which is behind the Ullstein building in Tempelhof. It can accommodate 8,000 persons at one time, and 380,000 persons have lived there. It is refugee industry, with long, bleak corridors and giant sleeping rooms. I talk to an old worker, who is afraid that he might utter dangerous words:

"Naturally, I belong to no party, I'm non-political. I have lived in Berlin during my entire lifetime."

He is a railroad worker, and has come over with his whole family. The others are already in West Germany. Despite the fact that he calls himself unpolitical he talks about political reasons for his flight, among other things his participation in the June uprising of 1953.

"That day I was working on Potsdamer Platz. A man came cycling along and said that we were about to go on strike. We quit working and joined the demonstrators. When the uprising had been put down we started to work again."

It was that simple.

"I am going to live near Bonn," he says proudly.

Only one of those with whom I speak has been searched for by the East German security police. The charge read: An anti-Soviet attitude and boycott propaganda. His wife came with him but his mother stayed in East Berlin. He is one of those who want to live in West Berlin so that he can see his mother. While we were talking a loud voice echoes in the halls from the intercom.

This is one of many German tragedies.

The others, too, have gone through the machinery of the Red Cross. For example, some 150 volumes are being brought out in a series, which contains the names of all Germans who were reported missing during and after the Second World War, but whose fate remains unknown. Emigrants from Poland and war prisoners from the Soviet Union are also received in Berlin.

"On the outskirts of Berlin we have seven homes for children who have been sent from Poland. Their parents are German and have never seen them again. The children have grown up in Polish homes. Most of them don't know a word of German."

This mass handling of human lives needs, of course, some organizational apparatus. I pay a visit to West Berlin's Office (Senat) of Labor and Social Welfare at Fehrbelliner Platz and am ushered into the office of Frau Scharfschwerdt.

She sits behind a desk as she talks.

Frau Scharfschwerdt is fifty years old, with a broad face and body, and somewhat resembles the idealized peasant mothers who sell picture postcards at folklore exhibits. Her dark blue dress is set off by a single ornament, a large silver-colored spider.

Behind her there is a wash bowl, a radio, and on the window sill a number of flower pots. There is a calendar on the wall in front of her, and in addition to the date it provides a little motto of no mean significance: "Be nice to one another."

The folders on Frau Scharfschwerdt's table are in good order. In addition to these there are some pencils, and the latest edition of *Berliner Zeitung*, which contains the latest revelations on Queen Soraya and her relations with the King of Iran.

I have plenty of opportunity to observe Frau Scharfschwerdt since I need hardly open my mouth, except possibly to gape in surprise. She is a living IBM machine, for whom the refugee problem has been reduced to a matter of statistics. She knows everything about the difficulties in West Berlin, about pensioners and the unemployed, about "the brothers and sisters in the East Zone," and about invalids.

A gigantic flow of statistics emerges from her.

She speaks about life in the free world.

"Even State Secretary Dulles and his wife visited Marienfelde. They were deeply shaken."

She talks about the old people in West Berlin.

"In West Berlin two employed persons must support six old folks, while in West Germany four employed persons need support only two old folks.

"The Communists refer to 'victims of fascism,' we to 'the politically and racially persecuted.' "

What she says would fill a novel. But it would be an extremely dull novel even though fully as long as Musil's *The Man Without Qualities*. I have no doubt that her feelings are genuine and sound. But she is a noteworthy example of the unhappy German fondness for transforming human and moral problems into technical and organizational ones. Thus I hear:

"So you see how well we have solved the problem of transporting and handling half a million refugees!"

While I had hoped instead to hear:

"Flight is always a tragedy." (Especially since the freedom to which one flees is not uncontaminated).

11   Otto John

Otto John is the embodiment of a German neurosis, the psychology of flight and betrayal. I refer to the tragic split in personality which is occasioned by the wish to serve *Germany*, and the simultaneous consciousness that Germany, in the old meaning of the word, no longer exists.

In the two German states of today there are emerging two different languages, two different cultures, two separate worlds. The neurosis springs also from the knowledge that neither of the Germanies corresponds to the faith and the hopes of those who believed in another new order after the collapse.

John was born in 1910 and from his early years became one of the many European intellectuals who saw the root of all evil in the military in general, and among generals in particular. His experiences during the war can hardly have diminished his loathing for the military.

He had been in close contact with the men of the July 20 attempt on Hitler's life in 1944. Warned in time of their failure, he had been able to flee at the last moment to Madrid. There it seems he was hunted by both the Germans and the English, until the latter won and immediately employed him.

His brother was executed in the big purge following the July 20 incident.

John returned to his destroyed Germany (which, in accordance with the victors' decision, had ceased to exist) as an English agent. He served his foreign employers until he became the chief for Verfassungsschutzamt (Office for the Protection of the Constitution) of the West German republic in Cologne. Neither the street nor the five-story house in which he worked had a name.

In the summer of 1953 an East German journalist wrote of John: "The true German patriots will see to it that Dr. John is brought to account before the court of the people for his crimes." According to the same source John had reestablished the Gestapo traditions of both Himmler and Kaltenbrunner, and improved them with American help. For East German politicians Otto John stood out as the arch-traitor, the personification of all the evil forces in Western Germany.

If one reads carefully the statement that John released in East Berlin on August 11, 1954, after his sensational flight, one can distinguish the various historic experiences which influenced him.

In June of the same year he had visited the United States and met, among others, Allen Dulles. He participated in the tenth anniversary ceremonies of July 20, and must then have reflected upon the execution of his brother and his own flight to Spain. He pointed out that the number of former Wehrmacht officers in the West German administration was noticeably high. He expressed his concern about the so-called Gehlen organization, which was later officially incorporated into the Bonn government. His speech was not full of hate. Many Social Democrats and Free Democrats in West Germany would have approved his views. But John's betrayal (this time against the West) lay in the fact that the statement was made in East Berlin, in the Haus der Presse on Friedrichstrasse.

I was a witness in Berlin to the tremendous stir raised by John's treason against the Federal Republic. His position had been so powerful that his flight at least reawakened the discussion about reunion.

What John had perceived was very simple: in the two German states and in the two Berlins all the best and worst aspects of Germanism are represented. But honor and guilt, goodness and evil, are by no means divided in the way that most Germans believe.

John is depicted as a schizophrenic, spilt by powerful tensions. He was cosmopolitan and German like many intellectuals who got their training during the Weimar period. The presence in him at the same time of two almost irreconcilable qualities occasioned some part of his anxiety for Germany.

A description from the summer of 1954 says:

Deep chasms and tormenting struggles were evident within him— at one moment a charming, warm humor, in the next moment a deeply pensive, almost depressive frame of mind. Like many thoughtful Germans this educated and widely experienced man . . . showed how torn he was between the Germany that could have been and the Germany that in fact is. He knew what the past had done to her, and what dangers the future might bring her. . . . He understood very well the disaster-fraught aspect of his country and its tendency toward delusions of grandeur, and he could speak clearly and unhesitatingly about them.

According to John's own words he wanted his flight to contribute to reunification. During his stay in the East (he lived in a house near Berlin) until December 12, 1955, he must have observed that the East German policy was wholly irreconcilable with the political liberalism to which he had paid homage at his

press conference in East Berlin. John saw two Germanies, both
of them on the way to military rearmament, both bound by the
irreconcilability of hate.

John did not want to harm anyone. He did not turn over the
names of persons who were living in East Germany as secret
employees of his former bureau, the Verfassungsschutzamt.

The "court of the people," of which the East German journalist dreamed as early as 1953, turned out to be the Administrative Court in Karlsruhe (West Germany), where, following
his return to West Germany, John was sentenced in 1956 to
four years in a correctional institution after being held a year
in prison.

His career has undoubtedly come to an end. But does this
mean that all the ideas which possessed him will die out and be
forgotten? By his fruitless effort to protest (possibly under the
influence of drugs), by his sudden and surprising decision,
John has shown that there is a doubt in Germany, a gnawing
concern for the political future of the country.

In the courtyard of a building on Bendlerstrasse in West Berlin, where the Wehrmacht once had its headquarters, there is
a sculptured figure of a man in fetters. This is a memorial to the
more than 2,000 Germans who were executed after the unsuccessful assassination effort of July 20, 1944. It is also a memorial
to John's brother.

If one passes Bendlerstrasse one can glimpse the monument,
modest and low, through the gateway of the courtyard. Most
of those who pass that way do not turn their heads, but they
surely know that the monument is there and that the figure is
shackled. Perhaps even these pedestrians, too, are ashamed;
perhaps there is uncertainty behind their broad, calm exteriors.

I know this to be true. All of these feelings, of flight and of
freedom, of anxiety and of helpless courage, are well known to
the inhabitants of Berlin. The positive quality of these citizens,

if one compares them to those of West Germany, lies in the honest hope that the division is temporary, a dream that will pass.

The capacity of Berliners to forget is not so well developed as that of their countrymen in the West. Nevertheless, they despise John. They see something disturbing in him: the possibility of treason. Treason is discussed often in Berlin. He who calls into question the absolute purity of the ideology of freedom is a traitor. He who doubts is suspected.

This interpretation of Otto John's fate is hypothetical and, furthermore, somewhat heroic. It clothes him in qualities which perhaps he never had. He was pardoned on July 27, 1958, by President Heuss. In the same year a trial was concluded in Karlsruhe, which was connected with John's flight in 1954. Specifically, he charged his former friend, the gynecologist Dr. Wolfgang Wohlgemuth on Uhlandstrasse in West Berlin, with kidnapping. John charged that Wohlgemuth had given him injections and then taken him forcibly across the border in the summer of 1954. But Wohlgemuth, who is an elegant and self-confident man in his fifties, and who had lived a strange life between East and West, was cleared. It is thus legally established that John went to the East of his own free will, just as he returned of his own free will. There was no third Germany.

12   *Bernauer Strasse*

A rewarding subject for those who like to explore the borders in Berlin: Bernauer Strasse, the dividing line between Wedding (French sector) and Mitte (East sector). The street goes through the workingmen's quarters; the sidewalk on the south side is East, while the street and the sidewalk on the north side are West.

I start from the North Station, formerly Stettiner Bahnhof, where the earlier long-distance train traffic is now only memory in the midst of rusty rails, unused warehouses, and ruins.

At this end of the street there is a brick wall on the East side (I am here using the political terms East-West). It does not conceal a prison, but only the graveyard of the parish of Sophie.

The destruction has eliminated a number of buildings. Many of the shops on the East side have HO-signs. The newspaper stand on the West side accepts subscriptions to Western newspapers, which can be picked up daily and for which East currency is accepted. The movable wooden sales stands which one can see frequently in West Berlin are here, too: the quality of merchandise is not very high—sort of beads for the natives (the residents in the East sector).

The pedestrians on the West side are more numerous, and the shop windows are filled with coffee and fruit, the consumer goods most in demand by the residents in the East. On some side streets I encounter stands where money can be exchanged. Currencies quickly acquire new owners.

There has been more construction on the West side, but the façades look just as dreary on both sides, the sidewalks give evidence of equally bad care. The police of two foreign worlds patrol their respective sides of the street. The only color one sees on Bernauer Strasse is on the advertising placards or in the illustrated papers on the West side.

That's the way it looks one foggy day.

The differences can take on shocking proportions when they are described by some persons. I have seen a Western newspaper story in pictures which very cleverly contrasts the two sides of the street. On the West side nothing but new buildings, advertisements for merchandise, gay magazine covers. On the East side HO's clumsy advertising techniques, gray news stands with gray papers (yes, they are actually gray), decay and poverty. The contrast between happiness and misery.

It is a well-known fact that both sides suffer from the partition, but the heightened picture story shows a serious one-sidedness in the presentation of facts.

This one-sidedness in describing the situation on the street is no less noticeable in Eastern descriptions. This is evident in Franz Kain's prize-winning miniature novel, *Romeo und Julia an der Bernauer Strasse* (Aufbau Verlag 1955). Kain seeks to describe the contrast between the two sides of the street at a time when a resident in the West could still go into a Bierstube in the East, and when the personal contacts were somewhat better than they are today.

A young worker on the East side gets acquainted with a girl on the other side of the street. To begin with it is not a harmonious association. It turns out that the couple's families are deadly enemies. The two fathers were co-workers and Social Democrats until 1946. Then came the break. The father in the East joined the newly-founded SED, but the other remained true to the Social Democrats.

The explanation given for the fact that there are more pedestrians on the West side of the street is as follows: these are the jobless of West Berlin who have time to go walking!

The acquaintance of these two young people consists at first of shopping together on the East side. He has an *Ausweis,* and she takes the things home and profits by the currency exchange but does not tell her staunch father that he is eating food from the East—for he would not hear of any such thing.

For the residents on the East side (but only for them) the possibility is conjured up that one can live without fear and without want. Heiner, who is Romeo in the story, saves his money and buys a motorcycle, while Helga, the drama's Juliet, is unemployed and sees no hope for the future.

The two young people begin to quarrel about politics. Heiner, who up to this time had been relatively ignorant of these matters, suddenly becomes an active defender of the system in the East. He takes Helga to Strausberger Platz to admire the white rows of buildings on Stalinallee. Imposing!

In Helga's circle of friends there is also a man who is engaged in smuggling large sums of Eastern currency to the West. Heiner hears of this and reports him to the authorities. The swindler is arrested.

So long as Kain confines himself to simple conversations, daily happenings on the job, or the free hours at the Bierstube, he is knowledgeable about his subject and his story has a ring of authenticity. But as soon as he feels compelled to construct a political explanation he becomes awkward and ensnared in the rhetorical flourishes of propaganda.

With just as much insistence as his counterparts in the West, Kain asserts the thesis that a reunion of Bernauer Strasse (by which he means Berlin and Germany) is possible only on *our* terms. Only our system can give the people the greatest happiness, the highest living standard, and the purest peace!

13   Borders

Berlin has four kinds of boundary lines.

The only unseen ones are those between the Western sectors. The signs have been removed, although the three Allied powers have their military establishments in their respective sectors.

The inner and visible boundary between East and West is in the heart of the city. There one can see the signs, the police, the barriers. But this boundary does not prevent freedom of movement.

Thirdly, West Berlin borders upon East Germany. Of the 156-kilometer boundary of the West city, 110 kilometers face upon East Germany, with 157 booms, barricades, and earthen walls. . . .

Finally, East Berlin naturally has its boundary upon East Germany.

The residents of West Berlin can leave their island and take certain roads to the West, or go by plane or train, without special permits. East Berliners can travel into East Germany. This is the extent of freedom of movement.

I am riding in one of the many radio patrol cars of the West Berlin police in order to see these boundaries. The police commissioner in my company is a tall, broad-shouldered man with a straight back. The Aryan experts would have called him a Nordic type. He was in the army for twenty years, but after his release from captivity he entered the police force, since at that time there was no German army. He has two children, and he has dreams of building a house with a garden, some apple trees, and a few berry bushes.

"All genuine Berliners have the same dream," he states quietly but firmly. But he himself hails from Pomerania.

He has no desire to own a car.

It is the lunch hour and the city is quiet. Our trip is not disturbed by any urgent alarms. Some petty thefts and auto accidents are reported but they are not in the district in which we are riding. Both the chauffeur and the police commissioner are proud of the technical equipment, of the fact that sixty radio cars patrol the city constantly, and that West Berlin has 19,500 policemen. Three thousand of these are in the barracks.

This entire force of uniformed men is, in the first instance, under the command of the famous police chief, Stumm, who was involved in the gigantic Oberjat scandal. But Stumm is still in office. In fact, and formally, the city Commandants of the Western Allies are the highest authorities over the West Berlin police. The city is still under occupation and obeys the instructions of the imaginary Control Council. A drunk and disorderly French soldier cannot be arrested by the police of West Berlin. They must call the French military police.

An item for observation on the boundary question: the Zehlendorf district in the southwest where the line between West Berlin and East Germany has been cut through an old area of Berlin and capriciously created a Western island in the middle of the East—the little Steinstücken with a few hundred inhabitants.

The residents must pass through a bit of East German territory before they reach their homes.

When the trees of Berlin are in foliage the boundary here is hard to see, so hard in fact that American soldiers who were putting up warning signs inadvertently wandered across the line and were arrested.

In order to reach Dreilinden, the last Western boundary control on one of the main arteries to the west, the radio car must make a long detour along the Teltow Canal, where middle-aged men are sitting peacefully with their fishing rods, unconcerned that their fish are Eastern fish in Eastern waters. The road continues on a narrow westerly tongue of land open only to official traffic. The main road is barred earlier by the East Zone. It is neither permissible nor advisable for Western police cars to drive over the enemy's territory.

Dreilinden is located on a high and pleasant spot near a bridge over the Teltow Canal. The stretch of road here which belongs to the West is only a few hundred yards in length. There is a parking lot, a café, administration buildings, and storehouses. During the rush hour there is a great deal of traffic, but now it is quiet. Western autos on the way to the Federal Republic may not stop or leave the main highway. It is forbidden to stroll for pleasure along the roadside.

At the control point there are a number of huge milk trucks (price: 100,000 German marks each) which furnish West Berlin with West German milk. It sells for 43 pfennig a liter, but without a state subsidy the price would be one mark per liter.

There is a sort of holiday atmosphere in the administration buildings. In the American office one soldier is trying to work while another has the radio going full blast: jazz. In the British office a soldier is sleeping behind the counter, with parts of his body strategically spread over several chairs. Nothing is happening.

It does not take long before one accepts as quite natural—and never again questions—the fact that young Germans in different uniforms stand on each side of a boundary which was laid out by the victors, but which has now been accepted by the Germans themselves.

Right next to the subway station Düppel-Machnow (also in Zehlendorf) is the boundary crossing to the little community

Border between East Germany and West Berlin, creating a no-man's land

Two faces of Berlin

Above, small gardens; below, Stalinallee

of Klein-Machnow, which political geography specifies as belonging to East Germany, but whose residents must ride through West Berlin in order to reach their jobs.

The East German administration is vexed constantly by the fact that the inhabitants of Klein-Machnow can do their buying in the West while going to or from their places of employment. Plans have been broached to close the passage and put in shuttle traffic with busses so that the residents will not have any excuse to go to West Berlin. But the more one gets to know these people the more one becomes convinced that such a measure would only swell the psychological deficit of the East German regime.

The People's Police are laying out barbed wire in front of the passageway. An entirely new set of barbed wire is being spun between East Germany and West Berlin. The guards check papers and peek into handbags, but otherwise the situation is practically normal. On the West side there is a promenade on which a few people are walking, on the East side the same promenade. If the signs were not there one would not suspect a thing.

The situation has become normal; the boundary is only a boundary. I visit some other outposts on the long boundary facing East Germany. In a little guardhouse surrounded by colorful flower beds there is an older policeman sitting by an open window. His colleague is at his post outside. Out in the flat one can see a barbed wire fence, and beyond that in the woods some buildings used by the People's Police. The two policemen here report that nothing ever happens, no one crosses the border. One day an officer from the People's Police had crept under the barbed wire and gone reconnoitering. When he returned he caught himself on the barbed wire and his companions had to clip him off.

At Glienicker See the boundary cuts right through farms, the walls of houses, and courtyards. Chickens may freely hop across the line, but people may not. They are watched carefully and are as far apart as on two separate planets.

The police in West Berlin must do more than watch the border. When the government in the East banned the import of Western newspapers the West retaliated, and East German brochures were confiscated. Demonstrators from East Berlin are arrested and their papers examined. And frequently they are given food.

I eat lunch at the police canteen in Tempelhof. The private automobiles of the police are parked in rows outside: how lucky we are, how rich!

At least that is what the commissioner from Pomerania thinks.

14   Humanism and Communism

The uninitiated may believe that "border-crossers" (*Grenz-gänger*) means deserters, runaways, or something else not very complimentary. But these are Berliners who live in the West and work in the East (12,000) or live in the East and work in the West (40,000). Their number has naturally been many times as great, but the blockade and the final partition has shrunk the number to a small per cent of Berlin's population of three and one-half million.

It is possible that the number of *Grenzgänger* will become even smaller. The East German government insists that the

40,000 who are working in the West are skilled craftsmen who are needed in the East. On the other hand, it is certain that East Berlin would not like to lose the 12,000 who are working there. Half of them are employed by the S-Bahn in West Berlin, but their wages are paid by the East German Reichsbahndirektion. The others are engineers, artists, and intellectuals who are sorely needed by the East regime—not alone for their prestige value.

Coercive measures have begun against the 40,000 workers. Some are being given notice on their apartments and thus presented with the choice of moving to West Berlin or of taking employment on the East side, where there is a labor shortage. Most of the unemployed in West Berlin prefer to accept employment benefits than take a job in the Eastern sector. Furthermore, most of the jobless are former white-collar employees of the former all-German government.

The 52,000 *Grenzgänger* have a common problem: the currency. The 40,000 who receive their pay in West Berlin must exchange everything over 500 Westmarks of their monthly salary to Ostmarks at a rate of 1:1. By this means the West Berlin Senate is enabled to exchange 90 per cent of the salary earned by West Berliners in East Berlin to Westmarks at a rate of 1:1. It can be said, therefore, that the border-crossers get no benefits from partition, at least not financial.

But there are some who find pleasure in it. For example, many convinced Communists look upon their service to East Germany as a higher calling, an act of grace.

This is true of H., for example, who in a slightly shaky voice confides his personal history to me.

"My father was a civil servant," he says gravely, "but he was also a thinker." H. invites me to share his Weinbrand Auslese. We toast to friendship, although I am somewhat puzzled as to what friendship.

"My father was a state civil servant," he goes on, "and a humanist. He had faith in Lessing's ideal of Germany, the humanistic ideal. My father was not only a humanist, he was also a Communist. He was arrested in 1934, taken to Buchenwald, and executed two years later."

Despite the fact that H. is discussing serious and tragic events, he seems to be excessively histrionic and maudlin.

"Ever since the day my father was executed I have known where I must stand. During the war, I was an officer. And finally I, too, was arrested and taken to Buchenwald. Soviet troops liberated me.

"I have not been a humanist. I am only a Communist."

"Can one not be both?"

"Unfortunately, no. No, not today. The dividing lines are altogether too sharp."

H.'s antipathy to what he calls humanism is presumably due in part to the fact that he identifies it with pacifism. He is dominated by a front-line psychosis, he is professionally geared to conflict. The boundary lines of Berlin are a part of his own personality. His very existence is premised upon their validity.

"Another Weinbrand? For friendship!"

Frau S., red-faced, sweaty, and with unkempt hair, is sitting in the S-Bahn train in the station on Friedrichstrasse. She has a bag in her lap, and is perhaps fifty years old. There is a hairy wart on her right chin. She doesn't stir, breathes heavily as though in wrath. She is angry. She begins to talk as soon as the train gets under way, and since I happen to be her seat companion she talks to me.

It seems that a member of the People's Police had come into the car when the train stopped in the Friedrichstrasse Station. He forced her out to the platform and began to search her.

"On the platform?"

"No, in the office of the SSD. These swine, these young

whelps, these fresh officials. To come right into *our* Berlin, and to search *me*. And with what right? After all, I am a free person."

I make no attempt to answer, since she herself ought to know why the People's Police looked into her bag.

"We don't have any freedom anymore," she says with a somewhat relieved tone as we enter Lehrter Stadtbahnhof, West.

"I should have gone home over the West sector, but this route is shorter. I was altogether too comfortable."

"What did you have in your bag?"

"Coffee, fruit, and chocolate." She empties the contents on the seat.

"Those devils never get to drink decent coffee except in West Berlin. That's why they're so greedy. But they didn't take anything from me. How nice," she sighs, "to be over on the West side again. It's ridiculous and humiliating to be searched in the middle of a city."

She complains about the boundaries, the division.

But there are many who see something positive in the fact that, though there is a boundary, it can be crossed. Better an open border in Berlin than an iron curtain.

This is undoubtedly correct. But the whole thing has an opposite and considerably darker side, which is discussed in West Berlin only in very fine print.

15   The Agents

An S-Bahn train on the way to Westkreuz. Serious old faces, women in black, and a number of men with worn caps, moustaches, and stumps of cigars. A German atmosphere, of sausages and cutlets.

Suddenly an alarm clock sends out a noisy clatter. A boy, perhaps thirteen years of age, gets up quickly and goes back to the baggage racks, and with shaking fingers opens a small bag. The noise ceases.

The boy goes blushingly to his seat. The old ladies in black seem somewhat astonished about the smiles which have cracked their dry, tired faces. Someone laughs out loud.

Then the train stops. Passengers get on and off. A teen-age boy dashes in with an armful of gaudy papers and shouts hoarsely: *"Tarantel, Tarantel."*

Little attention is paid to him, but he manages to hand some copies to two girls in their teens. They thumb through them quickly and then hand them back. The boy is angry.

At the next station he gets off and continues his huckstering in the next car.

I get out also and take a bus which goes down Kurfürstendamm. I get off at the corner of Joachimsthaler Street.

I have decided to visit the publisher of *Tarantel*, the Heinrich Bär Publishing House, Ltd., at Joachimsthaler Street 28, Berlin, W 15.

The company has large quarters but one cannot tell this from the outside. The main entrance is in a new building; above it is the Indian Consulate. When I ring, a cold eye stares me in the face. The door is opened and I ask to see the assistant managing director, Herr Klaus Kunkel.

It is early in the morning, but when I find myself in Kunkel's office a few minutes later there is a glass of brandy set for each of us. We toast, although I still don't know what for. I am handed a packet of *Tarantels,* a pile of political caricatures, and various news releases. The boss is unfortunately not available. I promise to come back later.

When I return to my pension on Grolmannstrasse, the help as well as some of the guests are busy. They are listening to the debate in the Federal Parliament on atomic rearmament. The radio is turned up loudly and between the various exchanges from Bonn I can hear *Jawohl* and *Nein.* Franz Josef Strauss is defending rearmament—with Bavarian energy and oversimplified demagogy. He links the question of atomic weapons in West Germany to the issue of unity within the Parliament, to the common front against Communism.

He gets applause, but not in my pension. I close the door to my room and bury myself in *Tarantel.* There is a taste of brandy in my mouth.

The magazine comes out once a month in an issue of eight to sixteen pages, with many colors and in pocket size. The number published varies from 200,000 to 250,000 per issue, depending on the political situation in East Germany. A certain number of copies is distributed free in West Berlin newspaper kiosks situated near the sector boundary; others are available on the streets where East Berliners do their shopping. The balance is sent to East Germany by various routes. *Tarantel* calls itself "The Satirical Monthly of the Soviet Zone."

I hope that this is not Defense Minister Strauss' dream of the perfect anti-Communist device.

Tarantel gives in coarse but rather clever form the so-called inside information from the Soviet Union and "the Zone." Important events in East Germany are recounted and life there is portrayed as hell on earth. Frequent emphasis is given to the theme that conditions in Poland, Czechoslovakia, and other People's Democracies are much freer than in East Germany.

Everything is presented in the form of anecdotes or drawings.

Insofar as I can comprehend it, such an activity as that of *Tarantel* can *possibly* have the effect of inducing in East Germans a feeling of unlimited insecurity, fear, and disgust. But isn't their own regime, in that case, a much stronger cause for their disgust? Can't the East Germans, if they wish, laugh at their governing authorities without reading *Tarantel?* What is the purpose of all this?

The Tarantel-Press (one of the company's numerous names) also publishes so-called special numbers of *Neues Deutschland* and of *Eulenspiegel,* the East German satirical journal. The quality of these copies is no better than that of the originals despite the fact that Herr Kunkel served as acting editor of *Eulenspiegel* before he shifted to Bär's.

Some people can change their colors in a day.

A special number of *Tarantel* was issued on the fortieth anniversary of the October Revolution. A million and a half copies were printed in many languages, and it was even translated into Hindustani (of all languages!) so that the population of India might receive the blessing of anti-Communism in the style of West Berlin and Heinrich Bär.

Sometimes in the evening on Kurfürstendamm I run into a stout teen-ager in a dark overcoat who waves a copy of *Tarantel* and offers it to me.

"This is *Tarantel,*" he said the first time we met. "It is a magazine directed against the East."

"I am acquainted with it," I said. "I have read it."

"You are obviously not from Berlin?" he comments. "You can

have *Tarantel* for nothing. But anyhow, Sir, is it possible that you have a few marks?"

"Yes, how come?" I am beginning to get interested.

"You understand, I am working against Communism and the East here in the West. But I live in the Zone, in Potsdam. I don't have a job. And I don't have any money for food. So I've got to beg."

"Can't you get a job in Potsdam and quit trying to sell *Tarantel?*"

"Well, you understand, I'm against the East," he repeats stubbornly, and waves his magazines again.

I fail to see any purpose in the whole thing. But he gets two marks. The next time he tries the same trick, but he is unhappy when he recognizes me.

I was grandly welcomed on my second visit to the Tarantel-Press.

I was taken to the founder, the chief, the fiery spirit, the drive shaft, Heinrich Bär—a small, dark-haired, swarthy, narrow-shouldered man with spectacles, a man with inexhaustible energy which is discharged about him in quick shock waves. He delivers rapid suggestions, which have all the earmarks of commands, after which his co-workers stumble out of the room with a sort of glassy stare in their eyes to act on the matter. Action is Bär's motto; he seems prepared either to jump on me with clenched fists or fall forgivingly on my neck.

After having sat in an East German concentration camp for three years he founded his press. He has seemingly a built-in propeller in his mouth. A small moustache gives him the appearance of a parlor hero—or a card sharp.

"It is better to get all your money from one source than to try to collect it from many. That is why we distribute *Tarantel* free."

This is Bär's fundamental view on the question of finances. He does concede that American and German money—*private, of course!*—is invested in the enterprise. As far as I know the capital comes from large German and American industrial concerns.

It must be terribly difficult to oppose Bär, what with his thrusting energy, his unconstrained temperament, and his go-getting spirit. I have a kind of sympathy for the man: he is undoubtedly an artist, but just as surely stark mad. If he has any irony about himself, the dark glasses effectively conceal it.

Work at the Heinrich-Bär-Verlag (another name for the company) is well organized and technically tip-top. On one wall I see maps of the distribution centers in West Berlin and East Germany. A large cabinet is filled with address plates for everyone from professors to agricultural laborers in East Germany. The enterprise has its own translation service, post office, photo laboratory, picture morgue, etc.

My tour of the place would be the fulfillment of the wildest dream of a member of the East German security police.

In Bär's work room I find awaiting me more brandy, Coca-Cola, coffee, as well as cigarettes propped in a gold-plated holder that resembles a Christmas tree.

"Do you think I'm a Nazi?" asks Bär.

"No, why?"

"Well, there you are. No one has ever charged that I was a Nazi."

Then he proceeds to elaborate upon another basic theme: "You must understand that we have a special task. Our writing is more ruthless and more caustic for the reason that we live *behind* the iron curtain. But we try for complete objectivity. The information and material we use is carefully scrutinized. We do not want to incite discontent. We spread factual information. We use satire in order to achieve our goal. Our goal is to redeem seventeen million Germans who are living in slavery. Our second goal is to win back the former German territories which are now administered by Russians and Poles. We want these stolen territories returned."

"That's no small order," I reply.

"No," says Heinrich Bär.

His enterprise suggests a giant, well-ordered nursery, where a boy has suddenly hit on the idea of conquering the world with a hand-painted toy elephant. Heinrich Bär is the man who, riding on his multi-colored hobby horse, *Tarantel,* is going to liberate seventeen million slaves and force Moscow to her knees. Can it be possible that his foreign employers believe this also?

Bär has really earned a medal from Walter Ulbricht, who has been presented with an excellent propaganda point; to wit, the Western policy of reunification. But the Heinrich-Bär Publishing House is, after all, not so childish as to think that its activities enhance the luster of West Berlin. This is the Cold Warrior division, indefatigable in its cunning, a generously underwritten branch of the economic life of West Berlin.

"Granted that the cold war campaign is being conducted brilliantly," writes Richard Crossman. "Granted that the Communists deserve no sympathy. Yet I still want to know what good this campaign does either to the Americans who finance it or to the West Germans who carry it out. Since we are not prepared to march our troops across the frontier and help the East Germans expel their Communist rulers, what is the point of organizing a resistance movement?"

But Heinrich Bär and Klaus Kunkel raise their glasses: "Skol, isn't that what you say in the Northern countries?"

16   Competing Enterprises

"The Berlin branch of U. S. Naval Intelligence was established a number of years ago, although no one knew exactly what the connection was between Berlin and naval espionage." This is being told to me by one of my friends, and if the story is not true, it is at least *ben trovato*:

"An effort was made to come up with some really flashy operation right away. And what is sufficiently flashy for American naval intelligence? It proved to be an effort to filch the *Fahndungsbuch* (list of those wanted) of the East German security service. This was an extremely interesting and extremely secret list. Through a combination of skill, American dollars (changed into Westmarks), and beginner's luck the office was actually able to get hold of the documents. Rival agencies just expressed surprise, and waited for a copy of the list. But their surprise was greater when U. S. Naval Intelligence, instead of permitting others to make use of the list, sent it to some unknown place in the U. S. A. far beyond the reach of competitors.

"Many of the bureaus here," says my friend, "work as though they were in a competitive sport. Furthermore, they are all convinced that a third world war is right around the corner. Peace is for them a transitory thing."

There has been a great deal of speculation about the number of centers for agents and spies in West Berlin. According to reliable reports they number more than eighty. Most of the twenty-four accredited military missions in West Berlin have their own espionage bureaus. Because of mistakes made by these bureaus the freedom of thousands of East Germans has been jeopardized or sacrificed for an end which is more than vague.

In June, 1959, the *Berliner Zeitung* in East Berlin published a long and detailed list of Western "spy nests" in West Berlin. Included in the list was the address of the Czechoslovakian military mission in West Berlin, Podbielski Allee 54.

All of this is a tragi-comical fact.

Who worries about the young East Germans, who are opponents of the totalitarian regime and are therefore induced to take bombs, poisons, and arms into East Germany? Is there any concern for human lives when refugees hear that they cannot be accepted as West German citizens if they do not first perform some dangerous mission on the East side? Some who have refused to participate in spy activities have simply been tossed into prison.

This is the dark side of freedom.

Out in Nikolassee, in a quiet suburb, at a safe distance from the boundary, there was formerly a house which was carefully guarded and enclosed by barbed wire. This was *Kampfgruppe gegen Unmenschlichkeit* (Fighting Group for the Struggle against Inhumanity).

It was founded in order to give advice and help to refugees. At first it had a kind of positive purpose. In the years around 1948 it tried to find out how many persons had been condemned to hard labor, especially in the newly reconstructed houses of correction, for example in the reopened prisons in Buchenwald and Sachsenhausen. What, in fact, happened when the Russians turned over the administration to the Germans?

KgU quickly lost its first chief, Rainer Hildebrandt, who was replaced in 1952 by Ernst Tillich, under whose leadership the organization developed some frightening methods.

Opponents of the West Berlin variety of the Cold War won their first victory in 1958 when Tillich was forced to resign.

During the previous six years KgU had been involved in "creating disturbances, and the transportation of explosives and secret drugs such as scopolamine and cantharadine." Members of the group were armed and were answerable only to Tillich. Efforts were made to influence the political development of West Germany by portraying the Social Democrats as fellow travelers, by sending anonymous, threatening letters, and by publishing falsified accusations against persons who were not in Herr Tillich's favor.

The Group, in short, had developed delusions of grandeur.

One of the leaders in KgU had arranged a meeting in a West Berlin restaurant with an alleged contact man from the East. This departmental chief, Baitz, took with him not only his false passport but also a list of his various informers in East Germany.

The contact man from the East turned out to be a charming woman: the pleasant evening was continued later in her temporary rooms, where Herr Baitz woke up the next morning without his papers, but with a hangover.

This kind of activity risks human lives.

Those who went to KgU in Nikolassee were primarily refugees from the East looking for help. Instead, they were probably entrusted with some kind of drug mixture. The authorities in West Berlin tried for many years to get information about the Group's activities and financing, but all inquiries were met by a wall of silence. It was known only that KgU financial support came primarily from the United States. Reason triumphed when the organization was dissolved in March, 1959.

The activities of the East German state security service are no less unscrupulous. But this does not give the West Berlin spy centers any justification for sacrificing the freedom of others. The best solution would be for the bureaus to pack up and leave their frontal outpost, this island in the Red sea. The value of these espionage activities is doubtful. The harmful effects are undeniable.

The man on the street in West Berlin knows this—but he doesn't pay the piper.

This is also the opinion of the Senator (Commissioner) for Internal Affairs in West Berlin, Jochim Lipschitz, one of the most colorful figures in the city's political life. He has set up a committee of experts which is checking the activities of the spy centers. But when I interview him in his office on Fehrbelliner Platz he is understandably very tight-lipped about the composition of the committee and its duties.

"I want to emphasize two things," says Lipschitz. "According to my observations there is *one Western spy for ten or fifteen Eastern ones.* On the other hand, I do not want to suggest that everything is perfect in the so-called camp of freedom. Espionage, remember, is something different from tickling piano keys or baking cookies. It is unforgivably irresponsible when an organization in West Berlin keeps its card file of Eastern contacts in an ordinary office in the city and then has it stolen by a break-in.

"The double-cross is also practiced," says Lipschitz. Next to Brandt he is the man in Berlin most hated by the Communists.

The double cross has been described by Irwin Shaw, who, in *The Man with One Arm,* tells the story of a certain Galbrecht, former lieutenant in the Wehrmacht. He goes and comes between the Russian and American information services in postwar Berlin. From a Nazi he gets the wise advice to tell his employers what they want to hear. No sooner said than done: the Russians are told about Nazi infiltration into the American information service, the Americans about Russian war threats.

Galbrecht gets a pay raise immediately.

Galbrecht is not around any longer. Mr. Norris, too, is gone.

He is the mysterious businessman whom Christopher Isherwood meets on the train to Germany, the man who joins the German Communist Party (KPD), who makes speeches on behalf of China, and at the same time sells information to the French police, a quivering conspirator in small format.

Mr. Norris has been succeeded by the serious "Eastern expert," who sits in his well-guarded room some place in West Berlin, the man who is personally not ready to sacrifice *his* freedom, but gladly permits his agents to take risks in conveying weapons and printed materials to the other side. The heads of these Bureaus for Eastern Affairs are heavily insured, but the agents in the East have nothing to win or lose, except their dirty jobs or their existence.

Mr. Norris' train left long ago. No more trains will leave from Lehrter Bahnhof, where he began his headlong flight to Mexico. Oftentimes, when going between East and West, I pass the ruins of the huge station.

In the spring of 1958 I can observe how wall after wall is being dynamited and disappears. Whole bricks are knocked loose, the others are crushed. Soon nothing will be left except the name of the S-Bahn station, Lehrter Stadtbahnhof.

Every time I see the destroyed station I cannot help thinking that the pavement on the platforms could tell me much about the millions of persons who have departed from there, whose experiences have been sad or happy. But when I go up on the platforms finally I see only a few birches, an empty beer bottle, rusty rails. A man comes running and shouts to me that I should leave. I leave as quickly and with as much dignity as possible.

17   The Iron Cross

I often go walking aimlessly. The city is so large that I can walk for hours before running into familiar streets and buildings. When I get tired I slip into a Bierstube, have some sausage and potato salad with beer, listen to the conversation on politics and yesterday's salary scale, about the weather and the new buildings, about everything which touches upon this city which we insist we like without understanding one another.

On one of the streets I go by a number of antique shops—small, dusty places with cowbells that tinkle just inside the door. The halcyon days for shoppers are over. But one can make a find. Behind the dusty windows I see Iron Crosses, Knights' Crosses and memorial medals of all kinds. One can also buy spiked helmets and all the other gaudy metallic junk which the Imperial Reich produced.

It is now permissible again to wear on the lapel of one's evening jacket the orders and insignia which date from the Nazi period.

I stand facing a man who does not have any wartime decoration, no memorial medal, nothing. And he tells me his story as though it had lost all its savor of newness and were worthy only of brief mention.

"How I lived through it?" he asks wearily. "From 1933 I did compulsory work, underground structures, you know. Then to Siemens. On February 13, 1942, I was arrested along with my family and relatives. We were separated. I was taken first to Auschwitz, then to Dora and Bergen-Belsen. I never saw my wife or children again, but I know that they were gassed."

This is the chairman for the Jewish community in Berlin, Heinz Galinski. Before Hitler, his community had 180,000 members. Only a few thousand were left in 1945; a hundred or so returned from the concentration camps, but most of them were those lucky enough to have stayed in hiding.

"Today, however, there are 6,000 Jews in West Berlin. Some have come from Israel, where they feel themselves endangered by the political situation. Paradoxically enough, West Berlin is considerably quieter."

As to the 6,000 survivors in West Berlin: they are what is left of the strongly Jewish, cosmopolitan element in Berlin's intellectual and economic life. What has gone can never be restored in the same form. The dead cannot be resurrected.

Heinz Galinski says emphatically: "There is no Jewish problem in Germany, it would be impossible. In all of Germany there are something over 30,000 Jews, of whom 2,000 perhaps live in the East. The extermination has been almost complete."

The Final Solution (the title of Gerhard Reitlinger's book on the Jewish persecutions) was a process which gradually increased in violence. From 1933 the Jews were boycotted. Two years later the notorious Nürnberg laws barred them from state service. The next turning point was the so-called Crystal Night, when Jewish shops and businesses were plundered and destroyed. A steady stream of Jews was poured into the concentration camps and gassed: total extermination was started and was carried out—almost.

"We are trying to give the members of our community new hope. Most of them are old and so deeply rooted in Berlin that they do not want to move. We have built new homes for the aged, repaired five synagogues which were destroyed, and have tried to take care of the indemnity payments. But it is impossible to restore property to the dead. The injustices cannot be rescinded."

"Is it not possible that within the strong drive for restoration in West Germany, and the dangerous tendency to forget or rationalize the crimes of the Nazis, that a new anti-Semitism might arise?"

"Anti-Semitism on a broad base cannot grow where there are no Jews," repeats Galinski. "But we are taking careful note of all expressions of anti-Semitism. I was plaintiff in the action against Lektor Zind from Offenburg. And he was found guilty."

Zind was one of those who thought that altogether too few Jews had been gassed during World War II. During one conversation that he had with a man in a pub, the latter admitted that he was half Jewish and had spent time in a concentration camp. Then Zind said: "Then you're a dirty Jew, too, and they forgot to gas you."

Yes, Zind was found guilty. But before sentence had been carried out he managed to escape to Egypt, and it is reported that he went from there to Afghanistan.

In Berlin during the year 1958 legal action was taken against eleven persons who were charged with making anti-Semitic statements either in speech or print. Justice moves quickly in this city. But I have heard the word "Jew" used as invective during debates in the Bonn parliament; yes, I have heard even Berliners, in both East and West, speak thus. Is it a term of abuse, and is the Knight's Cross a symbol of honor? Who is the victor, and who the vanquished?

In 1941 the Star of David was introduced, and all Jews were compelled to wear it. Is it intended that Herr Galinski must wear it on his evening jacket to balance off the Iron Cross? Is it just happenstance that I have seen the scrap metal of German honor in the display windows?

There are other scenes and other windows in Berlin.

18   *The Dancing Partners*

Christopher Isherwood writes:

And then there was a big dancing-hall with telephones on the tables. We had the usual kind of conversations: "Pardon me, Madame, I feel sure from your voice that you're a fascinating little blonde with long black eyelashes—just my type. How did I know? Aha, that's my secret! Yes—quite right: I'm tall, dark, broadshouldered, military appearance, and the tiniest little moustache. . . . You don't believe me? Then come and see for yourself!" The couples were dancing with hands on each other's hips, yelling in each other's faces, streaming with sweat. An orchestra in Bavarian costume whooped and drank and perspired beer. The place stank like a zoo. After this, I think I strayed off alone and wandered for hours and hours through a jungle of paper streamers. Next morning, when I woke, the bed was full of them.

The best-known Berlin dancing halls with table telephones today are: Altes Ballhaus (East Berlin, near Alexanderplatz), with ample opportunities for a young bachelor to find a fifty-year-old, gay and faithful East Berlin dance expert as a dancing partner, and where the atmosphere during the so-called Verkehrter Ball is clearly of the twenties; Rheinische Winzerstuben near the Zoo (West Berlin); Charlott on Stuttgarter Platz, which is frequented in large numbers by French soldiers and where the illumination comes from under the dance floor; finally, the inevitable Resi on Hasenheide (formerly at Alexanderplatz), which was opened to a big new renaissance on May 15, 1951.

Formerly, Resi was more folkish; now on Hasenheide it has

Above, censorer of the tube mail at Resi; below, bartender in Lichterfelde

become a "typically German" (fake German) dance restaurant, but this was presumably the intention. This part of my story deals with Americans. Hence I shall tell about Resi.

There is a central pneumatic-letter exchange near the entrance. The enterprising and the less enterprising can get in touch with one another by using one of the 250 table telephones. There is also a Klosterkeller (Monk's Cellar), likewise with telephones. Telephone connections are possible at the bar, although not in the toilets, which are constantly in use by grateful patrons.

It is dark in the big room when I enter. I get a seat at a table for four which has by chance been left empty, although the white table cloth is covered with glasses, bottles, cigarettes, and ashes. The waiter asks me what I wish to order.

"The least expensive."

"That's a small bottle of Henkell Trocken and beer."

"Together?"

"You usually mix the champagne with the beer. It's good."

"Can I order just beer?"

"My dear sir, we can't serve only beer all night. We have a fifteen-man orchestra. Our colored water fountains cost lots of money. It doesn't pay."

I order whiskey.

When the waiter leaves, a crew-cut, clean young man sits down on my side of the table, two girls opposite us. He is Bill, the blonde is Lisa, the brunette is Lise but calls herself Monalisa.

Bill is a warrior of the new age, world traveler, bombardier, at home in every city from Hongkong to Berlin. On his lapel he wears the Distinguished Flying Cross.

Lisa and Monalisa speak English, the former with an American accent. Lisa is older and has worked in England for seven years. She is now working for our American friends in Dahlem-

Berlin. Every other minute she gets a message in the pneumatic tube with an invitation to dance. The telephone rings incessantly, but when I answer it is for Monalisa.

"I'm a dentist," she says proudly. "I have my own practice in Berlin." Her eyes are bright with laughter and happiness. She *wants* to have a good time.

"I have a toothache," I say.

"My reception hours are between five and six. But you must come soon. In two months I'm leaving for Los Angeles."

"And for what, Mademoiselle?"

"To get myself an American husband." (She has gone over to German. Bill doesn't know German.)

"But there are Americans in Berlin. Won't they do?"

"They're different in Los Angeles."

Monalisa gets up and goes out on the dance floor. While we have been talking a tall man in a light-colored coat, with a bright red moustache, has been standing near our table waiting for her. Lisa leaves too, but before going she says to Bill:

"We go home the same way. I live in Dahlem, too."

He nods at her, but without enthusiasm.

Bill rests his head on his hands and says half apologetically: "I didn't come here with the girls."

We don't say anything for a while, just observe our surroundings: middle-aged men, Americans, tourists, German girls. The signal lamps on the telephones blink. There is a noise in the tube. On the wall Berlin's bear dances the dance of the seven veils with a half-nude girl.

"I wonder," says Bill, "how the Germans looked during the war, I mean in uniform." He yawns. "Such awful things they could do. Such mass murder. And here we sit together with them and are their allies."

"It's no fault of mine."

Bill, too, is a murderer in the technical sense of the word. He participated in the big terror raids on German cities, daylight attacks under an open sky, without danger from German fighters. He has dropped his bombs on Berlin and flown over mangled Germany. What is frightening about this type of fighter is that he who bears the responsibility for seeing that his load reaches its target never gets the smell of blood and death in his nostrils. The warrior becomes a technician and avoids meeting the enemy at close range. But doesn't this spatial separation mean that the conscience is destroyed? He is a professional soldier who has no acquaintance with the end purpose of his profession, death. He visits the more beautiful cities of the world, so long as they are on his side of the fighting front that winds around the earth. Bill talks about Venice and Naples, about the atolls of the Pacific, about Mexico and Paris. He is at home where he flies, and yet seems somehow out of place, imprisoned by doubt.

His life is perhaps empty, but he is well paid. He asks no questions. After a moment of hesitation he accepts this evening the German, the former enemy and murderer. It is only with slight surprise that he repeats his question: "I don't understand the Germans. Do you?"

When he wants to eat and the waiter suggests an Italian or French specialty, Bill says firmly: "When I am in Germany I want German food. Bring me something German."

Is this something to remember back home (a home that does not exist): to have eaten German food in Berlin, at Resi with its fountains and the music of Gershwin, with its table telephones and the slips of paper which come to us with a thud in the capsules of the pneumatic tube: "You are very Alone. Won't you Dance with Me. *Tisch Nr* 233."

We call table number 233, but an angry male voice answers that he is, by God, alone, and he hasn't the least desire to dance with us.

"Some charming English gentlemen have invited me to a late show," says Monalisa when she returns. We wish her well. She puts on the tired face of a blasé young dentist, takes her bag, and goes over to the English gentlemen.

Lisa has got the idea that we don't dare to dance. So she tries to order some girls for us. Meanwhile, she empties a few glasses of white wine. At the next table there are two gentlemen, each with his bottle of Henkell Trocken and beer. The orchestra plays in an unmistakably German way, even though the music is from New Orleans. My eyes are getting tired from the colored cascades of water which dance in the air.

Except for *Bier*, Bill doesn't know one word of German, but he is sitting with allies and friends. Berlin to him is a heroic city. It won't be long before he is back at his post outside of Paris, where he will regale his friends with tales of Resi. Right now he is yawning.

19   *Karlshorst*

I try to figure out why Bill and his government have had such fundamentally different attitudes toward the Germans and toward the Russians, their wartime allies. I want to understand the emotional gulf which exists between the American (who prefers to see the Germans armed, and who has helped them arm) and the Russian (who has also given Germans arms), who sees a mortal peril in the comradeship-in-arms between Americans and Germans.

Defense Minister Strauss in West Germany asks: Why should Russians and Poles fear the Germans? He has the right to ask, others the right to answer: the fear of German weapons, and of German death still lives on in Warsaw and Moscow. This is a psychological reality. It is also remembrance: the Russians lost 13.6 million soldiers and at least 7 million civilians. The Western powers, including the United States, lost 1.5 million soldiers. The Germans lost 3.25 million soldiers and 3.3 million civilians. Poland lost 5.9 million. Of all the losses in human lives resulting from Hitler's war the Russian share was over 40 per cent.

The Russians fought for their very existence. The Americans' existence was never threatened. While they felt a common solidarity with other nations, they did not carry on war at close range. United States losses in Korea were felt more keenly than those of World War II. The Russians were aware that a Nazi victory would mean annihilation of the Soviet Union. The Russians, in the mind of Hitler, were a slave people. The war for them was in truth "The Great Patriotic War," not in the first place a struggle for socialism.

What has been said here is borne out by Oleg, a Russian lieutenant, who participated in the capture of Berlin. He is no longer a soldier, but he speaks often of the war:

"I was called up in 1941 and had my basic training before the war started. I was sent to the front. When the German advance slowed up and we knew that we were not done for, I was made lieutenant and put over my own armored platoon. I participated in every battle until the end of the war. I lost my men several times but I got new men and new vehicles. Five times I was wounded, but never seriously enough to be sent home.

"One night I woke up in my armored car and heard a noise some place. I went out. A few minutes later my car was hit by a shell and started to burn. My crew perished in the flames.

"I could tell you a lot of stories, but what's the point? To make a long story short, I was in on the capture of Berlin. We lived for awhile in Karlshorst, then in Potsdam. We had some free time and could look around the town. We doled out bread to German women who begged us for more food. There were a lot of us, tired though we were, who couldn't withstand the temptation. The price of a woman was some cigarettes and a loaf of bread. We had become accustomed to living with the tension of death; now fatigue took hold of us. We had lived as soldiers for several years. My commander visited me in Potsdam and asked me to remain as an active officer. I managed to convince him instead that he should try to send me home so that I could continue my engineering studies. I haven't seen Berlin since."

The diplomatic spokesmen for Oleg's country have long ago abandoned the idea of a reunited Germany. They make ceremonial visits to Bonn and East Berlin. They have chosen a lesser evil (the fact that Western Germany is opposed to them) in preference to the greater one (that all Germany would be free to do what it wished).

Oleg's comrades fear nothing more than a militarily strong, reunited Germany. That's why they are willing to stay in Karlshorst until kingdom come, if necessary.

Street car number 69 goes from Alexanderplatz to Karlshorst.

Previously I had visited the American headquarters in Dahlem, Clayallee. The star-spangled banner flies in the open court, big cars with yellow registration plates whisk by. Some refer to Dahlem as an American ghetto. Others speak of the friendly relations between West Berliners and Americans. For West Berliners the American garrison is a moral protection. Of course, everyone knows that in case of war no one can protect West Berlin. The Germans do not begrudge their allies their five movie houses, three churches, two schools, twelve clubs. . . . As the old women said one hot summer afternoon in a pub in Steglitz: "If they were not here we would have had the Russians here long ago." Then she goes on gabbing. Every morning, she reports, the Americans awaken her when they go by in their armored cars. But she thinks they're there for a good cause and forgives them.

Tram number 69 is a noisy box that proceeds slowly and stops often. I ride through the workers' quarters, past factories, past houses with backyards, and backyards, and more backyards. Some new apartment houses are being built but they are still only white spots among otherwise dark buildings. In the more open spaces the ground has been parceled out into fenced plots. Vegetables and flowers are growing. On a summer Sunday one can see families out there sitting in front of their tiny huts admiring their plants. Just as Lichtenberg is the workers' Berlin, so the little gardens (*Laubenkolonien*) belong to the workers. Just as the dark backyards are a part of Berlin, the gardens, too, are a natural part of the city.

The trip to Karlshorst lasts a tedious half hour.

A number of long, broad avenues dominate this part of the city. Most of the houses show traces of their vanished splendor and upper-bourgeois life. They are largely two and three-story houses, with shady gardens, in which only the shrubs remain, not the shade.

People of means chose to live in Karlshorst even though it was not in the West because it has one of Europe's most attractive trotting courses. This they themselves asserted.

I wander around in the area one afternoon while the races are going on. Several thousand spectators are watching the events on the dusty track. There is nothing very elegant or festive about the crowd, but rather a drowsy and provincial atmosphere. Carriages, with shiny wet horses and dusty jockeys, roll past me en route to the stables. The races are over for the day. Business has been bad.

Berlin's Russian garrison is in Karlshorst.

I walk on the right sidewalk of one of the wide avenues. Alongside, extending from the railroad embankment near the race track, there stretches a high, rusty, iron net with gates where uniformed guards salute the military personnel who enter. Behind this net is the Russian Karlshorst, a city within Berlin with Russian cinemas and shops and with prices listed in rubles. A foreign world has put its stamp upon Karlshorst, where the German surrender terms were signed on May 8, 1945.

The fenced area was constricted somewhat after the size of the garrison was reduced. However, the contacts between Germans and Russians are minimal. While West Berliners take some pride in learning English, there is passive opposition among East Berlin young people to learning Russian. English is the language of the West, Russian that of the East. Even East Berliners consider themselves as belonging to the West.

The difference between Karlshorst and Dahlem is the difference between the proletarian world and one which is chrome-plated. Dahlem, with its new low houses, its lawns, sun balconies, its rows of automobiles, reminds one of an American college town, while Karlshorst is merely a run-down, bourgeois section of a city.

The Russians have a notably difficult time in making their world attractive and pleasing to the senses. There is an open, almost frightening contempt for them in the case of the East Berliner who points out houses to me and says:

"In this house the windows are clean; Germans live there. In that house the windows are dirty; Russians live there."

It is a cold, clear night when I take the tram back. Suddenly I hear some exciting jazz music coming from an open window, a short rhapsody which is drowned by the clattering of the tram and quickly loses its color. That side of the front represented by jazz is infinitely more attractive, neon-lit, promising for Berliners. On the other side, in the gray houses of Karlshorst, there seems to be no promise. This is a foreign world, the grayness from the East merging with that grayness which only Berlin can provide.

The two worlds are locked in helpless enmity; one of them cannot dissappear without the other doing so also. At Resi's, the predominantly heavy and sweaty German middle-aged frivolity is diluted by American matter-of-factness. But where Russians and Germans come together it is the Russian who predominates and he who influences the East German regime.

I have the impression of a dizzy dance which goes on and on since no one has courage to pull out.

The two enemies avoid each other as much as possible. Only a few dusty relics are left from the fraternization at the end of the war.

Of the 600 cells of the Spandau Prison in West Berlin only three are occupied. The remaining major war criminals, Hess, Speer, and Schirach, live there. The cost to West Germans to maintain these prisoners is 950,000 DM yearly.

The permanent personnel consists of eleven cooks, ten waiters, fourteen kitchen girls, three administrators and two laundry women. As regularly as clockwork there is a ceremonious change of guards between the American, Russian, British, and French companies.

This is one part of the tragi-comedy of four-power cooperation in Berlin.

20   "Die Hinterbliebenen"
(Those Left Behind)

The status of the literary cabaret in today's Germany is peculiarly ambiguous. This art form had its greatest flowering
during the twenties, and especially in Berlin. Today there are
only half a dozen good cabarets in the whole of Germany and
it was not by chance that one of the first of those to open after
the war called itself "Die Hinterbliebenen." These cabarets did
not feel that they had a new task under new circumstances;
they looked upon themselves as heirs of a tradition. It was
thought that the cabarets would flourish again in some future,
better day. That day has not yet come.

The cabaret, Die Distel, has its show in the Haus der Presse
on Friedrichstrasse in East Berlin. Here is the most popular skit
on one of the latest programs:

Upon arriving home the man surprises his wife in the arms of
another. Thoroughly aroused, he cries: "And here you lie! You
should be out of the house already. They have apples for sale
at HO!"

Even the People's Police in the audience, and the officials in
their correct dark clothes, laugh. They know how infrequently
the stores in East Berlin have enough fruit for sale. And they
know that many people buy fruit in the West.

The scene lasts only thirty seconds. But it is effective. Also
these three lines from a song:

> Le dernier cri geht um die Welt
> und wenn es der Welt nicht mehr gefällt
> kommt es in der H. O.

(The latest fashion goes round the world, and if it no longer pleases the world, it turns up at HO.)

It is only rarely that Die Distel scores so well. Its artists are mediocre. Its artistic leader, Brehm, was removed some years ago, and there were complaints that Distel was too free-spoken. Bonn is criticized and one number deals with unemployment in West Berlin. The American influence in West Berlin, and atomic rearmament are also criticized. It takes no courage for that, since these are part of the political ammunition of Ulbricht and his government. To be brave is not easy. It is easier to drift with the stream.

Both in its artistry and in its critical approach to the issues of the day, Die Stachelschweine in West Berlin is on a higher plane. It is located in small quarters on Rankestrasse near Kurfürstendamm. This is the red light district. Only fifty yards from the entrance to the cabaret there is a notice board which promotes a kind of public prostitution. Women are offering themselves as models, dancing partners, etc. Die Stachelschweine is a corporate enterprise owned by the artists themselves. When they started they had no salaries. The stage manager, Behnke, takes tickets at the entrance. On the walls one can see posters, and caricatures of the leading political figures of the world. Like its counterparts in Düsseldorf, Munich, and Hamburg, Die Stachelschweine plays primarily to a bourgeois public, against which most of its satirical barbs are aimed. They have also a few very effective numbers concerned with the diabolical East German dialectic, with bureaucracy, and with proletarian self-satisfaction. These help to obviate the complaint of being one-sided.

Conversation between a man and a woman: he tells about the biggest moment in his life, when he had the extreme good fortune of shaking hands with Der Führer. His voice quavers with emotion as he recalls the infinite strength that the Führer's presence gave him. He explains modestly that he served only as a Sturmbannführer in the S. S.

A little later the man is revealed as a rank impostor. He never shook the hand of the Führer. And he was only an ordinary SA-man, a very little Nazi. He is denounced as a big opportunist. But naturally he is one of those who fought on the eastern front in the common, historic battle against Bolshevism.

Die Stachelschweine takes a critical stand toward the follies and blunders of the petty-bourgeois federal republic. The political radicalism of the cabaret makes the gentlemen in the front seats grow pale. Their faces take on a serious attitude as though of self-examination, but it is probably not that. Die Stachelschweine dares to be itself, and even dares to put on special programs for the residents in East Berlin. This illuminates the best side of the Western system, its open-mindedness toward criticism of both persons and institutions. This is the basic difference between East and West.

Both Die Distel and Stachelschweine make a serious appeal to man's conscience: against atomic war. But such an exhortation in East Berlin has no significance as critique; it conforms to the political line. Yet it is necessary to disabuse oneself of the idea (in the West) that everything the Communists think is *a priori* false and foolish, and (in the East) that everything that the West thinks is *a priori* false and foolish. Naturally, it is idle to hope that the cabarets can break the habit of thinking in clichés, which has become deeply entrenched in a population, of whom only a few have ever attended a cabaret show. But even if we concede that today's cabarets are politically powerless and cannot pave the way to new conversations, we should also avoid exaggerating the political influence of their predecessors in the twenties. In their critique of the Weimar democracy the cabarets and radical art played unhappily right into the hands of Hitler. They rejected democracy but did not say what should replace it.

Unfortunately, art in today's world often is free only if it is at the same time powerless.

21   Freedom in Dahlem

As I step off a two-decker bus in Dahlem I see a young woman leaning against a fence. Unmindful of what is going on around her, she is reading *One Hundred Tips on Spain*.

Automobile traffic is limited to the city busses, American military busses, and large private cars with plates "U.S. Armed Forces in Germany." Near the bus stop there is a building which has survived from earlier days. I doubt that the former owner is there. Over each entrance there is a sign, in English, "Barber," "Beauty Shop."

This is the area around the Free University. Houses, quiet, the university's light, new buildings, a library, a large auditorium, a student restaurant, old buildings which formerly belonged to Berlin's real university.

I walk along Boltzmannstrasse for a bit and then stop in front of a small brick building of three stories. This is an old landmark that has been photographed hundreds of times, the building in which the Free University was founded, and today the quarters of the rectorate and the commission for external affairs.

I find myself finally with Dr. Rolf Hildebrandt, one of those who went along when the students revolted at the Humboldt University, and, with the help of professors and politicians, founded Free University. Hildebrandt is chief of the university's public relations office, otherwise known as commission for external affairs. He belongs to that generation of men who were called up in 1937 and did not wear civilian clothes again until nine years later. As a prisoner of war he was placed in the former concentration camp, Neuengamme, where he was put to work transporting cadavers.

"That was a good and necessary school. I learned to loathe the handiwork of the Nazis. I began to get apprehensive of the latent Nazism within myself. When we were set free we had been reeducated without the need of anyone making speeches about democracy. We had learned to try to be honest with people. We wanted to build a new Germany.

"Immediately after my release I began my studies at the only university in Berlin, the one on Unter den Linden. Today, more than ten years later, my comrades have wives and families. I have the Free University. It is my life."

This statement is not entirely free of rhetoric.

He is about forty years of age, wears glasses, and has a wide, boyish smile. He seems like something in between: scout leader or agitator? He emphasizes often that Free University is *different*. What does he mean?

"We are young. The traditional German university student corporations, the military exercises, the dueling are forbidden. F.U. is also noteworthy because 30 per cent of our students come from the East Zone. Many West Berliners would like to have their children study here but we want to give the first chance to refugees if they cannot move on to West Germany. But I hope sincerely that not all of the professors and students who oppose the East German regime come over to us. There are many who believe that they *should* stay where they are, even if they feel themselves threatened.

"It is true that the Pankow regime underwrites the education of its subjects. A student in East Berlin need not go hungry. We have many students literally living on the verge of starvation. But they are here, nevertheless."

This he says with proper confidence.

I have the impression that Hildebrandt tries to exaggerate the material difficulties of Western students so that he can emphasize more effectively the contrast between a totalitarian system and one that is free, a lack of system which enables the individual to escape too many urgent questions. Hildebrandt knows that anxiety is a concrete reality in the East.

"Unfortunately, our students are not as much interested in self-government as they used to be. Despite that, I think we have a stronger political consciousness than in other Western universities. The groups in East Berlin who reacted most quickly against oppression were the socialists and the Catholics. They wanted to be free."

"Are you free?"

"That's something you will have to judge for yourself."

Perhaps, I say to myself later, we have here a young generation which does not want to be duped by slogans. But in the midst of this freedom, this talk of freedom, and this freedom of action, I am perplexed by the way the suzerainty of the United States is taken for granted, accepted, and looked upon as an indispensable part of freedom. This is evident everywhere. A foreign power watches over the Free University.

One student comments: "It is better to have a good protector than none at all."

It is thus that the discussion of freedom suddenly becomes a question of the goodness or evil of the sovereign power.

The new Berlin University—an effort was made to avoid association with the old name, Friedrich-Wilhelm-Universität—
was opened under Russian sponsorship as early as January,
1946. It was considered to be Berlin's university, which, to begin
with, it was. Despite the heavy war losses the university had
managed to assemble a large number of excellent teachers on its
staff.

The first period was marked by a free and open clash between
points of view and ideologies. It was a happy time despite the
poverty, say the students who were there then.

But even before the first of May, 1946, a conflict had arisen
which was to spell the end of the trust between Communists
and non-Communists (the term anti-Communist was not yet in
vogue). The president of the student body was Georg Wrazidlo,
a worker's son from Silesia, freed from a concentration camp in
the spring of 1945. The Communists, who had supported his
candidacy, had assumed that he was party-less but weak. When
the university was decorated on the first of May with the flags
and emblems of the newly-founded SED, Wrazidlo and twenty-
nine other students protested that "flags and symbols of political
parties are shown at the university. The university serves
science and education and is not a party institution. We request
that the use of such symbols be avoided in the future."

It was only a short time ago that these men were freed after
a long jail sentence in East Germany. Their crime was a protest.

The situation at the university became intolerable for all of
those who could not swallow SED Communism. At first the
compulsory lectures in the area of politics had been looked upon
as extremely useful; there was great interest in studying German history, which had been falsified during the period of
Hitler. But the instruction degenerated into straight Communist
propaganda.

He who belonged to the Party or to FDJ (Free German Youth) was automatically a better student.

"Most disturbing, however, was the danger of demoralizing the students who were induced to join political organizations whose goals they rejected, nay, despised. What would become of the character-building task of the university if it looked on passively while a host of opportunists was bred?" So writes one of the chroniclers of the time.

The conflict within the university was merely a reflection of the increased tension in the general political situation as well as in Berlin. The Communists and their supporters were in the minority at the university. Police methods were then used against the majority; leaders of the opposition were arrested and disappeared. Violence became commonplace, enforced conformity set in.

Therefore the men at Free University, strictly speaking, do not need to talk of any other freedom than freedom from the pressure to adopt a point of view which made them rebellious and prompted them to leave East Berlin. All other considerations are for them secondary. Even in Dahlem there is not absolute freedom. It is possible that this freedom will lead to opportunism and silence. If that is the case it is an opportunism which the students accept, a road which they themselves have had an opportunity to choose.

22   *The Students of Berlin*

On April 23, 1948, the students of the opposition in Berlin
gathered for a protest meeting in the British sector. The ap-
parent occasion was that three editors from a student newspaper had been expelled. The more fundamental reason was a
thorough dissatisfaction with their studies. A student from Jena
opened the meeting and pointed out that Humboldt University
was still being treated with tolerance, when compared to the
other universities in the East Zone. This was not only a question
of the expulsion of three students but a question:

Of the practices of admission whereby members of the Socialist
Unity Party of Germany and other Communist organizations, no
matter what their qualifications, have been given increasingly prefer-
ential treatment;

Of the defamation of non-Communist members of the student
council;

Of the arrest of individual non-Communist students;

Of the advancement given to Marxist professors, whose lectures
have been made compulsory, in connection with which students
of all faculties are required to demonstrate every year their knowledge of the Marxist interpretation of our times;

Of arbitrary intervention of the "central administration" in the
teaching and the administration of the university and in the work
of the student council, which has protested in vain.

We wish an end to this atmosphere of encouraging denunciation
of those whose political point of view is different, of coercion,

And an end to this odor of undisputed supremacy of *one* state,
one party, *one* view of life, which once before rose in the nostrils
of many of the freedom-loving students of Berlin, as they called
themselves. . . .

That free meetings of freedom-loving students of Berlin demanded . . . the establishment of a university in one of the three
Western sectors of the city, a university in which—unencumbered
by political or philosophical tutelage—one could pursue one's
studies in peace. Politicians and respected citizens of Berlin made
the demand of the freedom-loving students (as they express it)
their own; and the Berlin city council, against the votes of the
Communist delegates and the abstention of two prominent members of a large party (of whom one was at the same time Dean of
the Law Faculty at Berlin University), concurred in the proposal
for establishing a new university.

West Berlin politicians and Allied liaison men both expressed
some reservations. One of those who supported the plans from
the beginning was Ernst Reuter. The founding of Free University, under these circumstances, became a political demonstration against the one-tracked intellectual outlook and the intolerance in East Berlin. The university took on a political
character. After twelve years of Hitler's dictatorship, and after
this new effort to apply intellectual coercion, German youth
had stood up to this evil and been strong enough to choose
their own road. "A German university should take a stand?
Why, that was unthinkable."

But the struggle over Berlin's university was part of a larger
battle in which the students, willingly or unwillingly, played
a symbolic role:

"Can the students help it if their wish to study in peace and
the wish of the professors to teach in peace grew into a myth?"

"A 'struggle for freedom,' a 'lighthouse of freedom,' a 'bastion
of human values,' the torch of free science?"

"German youth has frequently had to play a role which it
had not itself chosen. It has been used for ends of which it was
not always aware." So says the young man who has published
a novel about Free University, *Die Studenten von Berlin*
(1954). This is Dieter Meichsner, thirty years old, tall, broad,

and good-natured, one of the Germans who was born too late to participate actively in the war but who was conscripted into the Werewolves, the last troops with which Hitler believed he could "save" Germany. Meichsner was in the Hitler youth (he has written a novel about this period) and he, too, learned how to handle a submachine gun. The decisive early years of his youth were lived in a Berlin that was constantly threatened by new bombings and an even more thorough destruction.

I am riding with Meichsner in his new Volkswagen and we are headed for Wannsee, through the new Berlin which is emerging in the midst of the gray, the old. In the perspective of today all of the mad young people of the year 1945 seem unreal, a saga or a bitter legend.

Die Studenten von Berlin is Meichsner's greatest effort so far to paint a broad canvas of lost youth. His story begins at the end of the war in the midst of the anarchic conditions of defeated Germany, the ruins of the collapsed Third Reich. He chooses a group of young people from various milieus. They have one thing in common, they want to reeducate themselves. Gradually they come together at Free University. They live in Berlin, their inner conflicts take place there. Some of them were at Humboldt University during the first period, some come from Dresden, and some disappear into the maw of East Germany, either as prisoners or as functionaries.

Meichsner never stoops to agitation or gross propaganda. He has read his Dos Passos (which is evident from the quotation above) and readily admits it. It is the early Dos Passos whom he admires, the universality and journalistic down-to-earthness of his prose.

Meichsner's books have not suffered from this influence.

His novel is also a story about Berlin. It reveals how difficult it was for the lost young people of the postwar period to adjust their demands to the realities of the time. The book is a tragedy in that its characters, after having learned openness after the war, gradually begin to draw cynical and selfish conclusions from the partition of Germany and the policies of the occupying powers.

When one of the principal characters, disguised in civilian clothes, manages to slip into captured Berlin, he sees paintings on the streets with the well-known statement of Stalin, "Hitlers may come and go, but the German people, the German state, will remain."

The most interesting figure in Meichsner's book is Harald Momber, who is in some respects perhaps a projection of the author's own points of view and tendencies (to what extent is not important). Momber hesitates in his choice between the opposing sides and refuses for a long time to concede that Berlin is a front-line city where freedom and slavery stand opposed to each other.

Momber is nineteen when the Gestapo, in 1945, tosses him into jail. After the war he wants to believe to the very last that it is possible by discussion to bridge the chasm between the two Germanies. He not only stops and reflects, but actually changes, when he realizes that the Communists are using his name for purposes of provocation. But like many other Germans Momber still refuses to believe that the other side is lacking completely in honor. He follows the others to Free University, but he is a doubter, an oppositionist. This is a quality which, for the past seventy years of German history, has been looked upon as treason to one's country.

While on a trip to Dresden Momber is arrested as a Western agent, a too common fate in real life as well as in novels. Meichsner tells me that students who have been released from East German prisons have written to him and remarked upon the astounding degree to which his book describes their lives *as they were.*

Die Studenten von Berlin is Meichsner's last novel to date. He is now writing another whose setting is in West Germany. Since writing some pieces for the radio, as well as TV dramas, he has been busy. This is well-paid work. His play for television, *Besuch aus der Zone* (The Visitor from the Zone), attracted much attention and caused annoyance.

The play is about a private businessman, Reichert, from East Germany, who is visiting friends in West Germany. Hitherto they have imported 40 per cent of Reichert's production, but now they refuse to buy. Reichert discovers that they have started to manufacture his products themselves.

If his business does not continue to bring in foreign exchange Reichert runs the risk of being "expropriated." He is thus threatened on two sides—in part by his (former) friends in the West, who see nothing criminal in copying an Eastern product and renaming it, and in part by the regime in the East, which can use the halt in exports as sufficient excuse for getting rid of a troublesome private entrepreneur.

Reichert decides to return to the Zone despite the fact that his friends have offered him a good position, and despite the fact that both he and his family would prefer to stay in the West. Reichert is an integral part of the world in which he lives; he is loyal to his workers. By this device Meichsner wished to indicate that the choice between freedom and dictatorship, between East and West, in the Germany of today is not always as simple as Western propagandists of freedom would have us believe.

In both parts of Germany Meichsner's drama has been labeled untrue and fabricated. Is this a valid criticism of the play's quality? If so, the value of the work is extremely transient, which also means that the play can perhaps not be produced outside of Germany. For Meichsner the portrayal of political realities is never forced, but an inner necessity. No one can understand Germany and the Germans if he does not understand the kind of political policies pursued in both parts. Any prose which seeks to stand aloof from politics cannot claim to be describing Germany.

"Berlin, the city where I was born," says Meichsner, "compels one to take a stand. Berlin is Germany's real capital, no matter what the politicians in Bonn may say. I have lived here all my life, and without trying to seem like a romanticist I can say that I do not wish to live anywhere else in Germany."

We are sitting in one of the cafés along the Wannsee in early spring, looking out over the empty beaches and noting the suggestion of greenery and summer in the beechwoods. Love for Berlin. What is it? I begin to reflect on Harald Momber in Meichsner's novel, who becomes inexplicably happy when he arrives in dreary Berlin from Munich. The city was desolate and benumbed, in the grip of the first postwar winter, just like other cities which Harald had seen. "But when the train went from Lichterfelde across Papestrasse to the Anhalter Bahnhof, past the dimly lighted Stadtbahn stations, past the trams and the occasional street lamps in the suburbs, past the naked silhouettes of building façades, things became different."

I am sympathetic to Meichsner's frankness and his wish to write about Germany, of the time in which he lives. This is the same artistic principle which was formulated by Thomas Mann when he perceived that authors after the First World War could not write and create as before. A world had collapsed.

But these words were just as applicable after the Second World War.

For Meichsner Berlin is not only interesting, not only native city and place of residence, but also the open sore, the hidden tragedy. Berlin demands that one take a stand.

"How would Berlin and Germany have looked," muses Meichsner, "if the 20th of July men had come to power?"

"Better than now, in any case," I think.

It is Sunday. Families, with children decently quiet, are sitting near us. We are having coffee, with liqueur or brandy, and pastries. One can get here only by car. The glittering water beckons invitingly through the trees, there is the sound of an airplane, no one looks up. It is fifteen years since the end of the war, ten years since the airlift. Everything (almost) is as it was.

From the café we ride to the widened, majestic Königstrasse, with the Grunewald woods on the right and the sector line on the left. We drive out to a bridge which is on the way to Potsdam and is now called Brücke der Einheit (Bridge of Unity). The name has been given to it by the East German government, which is apparently unaware that there are two stout bars across the Bridge of Unity. This is the boundary line between West Berlin and East Germany.

We walk up to the West policeman who is standing guard and looking at the other side.

The widened Königstrasse behind us seems like something of a parody. It has little traffic, but it has been widened in anticipation of that dreamed-of moment when all the boundary markers in Germany will be taken down and traffic will move again toward Potsdam.

The Bridge of Unity will then get back its old name: Glienicker Brücke.

"This is where the world ends," says Meichsner with a sigh, and goes back to his car.

23   The Friend of Youth

It is not evident now that Berlin's old university was damaged during the war. The main building of Humboldt University looks as it did before. The two statues of the brothers Wilhelm and Alexander von Humboldt are still standing, one on either side of the entrance. In the surrounding area everything (almost) is as it was: the state Opera House (rebuilt), St. Hedwig's Cathedral (rebuilt), Zeughaus (repaired), the University (repaired), Unter den Linden (the linden trees are growing).

At the entrance, however, I note that the world has changed. A doorman asks for my *Ausweis*. Students who go past me show their identity cards. I pull a paper at random out of my pocket and continue on without saying anything. On the large wall above the steps across from the entrance there is a quotation from Marx. On the right in the corridor there is a red cloth banner with the words: "Support our national people's army." Under the text there are some pictures showing army life and training, guns and tanks.

I stop by a bulletin board in the nearest corridor. It is a wall newspaper of the SED organization, *Rektorat und Hauptverwaltung*. Seven new party leaders have been elected. They present themselves in words and pictures (passport photos). Two of those elected are women. Each one of them has written his autobiography on a quarter of a page.

The texts are painful to read. The new office-holders enumerate their merits and their mistakes. One of them at one time had had revisionist and petty-bourgeois views. Another had been a Communist during the thirties, when it was illegal. The seven autobiographies have the character of masochistic self-abasement before the Party, the highest court of appeal. Students pass by in the corridor, someone stops, takes a look at the texts, shrugs his shoulders and walks on.

The seven newly-elected persons promise to give their all for the cause of socialism. They promise struggle, hardness, sacrifice. They have made the cause of socialism their own.

But what kind of sacrifice do they make? For whom? And what?

I knock on the nearest door and enter a dark reception room.

"I am [and then I repeat the same story for the thousandth time] . . . and I would like some information about the situation in the university," I say to the sleepy woman sitting at the desk.

"You must by all means talk to Jugendfreund [Friend of Youth] Sommer," says the woman, looking me in the eyes. "He knows everything."

I blush, because I don't know what Friend of Youth means. Well, he is a trusted person in the FDJ and has an office in a nearby building.

Naturally I know what is meant by Freie Deutsche Jugend (Free German Youth). Doesn't the poet Johannes R. Becher in his diary write about FDJ's "blue flower" (their shirts are blue), which conveys some rather ghastly romantic associations? And is it not the custom for the young FDJ enthusiasts to greet each other and foreign "delegates" (one of the words which has become popular in the East German language) with the happy cry *Freundschaft, Freundschaft*? This is an old socialist greeting, but it seems to have lost its content and meaning, at least as far as FDJ is concerned.

Jugendfreund Sommer's office is on the bank of the Spree directly opposite the ruins of the Berlin Cathedral. Banners and flags are hanging in the corridor awaiting the next demonstration. The plates on the doors indicate that the SED and the

FDGB (the trade union) have their offices in the same building.

"Young people must be active," says Sommer, who is the university's Marxist, fighting dynamo. He is a sleek young man with dark hair, enthroned behind a large writing table, toying with a pen, answering the telephone, signing documents, being busy. He speaks in a cold, convinced tone, exudes hatred toward Fascism and love toward Communism. He is pleased with the way things are going and has adopted the characteristic East German official language, chemically free from all personal nuances:

"We have gone a long way toward building a truly socialistic university. The socialist evolution within our peasants' and workers' state is reflected in our university. Sixty per cent of the students are children of workers and peasants. They come here at age eighteen or nineteen, although we should prefer to see them somewhat older. In our opinion they should have worked in some socialized enterprise for a year before coming here. If they come here directly from their school desks they will have had no contact with real life. Neither do we want a trained scientist to begin his research immediately after his studies. We don't want cloistered scholars. The number of students in the different faculties is regulated by our five-year plan, which in turn is based upon needs. No one needs to be unemployed."

While Sommer is taking a staged pause and arranging the pencils in a new order, I take a cigarette.

"We have received remarkable support for FDJ," continues Sommer in a serious voice. He picks at his nails with a penknife. "Over 80 per cent of the students belong to our organization, despite the fact that many of them are bourgeois. And our students are active. Recently we had a big demonstration against West German atomic rearmament. We are watching developments in West Germany very carefully. Political consciousness is highly developed among us.

"We can't wait until the bombs fall," says Sommer threateningly, and tosses his pencil on the table. "We want to convert Berlin into a city of peace. And how do the police in West Berlin answer our peaceful appeals? Yesterday our students distributed leaflets in West Berlin and most of them were arrested. Three of them are still sitting there today. If they aren't released by this afternoon we will set up an even bigger demonstration. But I know that our students will be released. Those people over there know that our protest is strong and that opinion is firmly on our side. We are fighting for a righteous cause."

It could be, say I to myself, that you are fighting for a good cause. But *you* aren't the right man to lead the fight. That I know.

As I take my leave Sommer picks up the telephone to check if the arrested students have already been released. Presumably he has a new load of leaflets on hand in some closet.

So far as I can ascertain his vision of student loyalty is a thorough lie. Not one of the students with whom I have talked is an adherent of Jugendfreund Sommer's one hundred per cent SED-ideology. On the contrary, with the passing years they have become stronger opponents of party dictatorship. But they admit that 20 per cent of the students follow Sommer's line. This 20 per cent arranges demonstrations. They are the ones who go over to West Berlin to distribute leaflets. But for the other students the atmosphere has taken on a disastrous likeness to that of an insane asylum.

"We are socialists," says one student. "But we don't think that this is socialism." (A view which I frequently hear expressed in East Berlin.)

"The political pressure is such that one loses all interest in real study," says another student. "This kind of education is crap."

"If you want an education you have to make a formal submission. You have to belong to FDJ or the Party, participate in mass meetings and go to prescribed lectures. We are obliged to have a certain point of view on all questions. But mark my words, all of this begins to taste like sawdust very quickly.

"But what does submission mean so long as the possibility of going over to the West remains? Science cannot be independent of what is happening in the world. But it must be independent of parties."

The students give me a typewritten paper, a declaration which East German students must sign. Since the text is typical of the political methods employed, I reproduce it here in its entirety.

My socialist homeland is threatened by atomic rearmament in West Germany; our German Democratic Republic is a constituent part of the socialist camp.

Because of the threat of war by the NATO politicians in Bonn it is a moral consequence of my political convictions that I, as a young socialist, help to defend the achievements gained by the sacrificial struggle of the working class even to the extent of pledging my life.

I give my wholehearted support to the building of socialism under the leadership of the Socialist Unity Party of Germany and struggle against imperialism and the politics of NATO.

Therefore, at any time when it is deemed necessary by the Party and the government I will bear arms, since it is to my immediate personal interest to defend peace and socialism. To this end I will familiarize myself with the use of arms.

I declare myself thus ready:

To train myself as a reservist of the National People's Army (boys) or in the Red Cross and Air Defense (girls), to participate in the necessary courses of instruction at all times and setting aside all personal considerations.

I know that military service requires from me revolutionary discipline and unconditional obedience.

I am prepared to swear an oath of allegiance to the German Democratic Republic, and faithfully to carry out this decision.

Military Oath:

I swear faithfully to serve my Fatherland, the German Democratic Republic, at all times, to protect it with my life against every enemy when ordered by the Workers' and Peasants' Government, to give my unequivocal obedience to the military authorities, and always and everywhere to defend the honor of our Republic and its National People's Army.

24   *The Life of Galileo*

Atomic physicists from all over the world gathered in Berlin at the end of April, 1958, to commemorate the hundredth birthday of Max Planck. The festivities lasted two days. The commemorative speeches dealt with Planck's contributions and the development of modern physics.

What was strikingly abnormal about these festivities was that they were held in both parts of Berlin. The chasm between the two Germanies is so deep that occasions of this kind are exceptional. Three Western Nobel prize winners—Professors Max von Laue, Otto Hahn, and Werner Heisenberg—participated in the meeting which the venerable (now East) German Academy of Sciences arranged at the State Opera in East Berlin.

Max von Laue was one of the speakers. He referred to Planck's discovery that the harmonious, closed, ordered world in which scientists had previously believed was perhaps an illusion. He spoke of the need for further research in the physical world, of the curiosity of the scientist. Planck's discoveries, he continued, widened a gap which it has not yet been possible to close.

What is the chasm that is deeper than ever? That which separates the two German systems of government, the division between East and West. The physicists carried on their program despite this fact. Together with Walter Ulbricht they grew bored with the festival performance of Gluck's dusty *Iphigenie in Aulis* in the State Opera House. On the second day they assembled in West Berlin's Congress Hall, which is dedicated to the Western ideal of freedom and to the memory of Benjamin Franklin. The main speakers were Werner Heisenberg and Professor Gustav Hertz, the latter resident in Leipzig and the recipient of both a Nobel prize and a Lenin prize.

Throughout Berlin the Planck Festival was looked upon as a demonstration of the unity of science which transcends political boundaries. Nothing, not even a scientific gathering, is so normal and everyday that it cannot seem absurd in Berlin. The famous scientists did not mention one word about politics. But their anniversary celebration was a masterpiece of understatement.

I wonder if some of the Western Nobel prize winners didn't recall that they had signed a manifesto a year earlier which was addressed to all Germany:

We adhere to that freedom which today the Western world represents against Communism. It is undeniable that the common fear of the hydrogen bomb contributes greatly today to the maintenance of peace in the whole world and of freedom in a part of it. We believe, however, that this means of securing peace and freedom is in the long run precarious, and that the danger from its failure would be fatal.

These were proud words which aroused response all over the world, but not in Bonn. The eighteen scientists behind the ———— Göttingen Manifesto had perhaps realized that one can no longer conduct research only for the sake of research, but that new discoveries must be tied to a new sense of responsibility. Gluck's opera gives no answer to this question. But there is a play which poses these same questions. I refer to Bertolt Brecht's *Leben des Galilei* (Life of Galileo).

It was unfortunate that the Berlin ensemble, which had been playing this show, was out of Berlin during these April days. Had Heisenberg seen the play he would perhaps have understood why Berliners in both East and West received the backers of the Göttingen Manifesto with such demonstrative warmth. The fate of the world will not be settled in Berlin. But the fate of Berlin depends in the final analysis upon whether the powers of reason or of death prevail.

The first version of Galileo's life was written in Denmark in 1938-39. From friends among the atomic physicists Brecht had come to understand that German scientists, too, were conscious of the frightening perspectives suddenly revealed by their discoveries, the possibility of an explosive force hitherto unimagined. Faced by the threat of a German uranium bomb, the Western scientists cast their reservations overboard and enrolled in the bomb project. Werner Heisenberg was one of the scientists who had stayed in Hitler's Germany of his own free will.

Brecht's play was produced in Hollywood in 1947 with Charles Laughton in the leading role. It is probable that world events in the fifties and the ever darker perspectives of uninhibited scientific progress prompted Brecht to take up the play again in Berlin. He conducted about ten rehearsals during the winter of 1955-56 despite a serious illness, but the play as performed in Berlin was officially under the direction of his longtime associate and interpreter, Erich Engel.

At the very start of the play Galileo is depicted as a sensuous man, liking good food and a bit of bodily exercise to get his thoughts going.

It is the year 1609. Galileo realizes that he is on the verge of something decisive. He says to his young helper and disciple, Andrea: "But now we will move ahead with great speed. For the old time is past, and this is a new time. For a hundred years mankind has seemed to be awaiting something." A new day is dawning in which man is no longer the crown of creation. It is a great day, a joy to be alive!

Galileo wants time for his research and he needs money. From a wealthy disciple he learns that in Holland they have successfully tested out lenses that do not counteract one another's effect, but magnify. He recognizes the significance of the discovery, and sells it immediately as his own. The new lens then verifies the correctness of the Copernican system. Galileo excuses his theft of the Dutch invention by saying that he needed money: "And then I like to buy books, not only about physics; and I like to eat well. I am at my best during a good meal. The times are rotten!"

He wins his first victory when the papal astronomer, Christopher Clavius, confirms his interpretations. On the other hand Galileo is treated with complete indifference by the court philosopher in Florence. The skeptical thinker isn't even willing to take a peek into Galileo's telescope to check on the correctness of the new discoveries.

"There is a heavenly harmony, the divine Aristotle's view of the world," he says. "What is the use of trying to destroy that?"

The court in Florence finally gives in to pressure from the Inquisition, and Galileo is forced to go to Rome. Brecht points out that for the spiritual authority any other authority may be substituted. Thus the speech of the Inquisitor to the Pope, when he finally convinces the latter of the necessity of repudiating and rescinding the teachings of Galileo, acquires many meanings and becomes contemporary in a way that can only be construed as a criticism of all totalitarian claims to authority, including the Communist. "These people doubt everything," says the Inquisitor about the scientists. "Are we going to base human society upon doubt rather than faith?" Galileo's conclusions are right, but they are also dangerous, since they are aimed at the very foundation of the Church's teachings. The earth *must* be the center of the universe.

During a discussion in Halle the East German Professor Mathes made some remarks in the presence of Walter Ulbricht that could well have been taken right out of Brecht's play:

We men of science must, if we hope to achieve something significant, more or less question everything. Progress in science consists in questioning the past. When, however, we are told incessantly that the Mendelian laws are false, or that the world is infinite because Engels said so and that the physicists are wrong when they say that the world is finite—then one must answer that we scientists can exist only by questioning everything—Herr Minister-President, you can crucify me for what I have said here, but you should be grateful that you have still some professors at your universities who have the courage and character to speak out on matters as they are.

Since Brecht's play deals with freedom of the spirit, and not only with Galileo as a historical figure, the drama will always have relevancy. But it is hypocritical to think that Galileo's life has applicability only in the Eastern part of Germany. The freedom of the human spirit is constantly and everywhere threatened by churches which appeal to earthly or heavenly arguments.

Galileo becomes an easy sacrifice to the Inquisition. Without despising the martyr, Brecht also understands the traitor who buys his freedom on terms of shelter, food, and drink. The Pope enjoins the inquisitors to proceed gently; they are only to show Galileo the instruments of torture. The scientist will surely re-

cast his opinions: he knows what instruments can do! Regretfully, the Pope remarks: "He could not say No to an old wine or
a new idea."

Brecht understands Galileo's situation. But this does not mean
that the scientist is vindicated. Galileo is the last great man of
science whose discoveries became known quickly to the masses
and to those who lacked technical training. In his final mono-
logue to Andrea, who is now mature and himself a scientist,
Galileo achieves a clarity of vision which poses his problem in
sharpest relief. Science, says Galileo, brings knowledge about
everything, to all men. But it wants to make doubters of everyone—which is what both the earthly and the divine church fear.
What is the real goal?

In my opinion the only goal of science is to alleviate the hard-
ships of human existence. If men of science, intimidated by self-
seeking rulers, are content merely to store up knowledge for the
sake of knowledge, science can be crippled and your new machines
may mean only new oppression. In time you may discover everything that can be discovered, and still your progress will only be
progress away from humanity. The distance between you and them
can one day become so great that your joyous cry over some new
gain could be answered by a universal shriek of horror.—As a scientist I had a singular opportunity. In my time astronomy reached the
market place. Under these unusual circumstances the steadfastness
of a man could have had strong repercussions. Had I stood firm the
natural scientists could have evolved something like the Hippocratic
oath of the medical profession; that is, a vow to use their knowledge
only for the welfare of mankind. As things are now, the most that
one can hope for is a race of inventive pygmies that can be hired
for anything.

The Galileo of Brecht is a traitor to the people, not to pure
science. The scientific discoveries he had made could not be
halted by his repudiation. Brecht says in effect that Galileo's
betrayal meant that the opposition of the people to the Church
and to authority was smothered. Galileo was too weak to with-

stand the pressure. On the other hand there is double meaning in Brecht's presentation, and it is full of understanding for one who flees the pain of martyrdom. The ordinary person with ordinary senses is not created to be a martyr. This is the only point where Koestler's interpretation in *The Sleepwalkers* of the Galileo figure agrees with that of Brecht. Koestler speaks of "one of the most disastrous episodes in the history of ideas, for it was Galileo's ill-conceived crusade which had discredited the heliocentric system and precipitated the divorce of science from faith." Brecht is fascinated by the relationship of Science-People, Koestler by that of Science-Faith. Koestler looks upon Galileo as an irresponsible man, whose conflict with the Church was not unavoidable. While Koestler defends the Inquisition, Brecht compares it to all kinds of worldly authority.

The question of justice has always played a big part in Brecht's plays, which swing between the extreme of lust, sensuality, the mentality of a predatory animal, and the extreme of asceticism, resignation, obedience as Willy Haas has expressed it in his otherwise scandalously bad book on Brecht.

What the people understood about Galileo's discovery was that the authority of the Church was not infallible, that man was not the "crown of creation." The frightening scientific discovery of our own day, which can be understood by all, is that man is not only a being on the periphery but that he can be destroyed.

Brecht is undoubtedly correct in portraying Galileo as a traitor. By sacrificing his freedom as a citizen and by spending his last years as a captive of the Inquisition in return for his private, scientific freedom, Galileo became a forerunner of those scientists who later established a sharp demarcation between their private research and its political or social significance.

During the past twenty years physicists have seen the bitter consequences of Galileo's and their own betrayal. For hundreds of years they have been unscrupulous enough to serve masters

who were repugnant to them. They have sold their responsibility for the world. When finally they have come to realize that
a warning is in order they find themselves cut off from all chance
of influencing the course of events. Brecht has certainly read,
with recognition, the descriptions of the scientists' powerless-
ness in the face of the decision to drop atomic bombs on Japan.

As to what happened after Hiroshima Brecht wrote:

Then came the secrecy of the politicians and the military in regard
to this gigantic source of energy, which aroused the intellectuals.
Freedom of research, the exchange of discoveries, and the international community of scholars were suppressed by the authorities,
who were thoroughly distrusted. Great physicists fled the service
of their militaristic governments; one of the most famous took a
teaching position which compelled him to waste his time teaching
the most elementary principles, just to avoid working for these
authorities. *It had become a disgrace to discover something* [my
italics—J. D.].

The tremendous impact of still contemporary and understandable conflict that is conveyed by *The Life of Galileo* is
attributable to the masterly synthesis of details. The plastic
whole takes hold of one immediately, so that the spectator becomes unconscious that a technique is being used on the stage.
Near the close of the play Galileo's situation is projected through
a simple group picture. The half-blind scientist is sitting on the
stage. Andrea, the disciple who has been entrusted with the
manuscript of the *Discorsi* and who is to take it to Holland, is
on one side of him; on the other side is his daughter, Virginia,
who almost throughout the play has symbolized faith (in one
scene she is on her knees praying that her father will issue a
recantation) and who is now one of his custodians. It is to her
Church that Galileo has sold his freedom. It is in the presence
of her authorities that he has made his betrayal.

In his performance, Ernst Busch portrays Galileo as a person
of cunning and authority, sensually oriented, devoted to com-

fort but of penetrating knowledge—an ideal interpretation which emphasizes the many-sidedness of Brecht's language. Here, too, Brecht is mysterious, never fully ready to expose himself. The drama is clear and sharp, but it leaves the door open to many interpretations. It sounds a warning which the delegates to the Max Planck festival should not have missed. One of them, Heisenberg, has recently evolved a formula designed to restore harmony to the world picture that physics presents. But the most important task is to expel from mankind the fear of death, which is now more than ever threatened by discoveries whose uses no one knows.

25   *Brecht*

It is during the unusually hot summer of 1952. I have seen a guest performance of the Berlin Ensemble in the Deutsches Theater and am on my way to Brecht's rehearsal building. The outside of the theater has been landscaped—a park with benches, bushes, and sun-dried lawns. Just opposite Deutsches Theater there is a low, enclosed building in ruins, without windows. People go in and out. On the door there is a small sign: Berliner Ensemble.

I come into a little garden area with a lawn, lounging chairs, and tables. Empty coffee cups are on the tables, a manuscript is lying on a chair. Small birds are busy searching for bread crumbs. The garden is surrounded by high walls, the remains of a house. There is no one in the garden and I enter the building.

It is dark inside. There is a storage room for stage properties and a small auditorium with a few rows of theater seats. *Ur-Faust* is being rehearsed on the low stage. I take a seat and begin to feel the heat envelop me here in the shade and the darkness.

Brecht, dressed in his Chinese military gray coat, is sitting in the auditorium with the inevitable cigar stump in the corner of his mouth. A photographer in a cage high above and behind the rehearsal area is perpetuating each scene for posterity. Brecht's associates are standing at a respectful distance, ready to move in and act upon his signals. Neither the noise of the city nor Berlin's summer penetrates these walls. This is a theater laboratory.

Behind the auditorium there is another courtyard, but it is uncared for. Only weeds are growing there, plus some birch trees which have managed to send down roots through the stones. Brecht moves to the staircase in a posture as though he were waiting to be photographed. But I have no camera.

For many persons he has been a symbol of the dreamed-of *real* Germany, the cream of intellectual awareness, irony, and freedom. This dreamed-of Germany has been described in an English short story:

> But certainly it must be there. Something which was a combination of the rather weary irony of the refugees–, the bitter affirmation of the songs of Bertolt Brecht, the fighting passion of a Dimitrov (though, of course, Dimitrov was not a German); the crashing chords of Beethoven's Fifth. These qualities were fused in their minds into the image of a tired, sceptical, sardonic but thorough personage, a sort of civilized philosopher prepared at any moment to pick up a rifle and fight for the good and the right and the true!

For others who are convinced of the irreconcilability of ideologies Brecht has personified that which is most dangerous in Communism: its positive qualities.

Foreign Minister Heinrich von Brentano, on the other hand, has compared him to Horst Wessel.

Despite Brecht's composure I get the impression of an emigrant forever in search of a home. The East German state has given him generous support in realizing a long-standing dream: his own company, which is used as an experimental instrument under his searching eye. From time to time he is attacked from the East because of his formalism, and from the West for having sold his soul.

I tell him that I have translated one of his long essays, *Fünf Schwierigkeiten beim Schreiben der Wahrheit* (Five Difficulties in the Writing of Truth), which was written during his years of exile to describe the conditions of exile. But it is difficult to get it printed.

"This is the sixth difficulty," says Brecht.

Two years later I find him again in the Theater am Schiffbauerdamm, where he first won world fame. During the bitter winter days of 1954 I sometimes escape to the theater workshop on Schiffbauerdamm, away from the political theater played by the four foreign ministers alternately in West and East Berlin. The auditorium is decorated, as it was in 1928, in the nineteenth-century style, but a large troupe with a new spirit has come into the house. Brecht is sitting in the auditorium dressed as before, with the same cigar stub, and talks to his associates. He seems tired.

Another two years later, in August, 1956, I have just a brief talk with him in Buckow, where he is resting prior to the visit of his troupe to London. He speaks about meeting again, some other time, and appears still very tired.

When I get home I read in the papers that he died on the 14th of August. On the first anniversary of his death the East German post office released two stamps in his honor, valued respectively at 10 and 25 pfennigs.

He lived on Chausseestrasse, five minutes from the theater. He had just two rooms, one of them a former workshop with rough planks for a floor, simply furnished. There is a large and disorderly library, Chinese works of art on the walls. One shelf is full of English and American detective stories with gaudy jackets. The home is being used temporarily as an archive. His manuscripts, particularly the unpublished ones, are being arranged and photographed.

A crowd of police officers are on a visit. They look inquisitively at the books and at the manuscript, arranged with pedantic exactitude, of Brecht's lyrical interpretation of the Communist Manifesto. Any other questions?

"Yes," says one. "How could Brecht be satisfied with such a small, crowded home when he surely had opportunities to get something larger?"

"He had no pretensions. He liked the place, it was near the theater. And there are trees growing outside."

The People's Police bow and shuffle out.

"Better to be occupied with Brecht than with weapons?" says the chief archivist rhetorically, as we listen to the steps slowly echoing in the staircase.

From the window there is a view over the old and idyllic Huguenot churchyard where Hegel, one of those from whom Brecht learned his dialectics, lies buried beside his wife. Brecht insisted that the actors should read Hegel.

I follow a narrow path between the wall of the cemetery and the building and come to a grave outside the consecrated ground. There are a few pretentiously decorated graves, and near them, against a red brick wall, a single, uncut stone on which is Brecht's name.

It is still early spring and the grass has not become green. Someone has brought flowers to the grave.

His death united both parts of Germany, but there no two

commentaries agreed about his work. There is a classical and lyrical Brecht, contested by no one. There is also a theoretician of the theater, a politician and a Communist, who is controversial and will remain so. Despite the fact that Brecht's works have inner unity and consistency there are great differences between the universal message in *Galileo, Courage,* and the Communist, People's-Front ideology in his reworking of Gorki's *The Mother.* The evolution of Brecht into a poet who speaks to all has nothing to do with aging or resignation. Even at the age of twenty-one he was a great lyricist and a few years later a significant dramatist.

Brecht's work has become established not only because he is played with growing frequency in more and more countries. His plays have recently come out in a ten-volume set, but there will be four additional volumes from formerly unpublished manuscripts. And with typical German thoroughness a *historical-critical* Brecht Edition of thirty-five volumes is being prepared, as though he were a Goethe, a Schiller, a Kleist, a Fontane. Which he is, also, but even more: he is a poet of our times.

The two great interpreters of Brecht's theater are still Ernst Busch, the proletarian singer who first portrayed Mac the Knife in 1928, and Helene Weigel, Brecht's wife, who is manager of the Berliner Ensemble. These two have played the now classical Brecht roles, but in their footsteps are following a host of excellent players who have been schooled in strict but creative work by the Berliner Ensemble.

Dressed in black, matchlessly youthful, Frau Weigel sits at an old round table in her office on Schiffbauerdamm. Beside her is one of Brecht's foremost co-workers, Elizabeth Hauptmann. Both are chain smokers.

As so often happens when I want to meet someone, I have really nothing to ask. I want to see Helene Weigel's face, which

hovers between youth and old age, and to see the rustic furniture and to hear her voice. Her horsy face has become, if possible, even more wrinkled, her voice is as deep as ever. I know
that she gets furniture for the apartments of her players, that
she buys them burlap for their wall coverings. I know that she
has played Mother Courage more than four hundred times. I
have no desire to ask questions, but rather to experience personally a working laboratory which has done honor to the
theater by adhering to Brecht's formula: in socialist art, quality
must be paramount.

If it were only so always!

You artists who perform in the great houses under artificial lighting before silent crowds, seek out some time that theater which is
performing on the streets. That everyday, thousand-faceted and
unsung, but so very living, earthy, theater, fed on the common life
of mankind that plays on the street.

Thus Brecht admonishes his actors in 1930. It sounds like a
neo-realistic film manifesto, but, like other exhortations of
Brecht, it should not be taken literally. His production is rich
and varied; he has always tried to fit his direction to the character of the play, and not according to any rigid theory. But
when I see a number of similar stage settings in succession I
begin to think of his involved relationship to the past.

His reworking and stage production of Gorki's *The Mother* is
rightly renowned. The development of the mother, Pelagea
Vlassova, into a revolutionary is depicted in fourteen scenes.
His portrayal covers a much longer span of time than the novel,
and is therefore an original work, in which only Gorki's ideas
are utilized.

The performance, with its choruses (Eisler's music), its
dramatic actions and its vigorous, agitating rhythm brings
strongly to mind the Red proletarian theater of Weimar days,
with its simplifications and propagandistic knockout blows. A

viewer who is vacillating in his opinions will be overwhelmed. Together with some West Berliners and their West German guests I watch the play as the sixth person in a theater loge.

The West Berliners (who, too, are just as much Berliners as those on Schiffbauerdamm in the East) try to point out the strong points in the play to their friends:

"It's well *done*, isn't it?"

During the performance the emphasis upon *done* becomes even stronger. And at the end, not even that is said. They sigh.

It *is* well done. It is brilliant agitation, it is theater with the flavor of Red United Front and People's Front. It is like seeing a ghost out of the past, or—if you will—that part of Brecht's work in which the word "Party" is written with a capital letter. I cannot shake off the feeling of having experienced hollow declamation and empty rhetoric.

In East Berlin *Mother* is spoken of as one of the great Brecht stage mountings. One afternoon I come into the hall while the performance is being filmed. It is being preserved for posterity exactly as it was. Whether it survives as art remains to be seen.

I had something of the same consciousness of the past at the première of Vishnevsky's *An Optimistic Tragedy*. It too depicts revolutionary events, seeks to replace romantic clichés with reality, the reality of the theater. To this end it utilizes an anti-illusionistic prologue.

On the curtain one sees a cruiser at sea. On both sides of the stage there are suggestions of scenes: still other warships. A semi-comical act is played before the curtain. Three counter-revolutionary smugglers are sitting at a table. On the other side of the stage some girls are saying goodbye to the sailors, who are about to leave for battle. This is done with kisses and much pathos. Then the smugglers are overpowered and disarmed by the sailors. Suddenly one of them brings a halt to the act, stands in front of the others, and speaks directly to the audience: Let there be an end to such romanticism. The curtain, with its war-ships and side scenes, is torn down, both the smugglers and the sailors are tossed out. The real play, the real reality, the real reality of the theater can now be performed.

In *Mother,* and in the Brecht-inspired production of Vishnev-sky's play, an effort has been made to preserve the theater as a vehicle of agitation as it was in the thirties when it effectively reflected the times. Now it seems almost hopelessly passé.

26   Good and Evil

In the 1920's Berlin had more than fifty theaters; today there are exactly twenty, evenly divided between the two parts of the city. Piscator's former theater on Nollendorfplatz is now a movie house which offers American westerns. Reinhardt's Grosses Schauspielhaus is called Freidrichstadtpalast and has big variety shows.

The artistic predominance of the East side is indisputable, even though the Schiller Theater in West Berlin can compete effectively. Walter Felsenstein is working in East Berlin (at the Comic Opera) and is revivifying the style of the musical drama with brilliant performances. And at the Deutsches Theater with its *Kammerspiele,* at the new State Opera House, and at Volks-bühne one can frequently see nearly perfect performances.

With remarkably good taste West Berliners occupy the best and most expensive seats for a Brecht or Felsenstein performance, either at the State Opera or at the Deutsches Theater. Although the Berlin theater's center of gravity is in the East, one can find in the best from both sides a unifying element of critical realism which ignores sector boundaries.

I have chosen to describe Brecht as my single example because he remained true to Berlin, and because his influence has the greatest significance for the German and. European theater. Even the most critical partisan of Brecht since the twenties, Herbert Ihering, is working and writing in Berlin, while the competitor and enemy, Alfred Kerr, died upon his return to Germany in 1948. Ihering has written on Brecht with the same enthusiasm since his days as a critic with the *Berliner Börsen-Courier* in the 1920's.

Brecht's experiences as a medical orderly during the First World War, and his first-hand observations of the revolutionary efforts of the German workers, influenced his initial dramatic works. His attitude at that time comes very close to nihilism. Society—that is, capitalism—appears here as an expression of the unlimited struggle for power by antagonistic classes. Brecht fashions his conception of capitalism = the world, which never left him completely: anything is permitted, no norms exist, but the strongest wins. Or, in the words of the opera *Mahoganny*:*

> Erstens, vergesst nicht, kommt das Fressen,
> Zweitens kommt der Liebesakt,
> Drittens Boxen nicht vergessen,
> Viertens saufen, laut Kontrakt,
> Vor allem aber achtet scharf
> Dass man hier alles dürfen darf.

> * First and foremost, eating calls us;
> Secondly, the act of love;
> Thirdly, boxing oft enthralls us;
> Fourthly, drinking, as above.
> You can get away with any-
> Thing at all in Mahoganny.

This is one aspect of the times which Brecht hates and yet is fascinated by. It is typical of the mood of dissolution of the Weimar era. Even artists become involved in the polarization of political life. A conservative minority is driven to the right and ends up with Hitler. Others seek an ideal communism or socialism and end up in exile or in a concentration camp. Only at the end of the twenties does Brecht get close to Communism. Solidarity with the workers becomes a way out of the nihilism in society.

The inquisitorial elements in Brecht's productions become constantly clearer; trial scenes appear more frequently. From the question of society's coldness and enmity, the conflict between anarchy's "everything is permissible" and order's strict discipline, Brecht is led to the question of good and evil. Humanism and friendship are made exceptional in a world of barbarism. It is impossible to survive without cunning: the schizophrenic, split man makes his appearance.

This is the dramatic foundation of *Der gute Mensch von Sezuan,* which is being performed on Schiffbauerdamm under the direction of Benno Besson and with the unforgettable Käthe Reichel in the title role.

Three friendly gods want to intervene in the life of the world. They give money to the poor harlot, Shen Te. She buys a tobacco shop, but her goodness is irreconcilable with the demands of business. In order to extricate herself from difficulties she turns herself into her cunning male cousin, Shui Ta. Shui Ta is just as evil as Shen Te is good. He wears the mask of evil and suffering. The question which the gods ultimately put is typical for most of Brecht's productions: "Should there be another kind of man? Or another kind of world? Perhaps only other gods? Or none?"

From the dogmatic Marxian point of view (writes Volker Klotz) this question is purely rhetorical. *Another world,* that is the socialist reconstruction of society. But in the hands of Brecht the question ends in genuine irresolution. Not even Brecht knows the answer, despite the fact that as a playwright he strives to know the answers to as many questions as possible. Here, as in the rest of his great plays, he goes past the limits posed by dogmatic Marxism. His questions go beyond the narrow perspectives of class. Brecht knows that there is nowhere a refuge for goodness. It must be protected and preserved for another age, when hate will become the exception.

Background projections are frequently used by Brecht to help him overcome the drama's reference to a certain place, to extend the perspective of the action beyond the time and place shown on the stage. "The Sezuan of the parable," he says, stands for all the places where men are oppressed by men." And *Mother Courage* achieves its frightening effects because Germany's Thirty Years' War stands for all places and times where war is a reality.

Brecht was a jail-breaker, an outlaw, a traitor to German middle-class respectability. In his autobiographical and self-critical lyrics he emphasizes his revolt and his path to identity with the oppressed. At the same time as a poet and a person he is an emigrant, an outcast. As a refugee he is Germany's enemy. Both he and the working class are cast out of the bourgeois community, official society. The worker and the artist can join in a common posture of struggle; their goal is the same: to pave the way to a richer human life. Their methods are different. But art as "only art" is an absurdity to Brecht, even though in later years he frequently stressed that the theater is entertainment, a game.

Brecht has often been called dogmatic by his opponents. If he is, his dogmatism has enriched his productions and given them a striking power seldom seen in so-called undogmatic artists. He is always down to earth, close to concrete experience. That is why he condemns formal justice:

He makes this accusation against judicial procedure: its points of view do not correspond to the historical and social conditions, for they do not keep pace with historical movement. It does not penetrate deeply enough into the individual case and the social conditions which have given rise to it. It is in the hands of that social class whose well-being is dependent upon the maintenance of that social structure which bears the major guilt for the crimes. (Klotz)

In *Sezuan* the evil Shui Ta is arrested for having murdered the good Shen Te. Galileo is shown the instruments of torture as an inducement to recant. The *Caucasian Chalk Circle* reminds the people of that happy time when the judge, Azdak, in contrast to formal judicial procedure made decisions in the light of his own experiences: "You, however, you listeners to the story of *Chalk Circle*, pay heed to the opinion of the elders that each thing shall belong to those for whom it is best; that is, children to the mothers so that they will flourish, carts to the good drivers so that they will be properly driven, and the valley to the irrigators so that it may bring forth fruit."

Brecht repudiates the myth of heroism. Mother Courage lives cynically off the business of war until she reaches the naked and desperate loneliness of the final act. Only then does she merit sympathy. Galileo is a traitor and a pleasure-loving man. Puntila, the landed proprietor, is good only when he is drunk.

The difficulty in shaping these non-heroes lies in the actor's task of creating a detachment toward his role. It is a struggle between different layers of consciousness, which is played before the eyes of an audience. The part operates on three levels, that of the actor, that which indicates the actor's relationship to what is portrayed (to Galileo), and finally that of the part itself (Galileo himself). This requires an actor who has understood the role and the drama, and has not merely experienced and sensed it.

Without Brecht there would have been no living continuity between yesterday's Berlin theater (before Hitler) and today's, between the violent anarchism and artistic experimentation of the twenties and today's sick front situation. *The Threepenny Opera,* Brecht's break-through work, had its new première in the autumn of 1959 at the Berliner Ensemble. After the war the play was forbidden because its cynical lines were interpreted as criticism of the occupying powers.

Meanwhile, its theme song is now played in the night clubs and dance halls of West Berlin. Hither has it come after a long detour via America and Louis Armstrong.

27   *Exile*

Berlin is a real center of strength for East German literature only. West German authors prefer to live in the fatter, safer, and less political Federal Republic, where East-West questions are not discussed all the time.

The contributors to the famous anthology, *Hier schreibt Berlin* (1929) included Heinrich Mann, Ernst Toller, Lion Feuchtwanger, Georg Kaiser, Alfred Döblin and Erich Kästner. They are now either dead or no longer in Berlin. The leading German writers went into exile after 1933.

Max Zimmering, general secretary of Deutscher Schriftstellerverband (German Writers' Association) in East Berlin, is also an emigrant. He is not, however, a writer of significance, and publishes primarily SED-party poetry. His chief source of income has been his reporter's novel, *Phosphor und Flieder,* not quite as bad as his poetry and interesting for its description of Dresden in 1945 and afterward.

I make an appointment to meet Zimmering in his office on Friedrichstrasse. It is early in the morning. When I have taken a seat in his large work room there is a knock on the door and a secretary brings in a bottle of Weinbrand.

This is the second time that I have been served brandy in the morning in Berlin. The first time was at the Tarantel-Press.

Zimmering is about fifty years of age, speaks with a Saxon accent, and goes home to Dresden over the week-ends. I express surprise at the large staff in the offices of the writers' association.

Zimmering smiles modestly: "There are only thirty of us here. I think it's too few. We have, you know, two hundred members."

I do a bit of quick mathematics and discover that this means one office person for every seven authors. And it must be remembered that several VIP-writers have their own secretaries and chauffeurs.

As though he were reading my thoughts he says: "We have many responsibilities. In part we are a trade union and must see to it that the writers don't starve [which never happens among East German intellectuals] and are not treated badly by their publishers; we have, in addition, cultural-political and pedagogical tasks, and we cultivate our natural relations with the socialist countries."

The writers' association is also a sort of party bureau.

We drink a brandy. The sunlight streams in over a large writing table, a corner sofa, and some pictures. It is quiet—like the end of the world.

"I am primarily a political writer," says Zimmering.

I have not seen any nonpolitical writers in East Germany.

I ask Zimmering why so few of the returned emigrants have dealt with the new problems in Germany and—why not!—with "socialist reconstruction in the German Democratic Republic." My simple thesis is that the emigrant authors (despite the fact that most of them are Communists) really don't want to deal with these new questions, but prefer to confine their activities to warnings against the new Nazism in West Germany.

Zimmering has his answer ready: "It is not quite true that the emigrants have not written about the DDR; there are excellent examples to prove the contrary. And in the second place these emigrant authors are naturally drawn toward that period of their lives in which the struggle was most meaningful: Weimar, the First World War, the Spanish War, People's Front, the exile, and the struggle against Nazism."

I cannot escape the feeling that this is a dodge, an effort to put the best possible light on the situation. I look up Anna Seghers, one of the most prominent emigrants.

This is more easily said than done.

I know that she lives in Adlershof, but her number is not listed. Information service seems ignorant of her existence.

I telephone to the Writers' Association.

"Oh, you should call Frau Raffael. Here's the number."

"?"

"Frau Raffael is Frau Seghers' secretary and will know if Frau Seghers has time to see you."

I call Frau Raffael. We converse pleasantly for a while and Frau Raffael satisfies herself that I can be trusted. I get Frau Seghers' number. And when I call it is really she who answers at the other end of the line.

She lives on Volkswohlstrasse near the S-Bahn station in a house dating from the thirties. Her home is filled with books and art from Mexico and half the rest of the world. She is cosmopolitan and a Communist.

There is a Sunday quiet in Adlershof when I arrive. She serves me Starka, a Russian brandy out of an artistically shaped bottle designed like a cluster of grapes. The brandy is strong and good.

Like the other emigrants Anna Seghers can talk for hours about her adventurous life as an emigrant. .Germany lost over 500 writers through flight, concentration camps, or self-imposed silence—inner emigration—after they had been apprehended by the Gestapo and then turned loose.

Anna Seghers is almost white-haired, with wrinkles in her face. When she speaks her face is sometimes lighted up by a wonderfully attractive, yet tired, smile.

During our conversation she tries to assume a defensive attitude. I express my hope for the kind of change in East Germany which will assure greater freedom and security to the individual.

"And you say that you are not an enemy of socialism?" she says with annoyance.

No, I am not, but I don't call East Germany socialist either.

"When I got back to Berlin after the war," begins Anna Seghers, "Germany was not yet divided. One day I was sitting on a park bench and an old woman came to me and asked me to keep an eye on her bicycle. When she noticed that I didn't speak the Berlin dialect (my home is in the Rhineland) she asked me where I came from. From Mexico, I replied stupidly. Then the woman told me that I must send her a CARE package. I answered that I was here in Berlin and not in Mexico. The woman didn't say anything and left.

"Some time later I lost my way on a street in Warsaw, and asked a man for directions. He said: 'Where do you come from?' And I answered again, Mexico. Then the man said: 'You have a good president.' I didn't know what he meant until

he explained that he was attending evening school and had
heard there that the president of Mexico had nationalized the
petroleum industry.

"This shows the difference between two ways of life."

The story has an ironic double meaning which Anna Seghers
apparently had not noted. What she means is that socialism
(the present East German state) is building upon knowledge
and curiosity, it liberates man and is far superior to the "consumption mentality" of a CARE package. But East German citizens do not live on slogans about a freedom that does not exist
(even though the oppression in East Germany is less than com-
monly believed) but upon dreams of a better life in West
Germany. "They vote with their feet" (Willy Brandt) and flee
from what they consider a painful life to something they believe
is better.

I hear yet another story. An East German girl was asked by a
Western journalist why she had chosen to live in the DDR
(Seghers does not use the expression East Germany). The girl
replied that there were many differences between East and
West. But in the East everything is cleaner (*sauber*).

Anna Seghers means primarily a psychological cleanliness.
She believes that the East Germans have a future, a goal to
work toward. I have heard other East Germans say the same
thing. For them the West is shadowy, curtained night clubs
such as Petit Palais on Kurfürstendamm, unrestrained capitalism, militarism, dreams of revenge and restoration, while the
East is sacrifice, brotherhood, friendship.

I have the impression that Anna Seghers is talking about a
dream, an artistic illusion, and not about the reality to which
Marxists never tire of laying claim. I am not thinking here of
congresses and writers' conferences, of Walter Ulbricht and
SED party meetings or of Frau Raffael, or Anna Seghers' automobile. I am thinking about that spirit of *Angst* (fear) that one

finds in East Berlin despite the ease with which one can cross over to the West.

This fear has something to do also with the belief that the quality in everything is better in the West. An old woman whom I know rides over to West Berlin to dine on shashlik although she can get the same quality at the same price in East Berlin.

I ask myself if Anna Seghers does not live in a new—this time, unconscious—exile. Is she detached from the real truth about the state she praises? The answer is both yes and no, at least that is the feeling one gets when reading her last novel, *Die Entscheidung*, which has been published as the first part of a proposed larger work. The book came out in the late summer of 1959 and in it Anna Seghers reveals, in literary form (in some 600 pages), her ultimate position in regard to the East German "workers' and peasants' state."

She depicts the years between 1945 and 1951 and the events occur primarily in Germany, with flashbacks to the civil war in Spain, to Mexico, the United States, and France. The "determining" element in the story occurs in the life of Robert Lohse, the most fascinating figure in the novel. His hesitation and his individualism, his isolation and silence, are painted with the same psychological richness that gave Anna Seghers her earlier fame. Her description of a milieu is *as such* masterful. It is only when she wants to impose her political conclusions upon us that the whole structure comes apart. In the novel, just as in our conversation, she is convinced that East Germany is on the path of reason and brotherhood and that the doubters will gradually understand that the state needs their solidarity, as in the case of this Robert. His fate is linked to the industrial city, Kossin, where the workers on their own are rebuilding the ruined factories that once belonged to the Bentheim family, whose new West German enterprise is also depicted in the novel.

Those who flee from Kossin (Anna Seghers does not try to hide the fact) do so in order to avoid accounting for their Nazi past or because they have been recruited by Americans! West Germany is portrayed as a land of brutality and oppression where the really noble people must exist illegally.

We can read Anna Segher's novel as a work of art (and it is, partly) or as a contribution to, or taking sides in, the discussion on Germany. In the latter case it is a contribution to a discussion that never ends. Germans in the West and Germans in the East no longer speak the same language, and in the same way that Anna Seghers *sees* very little of the reality of West Germany the vast majority of West Germans see just as little of East German reality. The result is that an effort is made to idealize one's own world and discount that of the enemy. In his brilliant book, *LTI*, the Jewish philologist, Victor Klemperer, speaks of a breakdown in the German language, a corruption which influenced even the few surviving Jews from the Third Reich. (LTI = Lingua Tertii Imperii.) With the legacy of the pseudo-heroic, falsified Nazi language as background, Germany—split into two states—has also been split into two languages. It is not only the political terms that have numerous variant meanings and ambivalences, but the difficulties extend now to everyday speech.

In *Die Entscheidung* Anna Seghers glosses over the facts, dreams of a reality which does not in fact exist. But there are such writers also in the West. However, East German literature is devoid of works which try objectively to analyze conditions in West Germany. One Western book which looks at East Germany and the divided nation in a sympathetic, dispassionate way is the best-selling novel *Am grünen Strand der Spree* by the Berlin writer, Hans Scholz.

The book is a retrospective survey of the past. A group of

middle-aged and younger men meet in the Jockey Bar in West Berlin, where, during an entire evening and night, they tell about their respective lives and destinies. The novel is an artful mosaic of the so-called German Destiny, bewilderment and defeat, post-war hunger and prison camps, reconstruction and eventual partition. In most cases the individual stories have their beginnings during the war, when these men were scattered throughout Europe and discovered that it was too late to plan mutiny. The stories stemming from the Eastern Front and from northern Norway are particularly powerful.

A long section is concerned with East Germany and is also the occasion for the novel's happy ending, which becomes reality only in the morning when the gentlemen leave the Jockey Bar after having told stories about their own and others' lives.

Scholz' book is not a great novel. It seems in places frightfully naturalistic and much too wordy. At times I have the feeling that I am reading the transcript of a tape recording. On the other hand, Scholz has written an exact and believable story.

I am drinking tomato juice with Scholz at the Café Bristol and we are talking about Berlin. He is forty-eight years of age, a painter by profession. *On the Green Shore of the Spree* is his first—but not his last—book. Scholz is talking about exactness, that kind of precision which made his first book so good and sometimes so tiring:

"One must be careful when one writes about Berlin. What I mean is that one must know that American cigarettes cost 1,200 marks a carton, that some families during the blockade had to cook their meals in the morning between four and six o'clock while there was electricity. During the hunger years my family sold its last and only silver service to the Americans for fifty thousand marks. My parents lived many months on that money. I got cigarettes in payment for my paintings. If one does not know objective facts one cannot describe people, their fears and their hopes."

We walk together on the way to his residence on Fasanen-strasse. As we talk he seems open and free, not at all in exile, but at home in his city—Berlin. Unfortunately this is something that I cannot say about F., of about the same age as Scholz, also a writer, but living in East Berlin.

As a young man F. wrote successful comedies which were played on both German and foreign stages. He shows me some of them. They are commercial and strikingly free from intellectual aspirations. A number of years ago F. was recruited as a writer for the East German film industry in Babelsberg. He had lived earlier in Hamburg. F. defected.

He obtained a house to live in and moved his family and belongings to East Berlin.

He is a fast worker and writes two manuscripts a year, yet has plenty of free time. He drives around in an IFA. He lived through the Hitler era relatively painlessly. He has survived East Germany just as painlessly. He is just as unpolitical today as earlier. In contrast to the aging Hauptmann he never made any declarations sympathetic to Hitler.

He keeps his real treasure in a closet in his home—a complete, bound, well-read set of *Der Querschnitt,* the journal which, more than any other, represented the open, European-German culture during the Weimar epoch, and which Hemingway discusses expertly in *Green Hills of Africa.* When he has time on his hands it is F.'s habit to go through these volumes, sigh, and read further. It is a dream of a happy land, never found: the urge to experiment, impudence, freedom.

And F. continues to read.

When I see him now again after a lapse of several years he

seems more restless and close-mouthed, indisposed to discuss his viewpoints.

We are riding in his IFA across Alexanderplatz to the Café Warschau on Stalinallee. F.'s wife is along. I think she wants to get away.

F. is in a defensive position which is altogether too familiar to me. We get into an argument about the inevitable "June 17," even though my own point of view is far different from that of the one hundred-per-cent Western ideologues of freedom.

I make a few trivial comments on the façades and balconies on Stalinallee, and F. suspects it is a sly attack upon the *system*. Which, of course, it is.

I point out the strange paradox that East Berlin had earlier taken over a building style which flourished during the anti-labor era following unification—a closed, tenement-like style of architecture. I add that the apartments are wretchedly planned and badly constructed. And I insist that one does not have to be an expert in building construction to know that.

I concede that they seem finally to have learned from their mistakes. But were the mistakes absolutely necessary? On the other hand, I add, it seems paradoxical that the capitalistic, Americanized, war-crazy, and in every way despicable West Berlin builds *its* city of the future with light and trees and parks and detached housing units which are changing the face of Berlin. From grime and grayness to new freedom.

F. says nothing.

He is not silent because he does not know. He is silent because he can neither dispute me nor accept my point of view. He has a burden and a fear of words. We find that the coffee we are drinking and the cakes we are eating become hard to swallow. The situation becomes horribly painful.

As an author in the field of entertainment F. is very good; he is a technically skilled film writer, but his ambitions do not go beyond that day and that task which provide him with bread and security. Why should he hazard his security for a statement which serves no purpose?

I understand him.

And the worst thing about understanding him is that simultaneously I understand all those who choose warmth and food and clothing in preference to an uncertain freedom, an uncertain courage. The question of a man's point of view is ultimately the question of whether or not he can afford to be free.

Freedom too often demands—especially in our day—that one have either a large bank account or one's own desert island.

28 Damnation

On the first of October, 1810, a new daily paper appeared in Berlin, the *Berliner Abendblätter*, which declared itself "prepared in such special editions as this first one to cover everything that happens in the city and its environs, which, from the point of view of police activities, seems unusual and interesting, and to render prompt, detailed, and authentic reports upon them." The publisher-editor introduced some new journalistic principles. His paper became quickly known and its circulation increased rapidly.

The newspaper appeared six days a week. Advertisements for it appeared in other papers. The first number was handed out gratis. News of cultural interest was a secondary matter;

the population of the big city wanted sensational stories, police reports, and local news. The dominant Berlin newspapers of that day came out three times a week and their style was not appropriate for the new era.

The publisher of the *Berliner Abendblätter* made the big mistake of reducing the number of police reports and crime stories, as well as bar-room brawls and descriptions of intrigues in Berlin. In their place he put more and longer articles. The publisher even contributed some of his own short stories. The circulation went down. The paper had become altogether too high-brow.

Only a half year after the founding of the newspaper it printed an announcement as follows: "For reasons that cannot be given here I have decided to discontinue the publication of the *Abendblatter* with this issue. Elsewhere the public will be given a survey of what this publication was able to accomplish compared to what it believed itself authorized to promise, together with a historical reconstruction of the possible differences."

A half year later, on November 21, 1811, the publisher and chief editor of the newspaper, Heinrich von Kleist, committed suicide near the Wannsee.

It is said that he had doubts about Germany. This is true. But he had doubts also about himself and about his future. During his last years his personal and economic crisis grew worse. He blamed intrigues for the fact that the paper failed. The masses were not interested in the author, Kleist, who published some of his best short stories in the paper. They were interested in Kleist, the police reporter. He should have known this.

He had doubts not only about Germany, but about his own relationship to the nation. His sense of duty was mingled with revulsion against military discipline; his idealism, with a penetrating critical realism. Like his more recent successors Kleist sought faith and submission. The question of a double loyalty, which has bothered mankind in our times, was already a real thing for Kleist.

Of necessity his death had to be dramatic, idealistically histrionic. He acted in the same way as the futile heroes he had created. To continue living was impossible.

On November 20 Kleist took Henriette Vogel and rode out to a hotel on the Wannsee. It is said that the two had a pleasant evening. After dinner they wrote letters and went to bed. The next morning they paid the bill and ordered a messenger to take their letters into Berlin. Kleist wrote to his half-sister, Ulrike: "The truth is that nothing on earth could help me. And now farewell. May Heaven grant you a death even half as full of joy and inexpressible cheerfulness as mine."

The two drank some coffee and then went down to the shore. After shooting Henriette Vogel in the heart, Kleist put the pistol to his own mouth and pulled the trigger.

Today one does not ride to Wannsee in a carriage but on the Stadtbahn. The grave is only five minutes from the Wannsee station. Sightseeing boats dock here at the shore. They take Berliners out on the Wannsee, the Havel and the Tegeler See, the narrow reservoir of glistening water and freedom which the people of West Berlin still have. If you go by the Wannsee bathing beach in a boat during the summer you will see a mat of brown bodies but no sand.

I walk down toward the wide Königstrasse and then continue along a narrower road right to the embankment of the railroad. At the side of the road there is an American automobile graveyard and a garage, where soldiers in yellow coveralls are puttering with their cars.

The open strip of land between the road and the shore line, where the grave is located, is only a few yards wide. The houses are built snugly against each other on both sides of the road. A winding path leads to the grave. It is a simple stone in the shade of a tree. "He sought death and found eternity"—reads the inscription on the gravestone.

I look out over the shore and the water. There is no restaurant, only benches for the few visitors who find their way here. There is an endless stretch of time since that morning when Kleist committed suicide, but there is the same landscape, the same doubt about Germany, the strong and threatening.

Did not many have doubts about Imperial Germany? And about Weimar? And about Hitler? Today Europe awaits tensely what is going to happen to the two Germanies. What does it mean "to have doubts about Germany"? Is this a conflict that can be resolved only in death? Kleist could not know that Germany would cause the world more suffering than anyone in his day could imagine. He could not know that loyalty to Germany today is impossible, since there is not *a* Germany.

But Kleist's successors among the newspaper editors do not take their doubts and their loves quite so seriously. They are not prepared to resolve their problems by death. They have seen enough of death.

I know a young West Berliner who started a Sunday newspaper in 1956. It was called *Sonntags-Reporter* and came out during the newspaper-less Sunday afternoons. It had a good reception. It printed the latest football results, the latest political news, and the very latest film-star gossip. In short, the newspaper had every possibility of being a success.

But it received no advertisements and had to cease publication.

Today no one remembers *Sonntags-Reporter*. Except the publisher, W., and I.

There is reason to remember the paper—because not a word

in it was true. It was prepared in the middle of the week and printed on Friday, but was sold as the latest news two days later.

Surprisingly few of the many readers were aware that W. printed only lies. During the past 145 years since Kleist was a newspaperman the longing for news had become so strong, and faith in the printed word so widespread, that finally it was quite immaterial whether one printed lies or not.

No, W. did not commit suicide and he has no doubts about Germany. He is a prosperous businessman in West Berlin, he has read both Kleist and Goethe, and amuses himself by recording his telephone conversations on tape. W. has recently founded an advertising sheet called *Omnipost*, which goes to every home in West Berlin and advertises, among other things, bedroom furniture, TV sets, nylon stockings, pocket books on sex—all on installment payments (excellent terms).

It is Horst, political editor of *B.Z.*, the largest newspaper of the resurrected Ullstein empire, with a circulation of nearly 300,000, who accompanies me to W.'s villa in Steglitz.

Since Berlin was the capital of a growing state, the old Berlin press was influential. But only one of the Ullstein newspapers before Hitler, *B. Z. am Mittag*, circulated far outside the limits of the big city. What remain today are the former names, now divided on each side of the sector boundary.

Horst is twenty-nine years of age, W. somewhat older. We play cool jazz and talk about 1945. It is late at night and we are talking about Germany's collapse.

Why do we do this? It is because Horst and W. love to talk about that period. By a quirk of fate Horst had ended up in Czechoslovakia with his family. Since communications had been destroyed they decided to hike to Berlin. The party included Horst himself, who was a boy of fourteen, a small girl, a baby in a wooden box, and their mother. The trip took four weeks. They had managed to get a carpenter to fashion wheels for the wooden box so that it could be used as a baby buggy.

W. lived in Berlin and was a member of the Hitler Youth. He spent some time on a shooting range and drew beads on straw men. The defensive war of W. and Horst was without significance and shortly came to an end. When the Americans marched into their sector of Berlin both W. and Horst underwent re-education.

Each of them was named editor for his own youth newspaper, an organ of reeducation. Horst's paper was called *Wigwam*, it was mimeographed, and came out in 500 copies. W.'s paper was no more impressive. Horst had a jeep at his disposal and the editorial offices were set up in the work rooms of the physicist, Manfred von Ardennes. (The Russians had taken him to Moscow. He is now working in Dresden and is the chief of a large research institute.)

"For every number issued I received twenty bars of chocolate," says Horst with shining eyes. "When I was fifteen I made an interview with Bertrand Russell, who was then visiting Berlin. I poured out my admiration for his philosophy (with which I wasn't acquainted) and posed as tremendously well informed. 'A great democrat here on a visit,' I wrote."

From that date Horst has had a naïve, but genuine, admiration for everything Anglo-Saxon. He *was* reeducated. After editing *Wigwam* he was ready to conquer the world as a journalist. He got a position with *B. Z.* when it was started up again in 1954. His self-confidence, as well as his energy, is limitless. He has achieved what he has struggled for and he has no fear of any "restoration" which would force him to learn how to use an automatic pistol. With equal energy he attacks Nazism, Social Democracy, corruption, and Ulbricht. He believes in

Germany (West). He has learned his lesson, and he believes
that all Germans have learned their lesson—except the Pankow
government.

This description of my friend at *B. Z.* would not be complete
if I neglected to mention that Horst left his job shortly after
this occasion and moved to West Germany. He was, as I understood it, thoroughly fed up with Ullstein sensationalism.

But what does Frau H. say, who is eighty-two years of age,
one of the few who have survived from a period when Berlin
was the natural center for Germany and thus for the German
press? Frau H. is white-haired and has very positive opinions
that the past was better than the present.

"Once," says Frau H., "*B. Z.* was a decent paper. Now it is
only dung."

She serves me a glass of wine. I have a terrible hangover following my evening with Horst and W. in the villa in Steglitz.
We drove to a little pub in the vicinity, ate sausages and drank
schnapps, returned to W.'s house and played more cool jazz,
emptied his last bottle, and ended in agreement on almost
everything.

On the return trip Horst sang the praises of his Opel Rekord
and listed the weakness of all other cars. That's a weakness
among all automobile owners.

"It was wild, wasn't it?" he says as we part.

"Now there are no decent papers in Berlin," sighs Frau H.
"But before!"

She worked as the closest associate of the chief editor of
Tägliche Rundschau from 1914 to 1920. Like her newspaper
she belonged to the "national," that is to say, conservative wing
of German politics. *Tägliche Rundschau* reflected the thinking
of the upper middle class. Its watchword was the status quo.

"A heart ailment forced me to quit in 1920. The doctors told
me that I could continue working and die quickly or give it

up and live for another day. 'Frau H.,' said the Nazis to me, 'you must absolutely work for us.' That was in 1933. But I just showed them my doctors' orders."

For Frau H. the names Scherl, Mosse, and Ullstein are living legends: these were the three big newspapermen in her time. She lives now with her daughter in a small apartment in Wilmersdorf. One day she hands me some yellow newspaper clippings from the year 1918.

Why?

She likes to talk about the revolutionary period in Berlin, 1918-19, because she was still at that time an active journalist. Her eyes light up as she sits there motionless in her chair: "I recall the first balloon flights in Berlin. I remember the steam locomotive on the S-Bahn."

Yes, she remembers nearly everything.

I take the yellow pages from 1918 with me and start to read them. *Tägliche Rundschau* calls itself "the entertainment paper for the cultured of all classes;" its masthead is decorated with symbols of wisdom, art, and justice. On November 10, 1918, it reports that Berlin is in the hands of the Reds. In a long lead editorial the editor-in-chief enjoins his readers to close ranks around the common ideals of Fatherland and Nation. Of Potsdamer Platz there is the following account:

The throngs are immense. Trucks, loaded with armed workers and soldiers, laboriously press forward. Red flags are everywhere. And where in the world did all this red cloth suddenly come from? Certainly not much material is available on ration cards. Half-grown youngsters are hooting and flourishing hand grenades. Arms are as numerous as the sands of the sea; everywhere they have cleaned out military posts.

In those days there was terror throughout Germany. Fifteen years later the pendulum had swung to the opposite extreme—the black terror of Nazism. What neither Heinrich von Kleist nor the chief editor for *Tägliche Rundschau* understood, that there was neither a German Nation nor a united Fatherland, was what made it possible for the positive forces in Germany to destroy themselves in inner conflict.

On November 9, 1918, *Die Rote Fahne,* organ of the revolutionary Spartacists, states that the red flag is flying over the capital. This paper is edited by Rosa Luxemburg and Karl Liebknecht, who are shortly to see how their apprehensions about the results of the revolution are borne out. The newspaper was first printed in a bourgeois print shop, but was quickly thrown out. On November 18 Rosa Luxemburg describes the kind of attitude that is necessary:

> Not joy over what has been accomplished; not a triumph over the prostrated enemy is in place, but rather the most strenuous self-criticism and iron conservation of energy in order to carry on the work which has begun. For what has been accomplished is little, and the enemy is *not* prostrated.

The revolution was suppressed in all of Germany. The workers' movement was split and did not stand united in the face of coming decisions. The bestial murder of Luxemburg and Liebknecht, on January 15, 1919, confirmed the defeat of the revolution.

Frau H. could breathe again. The threat to *her* Germany had been removed, and the conservative forces were again in the saddle. The working class was again looked upon as traitorous to what was German.

Today's West German state looks upon itself as the legitimate heir of the German Reich which fell apart in 1918. Today's East German state looks upon itself as the moral heir of the testament left by Liebknecht: "And from every drop of this blood, of these dragon seeds of today's victory, will arise avengers for the fallen—new fighters for the noble cause, which is eternal, imperishable as the firmament. The fallen of today will be the victors of tomorrow. . . ."

In 1945 Frau H. was taken to a safer place, Breslau, but before the collapse she managed to return to Berlin via Czechoslovakia. She spent many weeks in a cellar, where she grew accustomed to hearing "Stalin's organs" (artillery), which began their program every morning at exactly six o'clock.

The war finally came to an end for her when a Russian officer walked into the cellar and greeted the women. One of them could speak Russian. The officer was polite and nothing happened. What Frau H. perhaps does not know is that the chain of events which began in 1918-19 with a victory for counterrevolution came to a logical end in an underground shelter when a Russian officer walked in as victor. Germany and the Germans have been responsible for much destruction and much terror in Europe. But I have the feeling that it indicates a tendency to self-destruction, conscious suicide.

This suicide did not occur in 1811, but 134 years later.

29   The Crippled Press

Only ruins are left of Berlin's former newspaper quarter. This section of the city lies abandoned astride the sector boundary, in the worst-destroyed part of Berlin. Only walls, and hardly those, remain of the publishing houses of Scherl and Mosse. On the former site of the Scherl building the big publisher of Hamburg, Axel Springer, has now begun to build a new bastion for his empire, which is held together primarily by the largest daytime paper of continental Western Europe, *Bild-Zeitung*. Significant for Springer's attitude is the fact that he laid the cornerstone of the new building on May 25, 1959—two days before the Russian ultimatum on Berlin was supposed to have run out.

One day I am wandering around in the cheerless silence near Koch, Zimmer, and Jerusalemer Streets. I encounter police officers from the East as well as the West, depending upon the side of the boundary on which I happen to be going. But it is silent, and it stays silent. Only the birds are singing. A bit further on are an excavator and a few empty trucks. It is the noontime rest period.

When Arthur Koestler came to Berlin in 1950 to participate in the "Congress for Cultural Freedom" his first question was about the Ullstein building on Kochstrasse. In his autobiography Koestler praises the progressive liberalism of the Ullstein interests during the 1920's. But in his Berlin speech of 1950 he preaches an intransigence which can hardly be reconciled with the Weimar ideal he says he admires: "I am speaking here of that category of our intellectual colleagues in the West who preach neutrality toward cholera. They are the victims of a strange intellectual perversion."

Twenty years earlier Koestler himself had become the victim of this cholera.

In September, 1927, he got a position as temporary correspondent for Ullstein in Jerusalem, which was the beginning of a brilliant career in this giant firm. He was transferred to Paris, and then came to Berlin in 1930. His colleagues were surprised that he went to Berlin of his own free will; they had dark suspicions of what might happen. Koestler continued his climb to

new heights of esteem and was soon science editor for *Vossische
Zeitung* and assistant editor of *B. Z. am Mittag*. The entire Ullstein press was at his disposal.

But in 1927 he was satisfied with his modest post in Jerusalem:

> The House of Ullstein was at that time at the peak of its glory.
> It was a kind of supertrust; the biggest enterprise of its type in
> Europe and probably in the world. It published four daily news-
> papers in Berlin alone. These were the venerable *Vossische Zeitung*,
> founded in 1704; the *Berliner Morgenpost* with the largest circula-
> tion of any newspaper in the German language; the *B. Z. am Mittag*,
> a midday paper which broke all news-speed records, and *Tempo*,
> a sensational evening paper. . . . To be a correspondent of Ullstein's
> was consequently every newspaperman's dream and placed you
> in the aristocracy of European journalists—or at least made you
> feel terribly important. Particularly at the age of twenty-two, as
> the youngest person on record to ascend to such dignity.

Koestler turned Communist in Berlin. He can hardly have
been of great help to his party. He has been equally ruthless
and one-sided in his arguments both as a Communist and as a
militant anti-Communist.

Koestler induced his closest associate on *B. Z. am Mittag*, a
certain von E., to pass on to him rumors and information concerning German diplomats and the military. Koestler then
transmitted this to the Party. Von E. quickly regretted his innocent activity as an informer and informed Ullstein of Koestler's duplicity.

Koestler was fired a few days later.

He went to the Soviet Union in 1932, firmly convinced of the
logical connection between the modernism of Weimar, the
liberalism of Ullstein, and the new Soviet state. He had occasion to revise this opinion.

> The motto of the House—that is to say, Ullstein's [writes Koestler]
> —was political liberalism and cultural modernism. It was anti-mili-

tarist, anti-chauvinist and Pan-European. . . . It was a political power, and at the same time the embodiment of everything progressive and cosmopolitan in the Weimar Republic.

That sounds like a report from some gray, prehistoric time. In the West Berlin of today Ullstein's has the same external position it had in the Greater Berlin of those days; but with changed circumstances the newspapers have also become different. *B. Z.* has been published since 1954 and is West Berlin's largest paper; the *Berliner Morgenpost* is the next largest. The big brick building at Tempelhof issues a constant stream of its own and other papers. Rudolf, one of the five sons of the founder of Ullstein enterprises, is now in charge of the operation.

But a war has swept over Berlin.

During the first years after the war there was open competition between the newspapers of East and West Berlin. As early as May 15, 1945, the Russians started to publish *Tägliche Rundschau,* but now as an organ of the occupying power. Somewhat later the *Berliner Zeitung* appeared, also on the East side. The name was filched from Ullstein's. One consequence of the partition is that certain newspaper titles appear on both sides of the sector boundary, *B. Z.* in West Berlin, *Berliner Zeitung* and *B. Z. am Abend* in East Berlin. Likewise, the largest illustrated newspaper of its time, the *(Neue) Berliner Illustrierte,* is published in the East.

The newspapers of West Berlin with good reason can be called provincial. But the press in the East has managed to create its special variety of dreariness and of German-Russian socialist provincialism which is at least as tiresome. While the West Berlin newspapers parade as courageous experts on the East, with detailed—and sometimes falsified or exaggerated—news items from "the Zone" or Pankow, the East Berlin newspapers play the no less heroic role of experts on the West.

A goodly number of the reports of corruption and stupidity in West Berlin are undoubtedly true, but the moral right of the press in East Berlin to criticize has been forfeited since it remains silent about shortcomings and mistakes in its own area and seems incapable of saying a good word about West Germany.

The greatest and most significant contribution made to the history of the press in postwar Berlin was made during the 1940's by *Telegraf,* the chief mouthpiece of the Social Democrats. In the ideological struggle for Berlin the publicist Arno Scholz played a significant role; people even talked in the city of the "*Telegraf* party." While vigorously attacking those in power in the East, Scholz turned his criticism toward Western politicians for lack of initiative on the Berlin question.

The press in West Berlin reacts with extreme sensitivity to any expressions that might damage the reputation of Berlin as a heroic city, but the East German press, on the other hand, has been converted into phrase-mongering nothingness. In both quarters there is lack of a living connection with the past. What became of the modernism of Weimar, the liberalism of Ullstein, the positive traditions of German socialism? Where are the remains of the influential, well-informed Berlin press?

Presumably where the ruins of the newspaper quarter stand.

The victor powers in both East and West have ceased publishing their own newspapers. Perhaps it might be worth the pains to visit a building which is a sort of parody of newspaper publication and yet goes under that name.

This is the editorial office of *Neues Deutschland* on Mauerstrasse in East Berlin.

This is a tremendous office complex, with endless corridors and an endless number of employees. One of the editors of the paper explains the situation candidly: everything proceeds by checking up on checking up on checking up; that is to say, a complicated network of security measures to prevent the small number of real editors from letting slip any unguarded word.

In such corridors, and in such buildings, with their meticulous doormen and cumbersome formalities for entering, I am reminded of K.'s question to the Herr Supervisor in Kafka's *Castle*: "In the castle you are acquainted only with the office arrangements?" And then the ironic answer: "Yes, but they are also the most important."

The press in East and West Berlin has one questionable quality in common: the tone of each is just as crude and blunt, the invectives rain down just as readily. The writers on both sides of the border seem to know that this world city is powerless, that its fate will not be determined in Bonn or Berlin, but possibly in Moscow or Washington, if even there. This feeling of being crippled leads to bumptiousness and provincialism.

The above thoughts come to me one afternoon at the Press Club in Haus der Presse on Friedrichstrasse, where it is my habit to eat, since the doormen and waiters are old acquaintances and are glad to exchange stamps, a common kind of German social intercourse.

Over the years my journalistic friends in the East have become a bit fatter and have acquired a broader self-confidence, while their colleagues in the West hunt up Eastern news just as hungrily as ever.

Only in this East Berlin Press Club have revolutionary changes taken place.

During the summer of 1952 I was privileged to eat my red cabbage under the watchful eyes of Ulbricht, Grotewohl, Pieck, Lenin, and Stalin. Marx and Engels, with their beards, hung there also, although in smaller format. During my next visit, in 1954, I noticed that all the political leaders except Pieck had disappeared, while the classical figures remained. And in 1956 only Marx and Engels were there. There were landscape paintings and industrial motifs hanging in the empty spaces. I remember especially a sunny, pleasant landscape, bathed in the positive sunshine of the creator.

Further, I thought to myself, the revolution cannot go. But now even some of the landscapes have disappeared. From one wall an old lady in a chair is looking out, with a face that is tired and free of illusions. The landscapes have been changed: a shipwrecked boat on the shore, although not Van Gogh's boat. Only Marx and Engels are left. From time to time they hang up the photo of some Communist who has been arrested in the West and for whose release an East German campaign is under way.

But the waiter who was collecting stamps is gone.

30   *A Single Journey to Potsdam*

The man sitting opposite to me has a glass of beer in his hand, froth on his jaw.

I am eating a late breakfast of bread, marmalade, and coffee. At the moment no one is playing the slot-machine. The man is in early middle age; beard and tired face reflect his poverty. The waiter is exchanging confidences with one of the guests about the latest bicycle races in the Deutschlandhalle. A girl is sweeping the floor. The windows are shaking from a power drill. The windows in Berlin will be shaking from these machines for another thirty years.

This is the tavern Zum Weissen Mohr.

The door opens and a woman enters. She is heavily painted and her face shows just as much evidence of drink as that of my table companion. She plops down immediately in his lap:

"Karl, give me a couple of coins. I want to play the machine for a beer."

Before he can answer either yes or no she has dug some money out of his coat pocket, signaled the waiter, ordered a beer, and started to play the slot machine. Surprisingly enough, she wins. In a couple of minutes she has 1.50 marks on the ,table (including her original capital). Then she sits down.

"Karl," she says as she smacks him on the cheek with her lips, "I'll buy you a beer, I've got money." He doesn't answer, but she sits in his lap again and pats and caresses him.

"Karl, Karl baby, how nice to see you here." She picks up a few coins from the pile on the table and begins to play the machine again. But now she loses. By the time I leave it is Karl who is buying her beer.

I take the 12:13 train for Potsdam.

For Karl and the other residents of West Berlin Honolulu is more accessible than Potsdam, the city of barracks, of Prussian militarism and Prussian culture. This despite the fact that the S-Bahn on the way to Potsdam goes through the West sector every twenty minutes.

During the ride out I get a reminder that "Potsdam," too, is a disputed political concept. A man in a dark coat and worn hat is standing jammed against the door of the train. He is speaking loudly and unpleasantly, almost in a wail.

"I come from the lost areas in the East," he whimpers. "I lost everything—my family, my children, and my belongings. Help me out, give me some money. Even Eastmarks. Look, I've got some pictures to sell."

A cluster of photographs is hanging over his stomach. Most

of them are pictures of dogs: sitting, lying, standing, well-clipped and cared-for dogs. The man is also carrying a small black satchel (much like that of the conductor), perhaps for money, perhaps for pictures. Right next to this beggar there is a man sitting and holding the hand of an old woman. At least he can be excused because he is blind and perhaps doesn't know where the beggar is standing.

Wannsee is the last stop on the Western side. Both the beggar and the blind man with his guide have disappeared. Our papers are looked over in Griebnitzsee. The People's Police and a Russian soldier go through the cars. The check is made quickly and the police are polite.

The impoverished face of Potsdam has not changed in the years since I was last here. It is a medium-sized city, and yet I have the feeling of gloomy provincialism. The *Residenzstadt Potsdam* (Potsdam the royal residential city) exercised its dominance not only over Berlin but over all of Germany for a long time. The big city, Berlin, is usually described as progressive, worldly, coarse, and ironical, but Potsdam is portrayed as reactionary, musty, and backward-looking.

It was this Potsdam spirit that Adenauer had in mind when he objected to Berlin as a capital. But in my judgment the slanderers of Potsdam are not entirely correct. There are two kinds of Prussian spirit; one is reactionary, military, and narrow, the other open and humanistic. Potsdam is not Berlin, that is true. But without the influence of Potsdam Berlin would lack an important nuance.

There are two purposes to my visit. One is the Potsdam of Frederick the Great. I want to refresh my impressions of his total planning and his efforts to create in Potsdam a world both uniform and civilized. But I want to go also to the more modern Cecilienhof, where something quite other than a uniform Gorman world got its start in 1945.

A description of Potsdam today can degenerate easily into a short chronicle about the little that is left. The old Prussian city was destroyed almost completely in a twenty-minute daylight bombing on April 15, 1945. Today the city lies in East Germany. And to demonstrate the humanitarianism of the Russians it is reported that a cultural officer was sent from Moscow whose responsibility it was to watch the park around the castle so that it was not overrun by the tanks or shot to pieces. There is a certain comedy in trying to protect Frederick the Great's creation from harm.

I can see the old residents, elderly ladies with black coats, fluttering around the streets. Others are standing in the little apothecary shop searching for a coin in their purses in order to pay for some headache powders. I have gone in to try to find some relief for a hoarse throat. But Potsdam is not only elderly ladies, or only the students who attend the nearby institutions of higher learning. A third Potsdam, wearing warm coats, can be seen going into the barracks with packages of food under their arms. These are the Russians.

Several epochs of time exist side by side. On the Brandenburger Gate situated on Platz der Nation (the terribly ugly copy of its namesake in Berlin—but without Schadow's quadriga or a red flag) they have placed a huge advertising poster for the Jugendweihe, the atheistic confirmation ceremony. Two young people are looking trustfully toward some distant future; that is, approximately in the direction of the S-Bahn train and West Berlin.

But in the little stationery shop just thirty yards from there, on Klement Gottwald-Strasse, the show window is filled with confirmation and birthday cards. A little further on I see a truck parked, loaded with new, unpainted coffins.

In the huge castle park around Sanssouci there is no trace of our times with its competing points of view. Except for a few

gardeners the place is empty. The traditions and legacy of
Prussia are being preserved here by an agency called "Administration of the State Gardens and Castles of Potsdam-Sans-
souci." Its office is housed in some old buildings below Sanssouci. Professor Willy Kurth, who is in charge of the work, is
an internationally known scholar.

"We are doing what we can," says one of his assistants, a
young art historian whose voice holds a note of slight regret,
almost of gloom. "We are trying to protect and restore the old
architecture. The city castle, Frederick's winter residence, was
destroyed in many parts, but it is reparable. There are many
people who want us to tear down the castle. Naturally, we don't
want to see that happen.

"And what should one do with the attractive old burgher
houses?" he goes on. "It is expensive to restore them. And who
is to live in them? We, too, suffer from the partition of Germany.
Let me give you an example. Both here and in West Berlin
there were memorial exhibits for Pesne and Knobelsdorff. But
the exhibit materials were entirely different. Couldn't one have
put the two exhibits together? Oh, no! And we seldom have
visits from West Germans or West Berliners. One can safely
say that it is impossible for them to come here."

Since then the situation has changed somewhat: The East
Germans have given permission for West Berliners to make
organized bus trips to Potsdam.

Today there is not the same effort made to dwell on the personality of the ruling princes. The individual artists who set
their stamp upon the castle are finally getting their due recognition. So far as possible Professor Kurth's staff is trying to remove the tasteless additions dating from the nineteenth century, and restore the original harmony, the pure beauty of the
eighteenth-century castles.

I wander over to Sanssouci, up the broad steps, past the

large pond with yellowish gold fish, past the marble baths with the quasi-Greek statuary, and past the orangery. And as I proceed I note again that Sanssouci is a pleasure house, not a cold castle. The free sculptures of the façade by Glume create the impression of lightness and free space, which never leaves me inside the building.

I shuffle through the rooms and listen to the comments by the excellent person whom Kurth's assistant has placed at my disposal.

"What would you like to know?" he asks.

"I don't want to know anything, just look."

He says regretfully that the rugs and the original paintings were removed during and after the war. Some are being held in West Germany, others have disappeared, some are in Cecilienhof. On the other hand there is a bust of Charles XII of Sweden standing in the marble room, the graceful central point in Sanssouci.

I renew my acquaintance with the special attractions of Sanssouci: the wing where the King lived, the dirty armchair in which he died, the circular library room with its French books, the flute, the Voltaire Room with the naturalistic wooden ornamentation of Potsdam rococo. In contrast to other castles in Potsdam, Sanssouci gives almost the impression of being a club for rich artists, for people with individual taste and refinement.

This is the humanistic side of Prussianism.

The pub, Zur Historischen Mühle, is in the midst of its quiet season, early in the year. It is strategically located one hundred yards from Sanssouci. An old man and I are the only guests. As protection against the cold the waiter recommends brandy-and-water. Above the bar there are a number of dusty champagne buckets, mementos from the good old days. There is a stuffy odor of food in the place. A large woman in a black costume, one of the service personnel, has taken a seat on the other side of the room and tries to engage me in conversation about the weather. We both decide that it is cold. On the hillside toward the "Ruinenberg," the product of a mistaken fantasy, I can see evidence that the Russians have been in Potsdam. There are inscriptions on many trees, names and dates after 1945.

Most grotesque is the still preserved artificial ruin: there are altogether too many real ruins in Berlin and Potsdam. Here is an edifice built to create a mood of decorative ruin. There is a round, deep pond in the middle.

In the open places between the trees boys are playing football.

31   *Cecilienhof*

This castle was built during the First World War but is now in the exact condition it was on the second of August, 1945, when the Potsdam Declaration was signed. Not a chair has been moved.

Cecilienhof is not for instruction in art history. Here one studies our own times as interpreted by the Museum for German History. It is one of the cult centers of the East German regime.

The castle was empty when the Russians came. Prince Friedrich-Wilhelm, with the help of the Fascists (I am quoting the guide), managed to move out the furniture in March, 1945, and ship it to the West. The only thing left was a library and a collection of securities in one of the desk drawers. The forgetfulness of princes is unfathomable.

With admirable speed the Russians filled the castle with valuable objects from other castles in Potsdam.

The miniature flags of the three participating nations are standing on a table in the dark conference room, the Russian in the middle. This was done at the suggestion of the Western allies, says the guide, because the Russians carried the brunt of the war. There are two photographs hanging on the wall, one of all the delegates to the conference and one of the Russian delegation, with Stalin, dressed in white, in the middle. "Up there," says my woman guide as she points out a gallery overlooking the conference room, "is where fifty journalists followed the negotiations."

First we visit the Anglo-Saxon wing. It is inspired by conservative English upper-class architecture, with dark paneling, low ceiling, relative freedom from pomp, intimate shadows.

We are in Truman's work room.

"It is in harmony with President Truman's imperialistic nature that the Prince's war literature, all kinds of imperialistic memoirs, and works on military history are preserved here. Look for yourself."

The collection of military literature is impressive.

As to Churchill's work room (later Attlee's) she points out that the desk chair was too narrow.

"The English Prime Minister was forced to sit on the sofa."

My guide takes out some maps, which have been pasted on paper, and which show the various Western plans for the partition of Germany: "These plans were abandoned during the meeting. As leader of the Soviet delegation Stalin alone defended the idea of a *democratic, united,* and *peaceloving* Germany. The chief result of the Potsdam Conference was that these Soviet principles were approved."

Frederick the Great's castle, Sanssouci, in Potsdam

Bernauer Strasse, showing the end of the French section of Berlin

After this little lesson we go into the conference room again.

I take note of the fact that German participation was confined to a carpenter who sawed the round conference table. We pass the bright salon where Marshal Sokolovsky, as host to the conference, received his guests, and enter Stalin's work room, which, like Truman's, is outfitted with books.

"Here we have the humanistic literature," says the guide (I can see now the diabolical calculation whereby Truman got the books on war). "Take a look on the shelves. Here are decent, bourgeois, humanistic books such as Brehm's *Tierleben*, and even the collected works of St. Simon."

"And Stalin sat there?"

"Yes, Stalin sat there. Can you see that the upper side of the desk chair has been whittled off? It is said that an American reporter took this piece of wood as a souvenir."

I am shown also the work rooms of the lesser Russian prophets. They are not especially pleasing for an explorer. But Princess Cecilie's boat cabin is one of the things really worth seeing.

She loved to sail, but during the World War she did not dare venture out into the Baltic. So she had Blohm & Voss build her a standard boat cabin in the castle. The windows are portholes, the walls are painted white, and the ceiling is low. In order to complete the illusion of a ship at sea a shaking machine was placed beneath the floor. When it was "under way" Dame Cecilie could sit in the cabin and look out the round windows toward the trees in the park (they must have disturbed her) while the machine created the illusion of a ship in motion. I understand that the Museum für Deutsche Geschichte takes sadistic pleasure in showing this room. One could really find no better example of Imperial German snobbery.

"My best wishes for a quick recovery," says the guide as I leave her at the exit.

"Thanks, the same to you," I answer and try not to think that she means my cold, not Germany.

Something obviously sickly hovers over this memorial, this meeting place of the world's great between the 17th of July and the 2nd of August, 1945. While East German propaganda never ceases to remind the people of the decisions made here, forgetfulness of Potsdam rests like a curtain over every respectable West German citizen. The attitude of each is determined by the usefulness, or respectively the harm, which an awareness of Potsdam might produce. This fundamental difference in the attitudes of the two states has not changed, even since the changed Russian campaign in respect to Germany.

It is now a depressing experience to read the Potsdam Declaration, a document which history has wiped out. The typical example is the question of Germany's eastern border (referred to in the Declaration as the western Polish boundary). While confirming the right of Poland to occupy the area east of the Oder and Neisse Rivers, the document says, "the final determination of the western border of Poland will be deferred until a peace conference has met." Since then the Soviet Union has considered the boundary as definitive, and the government of East Germany has dubbed it the "peace boundary." Even the Western Allies had nothing against the Oder-Neisse line so long as it could be assumed that the new Polish government might be pro-Western, even though neutral. In his speech to the House of Commons on December 15, 1944, Churchill did not raise any objections to shifting the Polish territory to the west as compensation for the areas abandoned to the Russians in the east.

The arguments whereby Churchill and his successors later justified a directly opposite solution are here conspicuous by their absence. To drive out the Germans from the territories

east of the Oder-Neisse seems to Churchill "the most satisfactory
and permanent method."

Today the question of the East German boundary has become a component in the German neurosis, just as unnecessary
as it is colored by propaganda. No West German map would
dare, or could, show the frontier as final; the eastern areas are
designated as Russian- or Polish-*administered*. East Germany
is frequently called *Middle* Germany, since the real East Germany is in Poland. On Mehringdamm in West Berlin there is
an imposing road sign which shows the distances in kilometers
to Königsberg, Danzig, Breslau, etc. Is this an effort to show
these cities are still German, that they are not called Kalinin-
grad, Gdańsk, and Wroclaw?

Politicians and newspaper reporters in West Germany and
Berlin, who, when speaking officially, never cease to talk about
"a mutually satisfactory boundary revision," concede privately
that the boundary question is a political chess piece, suitable
for use in future negotiations. Therefore, it is emphasized on
all public occasions that it would signify a new act of humanity
if the Germans, after many fateful years, were allowed to move
into these completely Polish areas.

All of this comes as a consequence of the Potsdam decisions.
The chief issue, however, is the question of German unity. German militarism and Nazism must be crushed, but it is "not the
intention of the Allies to liquidate or enslave the German
people." On the contrary: "The Allies wish to give the German
people the possibility of preparing themselves to rebuild their
lives on a democratic and peaceful foundation. If the German
people attempt unremittingly by their own efforts to achieve
this goal it will be possible for them at a suitable time to take
their place among the free and peaceful peoples of the world."

At the time the Potsdam meeting was held the troops of the
Western Allies had marched into Berlin and the brief period

of four-power administration was beginning. The Allied Control Council exercised supreme authority in Germany, but the Potsdam Declaration provided for five central German secretariats, which would function under the Control Council. This rudiment of a German government was torpedoed by the French, who never felt themselves bound by the principles of Potsdam. Their object was partition, which can be seen, among other things, by what the French representative in the Control Council said in December, 1946—at a time when the British and Americans had already joined their zones into one: "Those Germans who wish to see restored sooner or later a fatal union of the German Reich are Pan-Germans, not democrats, no matter how well-intentioned they may be."

Germany's unity was France's nightmare.

In the Potsdam agreement it was stated explicitly that the largest portion of the Russian indemnity of ten billion dollars should be taken from the East Zone, while the Western Zones should be responsible for the indemnities to the Western Allies. The Russians collected their demands by impoverishing the Eastern Zone, by dismantling factories and carrying off railroad tracks. For the English and French allies it was more advantageous to abandon the idea of unity and thus prevent the Russians from participating in the control of the Ruhr.

The French contribution to German unity was to act just as ruthlessly in their zone as the Russians did in theirs.

If the same policy of impoverishment had been pursued in Anglo-Saxon Bizonia it would have meant mass famine. The area was crowded with refugees from the East who had to be fed. But both the Russian and the Anglo-Saxon attitudes were conditioned by a tactical question: what is best for *us*? Small wonder that the Germans became cynical and took help from whatever quarter offered it.

The period down to 1948 is usually called the "years of the

Potsdam agreement." On March 20, 1948, when the Control Council met for the last time, the Potsdam Declaration was transformed into what it had really been during the previous period—a collection of worthless papers. Since 1946 measures had been adopted and carried out on both sides of the zone boundaries which had tended to deepen the cleavage between the different parts of Germany.

It is only in Berlin that the partition is so obviously an open sore that one cannot forget it. For two-thirds of the city's population a ticket to Potsdam would represent a foolish expenditure since the trip would end at Griebnitzsee, with consequent arrest and interrogation. Some Western newsmen have complained that there is a train which stops at Bahnhof Zoo and then continues directly to Potsdam; innocent West Berliners and foreign tourists can, through no fault of their own, end up in East Germany. This is a false picture of the situation: these *through trains* are announced several times over the station's public address system at Zoo. Only a foolish person would take this train. But foolish persons can make other mistakes in Berlin.

During my visit to Cecilienhof I have kept my taxi driver waiting outside. The chauffeur laughs heartily as we drive away and pass through the gate several kilometers from the castle. The female guard is polite and respectful. When we had entered she wanted to see our papers and register us. I ask the chauffeur what has changed her attitude.

He tells me that while waiting at the castle he had picked up the telephone at a moment when he wasn't being observed and had called the gate.

"I disguised my voice and bawled out the porter for causing so much trouble for an important foreign guest. She answered that the chauffeur had been impolite, but I said that that was impossible, since the chauffeur is a respected and well-known person in Potsdam.

"So now she's polite," he adds. "When I called, she thought it was someone in the administration of the museum. We Germans are like that. As soon as we start talking to a superior we begin to crawl. But if we encounter an underling whom we can boss around, we do it gladly."

I feel confident that that man knows more about Germany than many of those who participated in the Potsdam meeting. In both parts of Berlin I feel the presence of a protector, a higher potentate, which is not only localized in the military encampments at Karlshorst and Dahlem, but which hovers like a gas over the city.

My chauffeur, who gets me to the S-Bahn admirably on time, would perhaps concur in the final words to be found in an excellent book dealing with the partition of Germany: "Since both [German states] equally assert claims, authorized by their momentary protectors, to speak solely and exclusively for all of Germany (although each is only a part), they avoid each other like the plague."

32   Darkness in Berlin

"Well," says B., "so you have been in Potsdam. That town has always been a threat to Berlin, but not today's Berlin, of course. The glitter of monarchy and the hardness of the military came to Berlin from Potsdam. But Berlin has always managed to defend itself against outsiders and to live by its own strength."

We are sitting in the new pub, Berliner Kindl am Hansaplatz, from which we can see the new buildings in the Hansa Quarter, the clean lines of Aalto's and Niemeyer's apartment houses, the Catholic church with its three bells, and the sky with its shifting hues from bright sunlight to the ominous gray which precedes a rain. The façades of the buildings do not tell everything, and the unity of lines can be deceiving. In some of them here in the Hansaviertel there are some idiotic solutions to problems— toilets separated from the living room only by lattice work, dwellings made for machines, not people. But even at that, B. insists, it is a daring and on the whole successful experiment, and as a contrast he cites Rilke's description of the misery of housing in the nineteenth century:

From these walls, once blue, green, or yellow, and now framed by the scars of parti-walls which had been destroyed, emanated the air of this life—the sticky, inert, foul air, which no wind had dissipated. Here was the odor of food, of illness, of exhalations, the smoke of many years, and of sweat which exudes from armpits and makes the clothes heavy, the stale human breath and the fermented smell of dirty, sour feet. Here was the acridness of urine, the sting of soot, the gray vapor of steaming potatoes, and the heavy, slick smell of old grease.

B. is a journalist and author. His best book, *Thomas Mann und die Krise der bürgerlichen Literatur,* came out right after the war. B. writes reviews of the theater, observations on cultural history. And B. writes about Berlin.

"This is a job in which you'll never get rich. But I am a bachelor and live cheaply. Once in a while I save a little, but from time to time I fall sick and am unable to write. But I make out."

He has managed to make out through Weimar and Hitler, as well as the dreariness of the postwar period.

We talk about Weimar. We are agreed that the social prerequisites for a cultural renaissance like that of the 1920's are missing. The Jews, who, by their openness and cosmopolitanism, dominated the artistic life, have either been killed or have fled. Berlin during the Weimar era had social fluidity and maintained an explosive balance that could fly apart at any time.

"There was something very sick about the times," admits B.

Berlin experienced a deluge of new talent which revolted against nationalism, against authority generally. Berlin had wide-awake journals, a daring theater, new music, new literature, new forms of artistic dancing, new, new. Willy Haas, editor of *Die Literarische Welt*, writes in his memoirs about the special atmosphere which attracted the intellectuals of Europe:

Berlin was the joy of my life. I loved the quick, ready answers of the Berlin woman to everything, the sharp, clear reaction of the Berlin audiences in the theater, the cabaret, on the street, in the coffee house, the irreverent and yet serious approach to matters, the beautiful, dry, cool, and yet not cold atmosphere, the indescribable dynamism, the love of work, the spirit of enterprise, the readiness to endure hard blows—and to carry on.

"Darkness does not descend all of a sudden," says B. abruptly. He seems drawn in the face, thin-haired, emaciated. He is not thinking only of the cool Berlin evening, of the contours of the buildings around the Hansa Platz, or of the low building in which we are sitting, where the movie house is playing "Smiles of a Summer Night" and in which the boxing idol, Bubi Scholz, has opened his own perfume shop.

"I have lived through two kinds of dusk and darkness. The first time was in 1933. It wasn't like many foreigners think. I wrote frequently in Theodor Heuss' magazine, *Das Deutsche Wort*, a successor to *Die Literarische Welt*. To be sure, I was hauled in by the Gestapo for helping in the preparations for high treason, but when I was released I wrote under the names of friends and acquaintances. We began a dangerous game of duplicity that was well known to all German intellectuals who were even slightly honorable. The journal printed articles which praised Nazism, but there was also other material which was strongly critical. Out of it developed the harmful attitude of the juggler."

"Why didn't you leave then?"

"I had my opportunities to do so. I was even an official representative at a meeting in Brussels in 1936. In part I wanted to stay in Berlin, in part I couldn't leave Germany. Altogether too few foreigners have understood that most Germans chose to cooperate rather than land in an uncertain exile."

"Out of some mystical love for Germany?"

"Twice I was taken in by the Gestapo. But we had a circle of literati who could associate with one another and speak freely. It was not these friends who turned me in, but I had connections with the illegal Communist Party, which was swarming with Nazi spies. I was not the only so-called resistance fighter who remained. Think of Erich Kästner, whose books were burned on the Opernplatz on May 10, 1933. He lived in Nazi Germany as a rentier, and even wrote the manuscript to UFA's jubilee film, 'Münchhausen'—under a pseudonym, of course."

Then later he defended the non-martyrs, I remarked, somewhat as Brecht defends Galileo:

"The hero who fights the microphone, and has no support in the newspapers, becomes a tragic clown. . . . He joins the martyrs. He dies officially of pneumonia. He turns out to be an anonymous obituary." Does Kästner mean that the death of an Ossietzky was in vain? Or is he thinking of his friend, the actor Hans Ott, who, before the murderers threw him out the window, with blood running down his face, cried out to them: "This is my finest role!"

"You must understand that a dictator has all kinds of opportunities to change people and destroy their external opposition," says B. after we have ordered another beer. "For an artist the choice between prison and silence ends usually in silence and self-contempt. Like small children we were delighted with every hole in the cloud over Germany. For a short time during the 1936 Games Berlin became again a free city, open to the world.

"A Swedish writer whom I admire visited Germany in 1936. He wrote a little book which was remarkably ambivalent toward Nazism. Among other things he asserted that Berliners were more open than formerly. Berlin, which formerly 'had given in many respects the impression of being lost,' with marked contrasts between luxury and poverty, had, according to him, changed for the better.

"Yes, to order and silence.

"He described how 'modern German justice does not hesitate to remove unbecoming and disfiguring faces from the streets.' But though he knew that these faces were now in prisons and concentration camps, he meant obviously that it was effective.

"One can be fooled easily by façades. Do not judge Berlin by its façades. The Hansaviertel is a façade. No, go to Aschingers."

"I eat at Aschingers. There the people are anonymous."

"They are Berliners just the same. But notice now how the colors of the buildings change as it grows dark. I am accustomed to going out in the evening, but my doctor tells me that I need to get out in the sunshine; it's healthful. I am a night person. Sometimes I get afraid of the sunlight."

"You spoke of two kinds of experience with darkness?"

"Spiritually, yes. In 1945 I managed to escape imprisonment by talking French to all the 'occupiers' I met on the street. This was right after hostilities ended. Berlin was to be united, democratic, and so forth. Johannes Becher flew in from Moscow and became chairman of the Kulturbund. And then they opened the Club der Kulturschaffenden, where all of Berlin's hungry intellectuals could eat."

"And this was the most important."

"Just then we thought it was the most important. The cream of Berlin's intellectuals ate dinner at the Club der Kulturschaffenden—Kästner, Edwin Redslob, one of the founders of Free University, Erich Reger, soon to be a cold warrior. We became satisfied and democratic, and felt grateful to the Russians. We wrote in the Eastern journals since there were no others. But it was not long before the new twilight fell. One after the other disappeared, there were rumors of arrests, the party line in the Eastern papers was sharpened, and the bourgeois liberals began to feel the heat. The pressure was not visible and not so brutal as in the days of the Brown Shirts. But we had had enough of silence."

"The Russians missed their golden opportunity?"

"It wasn't only the Russians who did that, but primarily the idiotic German émigré Communists, who didn't seem to have the least idea of what had happened in Germany. Stupidity isn't any better just because it's called Communism. But remember: we had a choice between two Germanies. We didn't have to leave our country in order to escape. I am thinking of all of those who ate their fill on Jägerstrasse and shortly thereafter were sitting in the front city of West Berlin—like me."

It is dark when we pay our check. On the horizon the Siegessäule looms like a black, unlighted giant cigar. We walk toward Zoo, stop near the water and listen to the Tivoli music beyond the railroad embankment. Large trucks are hauling away the remains of the giant Zoo bunker, which are then crushed into building materials for better houses than this concrete colossus out of the past.

"But why is darkness settling over Germany?" I ask B., who is walking silently beside me. A passing S-Bahn train drowns

out my question. Lines of blurred faces behind steamy windows
flash past.

We part at the gate of the amusement park, where I get in
line for a merry-go-round in order to mingle with the German
people. B. is a mystery. A Weimar-era cosmopolitan who is
clear-eyed enough to see the weaknesses of his country and yet
stays in Berlin of his own free will.

33   *Communist and Ex-Communist*

"The heroic poem about Berlin will be written during the coming epoch," wrote Heinrich Mann in the 1920's. Is the life of
Ernst Reuter a heroic poem about the big city?

In the middle of the wide East-West Axis in Berlin five
streets merge in a huge traffic merry-go-round. New buildings,
their façades shining with tile and aluminum, are going up
in the area.

This is Ernst-Reuterplatz.

Until Reuter's death it was called Knie. It is still called that
by the newspapers in East Berlin, who are particularly sensitive about the name Reuter. During his lifetime Reuter would
not allow any squares or streets to be named after him. Today,
five years later, I see his name in many places in the geography
of West Berlin. But the concept of West Berlin, the front city
and heroic city, is unthinkable without Reuter. For the simple
reason that Berlin's two parts would certainly not have been

such entirely different worlds had not there been a Reuter. The prophet of unity became the man responsible for the partition.

Ernst Reuter, born in 1889, received a Protestant, bourgeois education, but became a Social Democrat during his student days. When he first arrived in Berlin he was oppressed by the dreary expanse of the city. "Dust, and frightfully many people, who are all running, as though every minute cost them ten marks." At that time he was a traveling speaker and writer, and like many other colleagues of his generation he viewed the attitude of the Social Democrats toward the war of 1914 as a betrayal of the internationalism of the workers' movement. For Reuter "the German nation" was the oligarchy of the military and the bourgeoisie.

Reuter was captured on the eastern front in 1916. He was badly wounded, and limped for the rest of his life. The beret and the cane are external elements in the Reuter legend of later years.

In the new Soviet state the anti-militarist Reuter had an opportunity to do practical, organizational work. It is not surprising that he and Lenin felt mutual sympathy. Reuter was an oppositionist Social Democrat, a prisoner of war who learned Russian quickly and won the confidence of his fellow prisoners. Just as quickly he impressed Lenin with the strength of his own personality. A new day had dawned, a new kind of social order was being created. Reuter became a Communist.

He was named leader of the so-called Volga Germans, the descendants of the colonists who had been brought to Russia during the reign of Catherine II. Lenin's state was in chaos and was threatened by the armies of the interventionists. The fertile land of the Volga Germans was indispensable to the Soviets as a grain reserve. Reuter succeeded in his hard task. He reorganized the administration and acted as a mediator between Germans and Russians. He looked upon his work as a natural thing; this is characteristic of his attitude toward life. He adjusted himself to the realities of the situation and did the best he could.

He was sent as a Soviet Russian representative to Germany in order to establish contact with the revolution in his home country. He arrived in Berlin about Christmas time, 1918. By this time the German revolution had already been defeated.

As a German Communist Reuter represented at times an extremely militant and aggressive revolutionary doctrine. "Comrade Friesland" belonged to the left wing of his Party. He conceded later that the Russian Communists had been right in many respects when they opposed the fruitless revolutionary efforts of the German Party. The Party's chief task must be "to win the confidence of the toiling masses by participating in the day-by-day battles. But for this task there was needed some other form of national and international Party structure than the central apparatus of the Comintern."

This was the real reason why "Comrade Friesland," the general secretary of his Party, left Communism. He did not wish to take orders from Moscow; he disliked the Party apparatus and Party bureaucracy—he did not abandon this dislike even as a Social Democrat—and above all he wanted to *act*.

It was not a faith that he sought in Communism, but an instrument for political action, and since he aimed at Absolutes he felt compelled to draw closer to the Bolsheviks and Spartacists than to the more moderate Social Democrats in the chaotic years from 1917 to 1920. . . . Less an ideologue than a politician, not a theoretician but a practical person, never really without a home even when in exile, and ever the rationalist for all his passion, and even in hatred, he possessed that kind of physical and intellectual health which in our century only the few enjoy who were already full-grown human beings before the First World War. (Margaret Boveri)

Reuter never preached political truisms which were contradictory to his own experiences. In his speeches in blockaded

Berlin he assumes an Old Testament eloquence, but on those occasions he is in the role of spokesman for public opinion and for the struggling city. He was never a Christian in the church's meaning of the word, but he did not lack faith.

Despite the fact that he was an apostate from Communism, he carved out a speedy career among the Social Democrats in Berlin. As a city commissioner he laid out the traffic plans for the capital; he founded the Berliner Verkehrs-Gesellschaft (BVG) as the unifying organization for all means of transportation; and he became the chairman of the company's administrative board. He planned and directed the extension of the subway network. This work was continued twenty years later when Reuter was Mayor of Berlin.

When he was arrested by the Gestapo in 1933 he was Bürgermeister of Magdeburg. He was taken to the camp at Lichtenberg, where the Communist journalist, Friedrich Ebert, was already incarcerated. These two, Reuter and Ebert, could have had no premonition that sixteen years later they would be mayors, each in his respective Berlin.

Reuter was tortured by the Gestapo, but was let go. He knew that his days of grace were limited and so fled to Turkey. Again the accommodation to a new environment, a new language. He had learned Russian and become commissar for the Volga Germans. He had become a Social Democrat and planned the traffic pattern of Berlin in the 1920's. He had been elected Bürgermeister of Magdeburg and tackled the problems of a strange city. Now he became a teacher, a city expert, the author of practical handbooks, and received the title of professor. He had learned Turkish perfectly.

34   *The Hero of the Heroic City*

On November 30, 1946, Reuter arrived in the ruined Berlin by train; six days later he was elected to the City Council. His election was approved in principle by the Allies, but a final decision was reserved.

Reuter wanted to stand firm against all pretensions to power by the Allies. He shared none of the guilt for Germany's tragedy. He knew that Germany could regain the confidence of the world only under freedom. When someone insisted that man does not live by freedom alone, Reuter answered that neither does a fish live only by water, but rather *in* water. No people could feel any more intensive longing for freedom than the Germans, who had just lived through the inhuman tyranny of Hitlerism.

The Russians and the German Communists who began to create a new order in the East Zone did not take this elementary need into consideration.

Reuter had a clear notion of the task that lay ahead. He wanted to help his country. But he did not want to act like a vassal of the Allies. Experience had given him a deep distrust of the Communists, and he did not hide his antipathy for them.

On June 24, 1947, he was elected mayor of all Berlin by a vote of 89 for, 17 SED against, with two votes not cast. After long hesitation the Allied commandants decided in August not to validate the election. Formally speaking, the decision was unanimous. In the eyes of the Russians Reuter was not only anti-Communist (which was true) but anti-Russian (which was a lie), a simple "traitor."

The election of Reuter was interpreted by the Russians as a "demonstration."

In the spring of 1948 the fate of Europe was in the balance. The coup in Czechoslovakia showed that the Communists were ready to destroy a democracy when it suited them. There was talk about a coup in Finland. The cold war picked up. Berlin was still undivided, despite the sector lines. The city administration operated as before, but both sides prepared themselves for ultimate partition. Reuter knew that Berlin could be easy prey for any Russian annexation plans. In the spring of 1948 the Western Allies were not at all certain of their attitude toward the Berlin question. But Reuter did not want to give up Berlin: "We must fight for this city with utmost tenacity, and make it impossible for others to abandon it."

The alternative to opposition was surrender. Reuter looked upon this as suicide.

The expected explosion in the Control Council came on the 20th of March. A meeting was held in the building on Potsdamer Strasse under the chairmanship of Marshal Sokolovsky. The Marshal demanded an explanation about the Western foreign ministers' meeting in London. When he did not get it, he read a prepared speech in which he summarized the Russian complaints about plans of the Western Allies to split Germany. When the English representative on the Control Council tried to answer Sokolovsky's charges, he was interrupted by the Soviet delegation, which got up as one man.

"I see no purpose in continuing this meeting," said the Russian Marshal, "and I hereby declare it adjourned," and he and his compatriots left the conference room.

General Clay has something more to say about this last meeting:

It had never happened before that a chairman of the Council tried to adjourn a meeting without the approval of his colleagues.

Neither had it ever happened that a chairman had adjourned a meeting without agreeing upon a time for the next meeting. And it is significant that no chairman had left a meeting without first inviting his colleagues to coffee or refreshments. We understood that this was no accident. This was the last effort made to sow doubt among the western powers as to the advisability of continuing with their program for western Germany.

Every expert on foreign policy in Washington and Moscow knew then that Germany's partition was a fact. Thus, the Control Council also had to cease its work.

Despite the fact that Reuter was not officially the mayor of Berlin he became the spokesman for West Berlin, self-appointed, self-advised. He conducted a two-front battle. Under no circumstances did he wish to make concessions to the Russians. He wanted to convince the Western Allies that the proposed currency reform in West Germany must be extended to West Berlin. He considered a West Berlin with Eastern currency unthinkable.

The West German currency reform was extended to West Berlin on and from the 24th of June. On the same day the Russians began the complete blockade of all land routes between West Germany and West Berlin. The euphemism for the blockade was "technical difficulties."

Reuter was not responsible for the blockade or the partition of Germany. But his uncompromising activities contributed to the sharpening of the East-West conflict. This was the necessary price for the freedom of West Berlin. Reuter played a dangerous game and because he was successful he was called a hero, his city a heroic city. Reuter could not have been a hero without American armored divisions at his back.

He was the incarnation of defeated Germany's will to resist:

With every means at our command we shall resist to the utmost any effort to impose the kind of authority that would turn us into the slaves and helots of a party. We have lived through that kind of slavery in the Reich of Adolf Hitler. We have had enough of it. We want no return. As a four-power city our Berlin has up to now remained what it always was: not a provincial town with a provincial character but a world city. . . . Today the whole world knows that we are not the secret, but rather the genuine, capital of Germany.

Historical writings on both sides of the sector boundary accuse the other side of being responsible for the events of September 6, 1948, when Berlin was finally partitioned.

It was an entirely normal day, and the city councillors were to meet in East Berlin. Both East and West demonstrators had collected at the place, also the official (East) police and the newly-trained West Berlin police. After the uproar in the meeting hall had died down it was evident that only the SED council members were in their seats. Already on the same day a Western parliament was meeting in the student house on Steinplatz near the Zoo. Reuter and his colleagues had anticipated the inevitable by shifting the bulk of the documentary material to the Western sector. That Berlin was partitioned, that the tragic split became reality, was for Reuter more necessary than to continue formally and fruitlessly to "cooperate" in the city council.

And the Russians, too, were satisfied. Better to be able to dominate a part of Berlin than none at all.

Reuter knew that a Russian push to West Berlin would have meant world war. His role as hero is undeniable, but the director stood in the wings and protected his life. It is uncertain if the Western Allies would have gone so far in their policy had they not been dealing with a man of Reuter's incontestable moral conviction. Because of his determination he became one of those who worked most strongly for the coming West German state. On the other hand, one is gripped by a sense of fatalism when one reads the history of this period: it had to go as it went.

Reuter's personal tragedy was that West Germany, in many respects, completely disappointed his hopes. Berlin did not become the capital (Reuter did not take much stock in the formal objections posed by the Allies) and the new republic did not turn its attention in the first instance to that task which Reuter thought most important: that is, efforts at reunification.

Reuter interpreted West Berlin as a symbol of Western freedom; he pleaded with the Western world: we have done our duty, we will continue to do it in the future. Help us, not alone by airplanes and transportation facilities, but by fighting for those ideals that can guarantee our future, as well as yours!

The population of West Berlin began to look upon the Americans as closer allies and more faithful sympathizers than the West Germans. But what was right in the Berlin politics of 1948 need not be so ten years later. I have the feeling that the politicians in today's Berlin have stared themselves blind by following Reuter's uncompromising, dated conceptions, and have forgotten that conditions today are different. Like Reuter they dream of the day when the powers of darkness will be crushed. Like Reuter they employ a kind of rhetoric—which was justified in the days of the blockade, but sounds a little hollow today. Reuter spoke of the day of unification: "We will celebrate this day here in front of the old Reichstag. Then our trains will take off for Frankfurt and Munich, for Breslau and Stettin, and in the wretched railway stations the second railway track will become the symbol of regained freedom."

This note of victory in Reuter's speeches created an atmosphere of strength and security.

It must have been bitter for Reuter to observe how Berlin ceased to have the same significance as a symbol of struggle after the end of the blockade. On both sides the blockade was a prestige matter, and when the West had won its battle the distant island of Berlin could be relegated to a secondary position, a relic from the days of struggle. Subventions were paid out in order to escape dealing with the moral issue of Berlin.

For Reuter, as well as for his successors Schreiber, Suhr, and Brandt, Berlin was not only a front city, but also the last open connecting link with the seventeen million East Germans. On June 17 Reuter said that he could go entirely alone over to the City Hall in East Berlin and take over the office of mayor for all of Berlin with the approval of Berlin's entire population.

If the Russians were not in Berlin.

Reuter did not want to negotiate with the other side; he wanted to occupy it. This attitude has been inherited by his successors. But they have overlooked the fact that the East German system, despite its development toward an ever stricter dogmatism, has an undeniable inner dynamism.

Without doubt Reuter was a hero and his people very brave. But it is possible that his stand could become a stumbling-block for Berlin. Too much heroism is often equivalent to foolhardiness.

But every day West Berliners make pilgrimages to his grave in the Waldfriedhof in Zehlendorf, and pass houses or places which are reminders of his life. Just how strong the myth around his person has grown can be seen in the sharp protests that were registered when the West Berlin Senate decided to sell his old, worn-out automobile, which now, several years after his death, seemed no longer necessary.

People wrote: "It should be preserved in a museum."

35   *Pankow and Bonn*

"Berlin," muses Hitler during his table talks, "will some day be comparable only to ancient Egypt, Babylon, or Rome as a world capital. What is London or Paris in comparison?" The name Berlin was to be changed to Germania, and it was to become a showplace for the masses of people in both East and West. Great autobahns would feed into the world capital, Germania.

In our times Berlin has had to be satisfied with a somewhat more modest position. The city is East Germany's capital. But this fact was so thoroughly distasteful to all Western propagandists that they began to use the name Pankow as a designation for the capital in the east.

Pankow is a section of the city in northwestern Berlin. It is not very different from other Berlin suburbs. It is not a typical workers' section; neither is it one of the richer villa-suburbs like Wilmersdorf in the West. The Polish and Rumanian embassies are located in Pankow. Pankow has pubs, antique shops, schools, factories, and parks. In the rest of Berlin one can also find pubs, antique shops, schools, factories, and parks.

Pankow also has a night club which is called Rialto. Discreet dance music is played here until five in the morning. Pankow has a city hall and a Ratskeller, where one can eat good food. I met the former manager of the restaurant a few years ago in a small pub in West Berlin, where he was now a waiter.

"My goodness, do you know Pankow!" he said, and sighed.

Pankow has trams, and it has tenements for rent. It borders upon West Berlin. But in all my wanderings in Pankow I have not found anything which would justify Western newspapers in treating this section of the city as though it were the whole of East Berlin.

After Western politicians and newspapers had so neatly cleansed the name Berlin from its uncomfortable association with the East, one would think it only natural to locate at least some of the Federal Republic's ministries in Berlin. But Adenauer and the CDU (Christian Democratic Union) have had very little understanding for Berlin. It is reported that they are not happy in the city. According to the Chancellor Berlin is a heathen—that is to say, non-Catholic—city.

Berlin is looked upon as altogether too radical, too Social Democratic, worker-dominated, ironical, impudent. Solemnity is not highly regarded in Berlin.

Adenauer also seems to think that Berlin is Prussian. And "Prussian" is a kind of red flag for him.

Compared to Bonn, what other drawbacks does Berlin have? Bonn is situated in the west, on the Rhine and near France. When Bonn became the capital, the political center of gravity of Germany was shifted westward. Bonn has no political past worthy of mention. Berlin is defiled by associations from Hitler's days. Bonn is a better symbol for Western European cooperation. Bonn is dominated by the institutions of the Federal Republic. Berlin would dominate the government. Bonn is provincial, purely and simply. It is easier to be a big man in Bonn than in Berlin. In Berlin one cannot avoid talking about reunification. In Bonn one can peacefully discuss Western European cooperation.

Bonn has many advantages.

The Federal Parliament has naturally voted several times that Berlin is to be the coming capital of a reunited Germany: "The Parliament supports Berlin as the democratic outpost of Germany. It declares solemnly before the whole world that accord-

ing to the will of the German people Greater Berlin is to be a
constituent part of the Federal Republic of Germany and its
capital."

This decision was made on September 30, 1949.

Later it was announced that Berlin would become the capital as soon as universal, secret, and free elections were held in
East Germany.

But even at that Berlin is a sore in the conscience of the West
German parliament. Dr. Gerd Bucerius (CDU), owner of the
magazine *Stern,* influenced by the events in Hungary, wished
to submit a motion to make Berlin the capital of the Federal
Republic. There should be a budget appropriation for "the construction of a German parliamentary building in Berlin." After
some little time Bucerius let it be known that he had decided
not to submit his motion.

The Federal government had reiterated its earlier arguments:
in its own interests West Berlin was still subject to the three
city commandants representing the Western Allies. The capital
of the Federal Republic can be situated only in an area where
its sovereignty is unlimited, which is not the case in Berlin.

On the question of unlimited sovereignty Berlin politicians
of all parties are quick to point out that West Germany did not
get full sovereignty until the German peace treaty came into
effect on May 5, 1955. The security of Berlin is guaranteed from
all attacks by the London agreement of October 3, 1954. The
Federal government knows very well that Berlin cannot be lost
without world war.

The Western Allies did not raise any objections to making
East Berlin capital of the East Republic. Should they then
object—argue the West Berlin politicians—if the Federal gov-
ernment, a friendly state, establishes its capital in West Berlin?
Hardly. The Control Council has not had a meeting since 1948.
Consequently, the Western Allies in the Control Council have

sovereignty over West Berlin and the Russians over the East. Or: West Berlin is subject to three-power control and East Berlin to one-power control. The respective powers have the right to do as they wish in their part of the city. What they may not do is to change the status of Berlin as a whole.

Four-power control still functions in the Spandau prison, in the air safety service, and in connection with certain technical agreements. In addition, the flags of the four former allies fly in front of the Control Council's building on Potsdamer Strasse. The red one is furthest to the right, which signifies that the chairman is a Russian. The military missions accredited to the Control Council are fossils from a gray, long-past day.

West German government circles do not fail to point out that some central offices are being moved, or will be moved, to West Berlin, and that repair work was begun in 1954 on the Bellevue Castle in the Tiergarten, which is intended to serve as a residence for the Federal President during his visits in Berlin.

This is entirely correct, but before the imposing castle had been finished in 1958 the Berliners had nicknamed it Bundes-schnellbau (the Federal's Rush Construction).

An architectural competition has also been organized for the re-planning of the former center of the city, most of which lies in East Berlin. The Finnish jury member, Professor Alvar Aalto, tells me that this was a propaganda maneuver (so, we have plans for Berlin!) which was completely devoid of value or new ideas.

One can also hear the sound of workmen in the Reichstag building.

The Federal government has imbedded itself in Bonn for an indeterminate time. But there are other German capitals. For example, Vienna. Or Prague, which many Germans still consider theirs. Or Budapest, which is conceived of as German by some people because you can still order beer in German at the

Hotel Gellert. Or Bern, which is quite German. Or East Berlin.

I take a ride through the Brandenburg Gate in order to look over the East German state.

36   Calendar of Abbreviations

The German Democratic Republic, shortened to DDR in the language of the East Germans, and to GDR in English, and called Pankow in West Germany, was founded a month after the West German state had become an official reality. This was on the 7th of October, 1949.

For some years the three highest officials remained the same: Wilhelm Pieck as President, Otto Grotewohl as Prime Minister, and Walter Ulbricht as the regular proxy for the Prime Minister.° Changes took place in other positions. The Christian Democrat, Otto Nuschke, died, others were dismissed, some were in correctional institutions brooding over their crimes.

The parliament of the Republic, called the People's Assembly (Volkskammer) meets in a building on Luisenstrasse 58/60 just opposite the university clinic, Charité. When the Assembly is meeting I see cars in East Berlin with large red and white slips of paper on the windshield, which read: *Freie Fahrt. Volkskammer* (Priority Transit. People's Assembly).

° After the death of President Pieck in 1960 no new president was elected. Walter Ulbricht confirmed his leading position by letting himself be elected chairman of a newly instituted "Staatsrat der DDR" (State Council of the German Democratic Republic).—J.D.

In order to be elected to the People's Assembly it is necessary, among other things, to belong to the National Front for a Democratic Germany. In order to be elected to the National Front one needs to be a member of some mass organization. In the elections to the People's Assembly the National Front presents a single list which the faithful population in the DDR accepts almost unanimously. In the three elections which have been held since the founding of the state the single list has received respectively 99.61 per cent (1950), 99.46 per cent (1954) and 99.87 per cent (November, 1958) of all the votes. One-fifth to one-half of one per cent of the voters have had courage to vote against the single list. In 1946, when the Communists' defeat in the Berlin election surprised not only them but also their opponents, the following conversation took place between the gifted Communist, Wolfgang Leonhard, and a Soviet officer:

Imagine, Comrade Leonhard, that an entirely free election were to be held in Berlin and in the Soviet Zone—no propaganda and no particular distribution of papers—and say all the eligible voters were asked to answer a single question: "Are you for the East or the West?" In your judgment how would such an election come out?

Comrade Leonhard is hesitant about giving an answer, but when the officer begs him to give an honest answer he says that under such circumstances about 15 to 20 per cent of the votes would be for the East and 80 to 85 per cent for the West. Smiling imperturbably the officer replies: "You have a good sense for mass feeling. Our own calculations are about the same." Leonhard is of the opinion that the Russians knew by that time that they could not win the Soviet Zone by democratic methods. The dictatorship of the proletariat was the only alternative.

In actuality the Party composition of the People's Assembly, with its 400 members from East Germany and 66 from East Berlin (without voting rights, but voting is a mere formality) seems very Western, with factions and splinter parties. This gives the form of sham democracy and formal parliamentarism which East Germany, like the people's democracies, has appropriated. Outside the Soviet Union the most faithful heirs of Marxism-Leninism-Stalinism are the German Communists, and Walter Ulbricht is the highest prophet of the faith. Hegel's dialectic has come the long way over Moscow to East Berlin. It has hardly been improved upon by this detour.

The composition of the Assembly is as follows:

The Socialist Unity Party (SED) of Germany has the largest number of deputies, 117 in all. The rest are distributed as follows:

- 52 LDPD (Liberal-Democratic Party of Germany)
- 52 CDU (Christian-Democratic Union)
- 52 NDPD (National-Democratic Party of Germany)
- 52 DBD (Democratic Peasant Party of Germany)
- 53 FDGB (Free German Association of Trade Unions)
- 29 FDJ (Free German Youth)
- 29 DFD (Democratic Women's Association of Germany)
- 18 Cultural Association for the Democratic Renewal of Germany
- 12 VdgB (Union of Mutual Peasant Help and Peasant Trade Association)

If the list is long it is not my fault, but rather that of the East German regime.

In West Germany it is denied that East Germany is a state. It is, however, to the very highest degree a state. It has a government which exercises supreme authority over a significant part of Germany.

According to every definition in political science East Germany is a state.

The only difficulty is to determine where power lies and what its nature is. The word "democracy" is used with conspicuous frequency. The Republic is democratic, most of the parties (except, significantly, the SED) are democratic parties.

It is difficult to discuss the socialist government unless one is well versed in the various abbreviations which are used. I have therefore selected a few typical examples from the yearbook, *Jahrbuch der DDR*:

DEFA. After the war the Russians took over thé Goebbels/ Hugenberg-UFA's film studios in Potsdam/Babelsberg and founded the DEFA. This is now the state enterprise for the production of entertainment and documentary films. Meanwhile, UFA has been resurrected—in West Germany.

DM. East German denomination of the German mark, printed and issued by the Deutsche Notenbank. The official exchange rate with the Westmark is 1:1, which is as far from being right as is the 1:4 rate used by West Berlin exchange offices.

DR. Deutsche Reichsbahn, or State Railway. Not to be confused with Deutsches Reich, the German State which ceased to exist in 1945.

GST. Gesellschaft für Sport und Technik (Association for Sport and Technology). Sport and technology in this sense means quick training with rifles. In addition to the People's Army, the GST, and the People's Police there are the SED's Kampfgruppen in East Germany, which are worker groups organized on military lines and armed with automatic pistols. I see frequently groups of men with red arm bands on their way to shooting exercises somewhere outside of Berlin. I have also been present when new Kampfgruppen take the oath by which they bind themselves: "To regard my orders as commands of the Party and our state, and to carry them out with a sense of responsibility—side by side with the other armed forces of the DDR and with the Armies of the socialist camp to take my stand unreservedly for the defense of our homeland and the victory of socialism."

JP. Junge Pioniere (Young Pioneers). A child becomes first a member of Young Pioneers, then an ordinary Pioneer, thereafter a member of FDJ, and at the age of thirty he is considered ready to belong to the SED. A double membership in both FDJ and SED is possible.

LPG. Association of Agricultural Producers; that is to say, a kolkhoz, or collective farm.

MTS. Machine and Tractor Station.

NAW. Nationales Aufbau-Werk (National Construction Work). In order to qualify for new housing one must work several hours for NAW, for example cleaning bricks or removing rubble.

Pf. Pfennig, unit of money.

SAG. Soviet Corporation. A euphemistic designation for East German enterprises which have been, for many years, delivering the whole of their production without cost to the Soviet Union. The East German state has now got back the largest proportion of these SAG enterprises.

VEB. Volkseigener Betrieb, or enterprises which are "owned by the people." Private enterprise still plays a significant role only in handicrafts and in retail business.

VP. Volkspolizei, that is, People's Police. In West Berlin called *VoPo*.

ZK. Central Committee, the most important of which is naturally that of the SED.

Strangely enough there are two abbreviations which are left out. One is HO, or Trade Organization, which is rapidly dominating both the production and the sale of consumers' goods. The other is SSD, or State Security Service. This latter abbreviation I have heard used only in West Berlin.

East Germans have also taken over the party lingo of the Russians and turned it into a German which is called in West Germany "Party Chinese." This language is distinctive for its long sentences, its chancery diction, and its way of expressing things, which is an immediate reminder of the fact that several of the German émigré Communists were formerly school teachers.

I am selecting an excerpt which throws light on the East German party jargon and the political goals of the ruling party. It is taken from a communiqué regarding the negotiations between "the delegates of the party and government of the German Democratic Republic and the People's Republic of Bulgaria." The communiqué was signed in Berlin on April 18, 1958, by, among others, "the first secretary of the Central Committee of the German Socialist Unity Party and the First Vice-Chairman of the Council of Ministers Walter Ulbricht." Here is a selection:

> The consistent and successful struggle against revisionism, which is presently the chief danger to the international workers' movement, has led to a significant ideological consolidation in the ranks. As experience shows, revisionist "theories" at present are directed primarily at slowing down the tempo of socialist construction, at abandoning the socialist reconstruction of agriculture, and at weakening the state power in Socialist countries and the unity of the Socialist camp. Both parties are struggling simultaneously against dogmatism and sectarianism, which are foreign to Marxism-Leninism.

The quotation suggests a fact which the People's Assemblies, bourgeois parties, mass organizations, the government and parliamentary forms are designed to disguise; to wit, that real power in East Germany is wielded by the Central Committee of SED.

Despite concessions on details, despite setbacks and difficulties, the government has steadily hardened its ideological position; it has armored itself in genuine Stalinist style. East Germany's Gomulka has not yet been born. Or perhaps he was born, but the Gomulkas of East Germany are all in prison, in exile, or dead. The SED government rules East Germany with a hardness that disregards reality and with a ruthless speed in arresting revisionists and other transgressors.

The East German Republic wishes to win international recognition. But when I try to find out just what the government wants, and request a few simple interviews, I am told:

"We cannot grant interviews to our enemies." "We do not know for what purpose you will use your material." "Don't you realize that the political situation has grown more tense? We must be more careful. We must watch out for enemy agents." "It's not our fault that West Germany is rearming. We can't remain passive."

It seems to me that Adenauer has here an appropriate answer to his policy of strength. The more opposition to West Germany sharpens, the more uncompromising and tough will the East German regime become.

I am standing in Reichskanzlerplatz near the fair buildings in West Berlin and am looking at the gas flame which is burning in memory of those who fell in the cause of freedom on June 17, 1953.

This flame, they say in West Berlin, will burn until German unity has been achieved. This is a pleasant thought, but is there enough gas to keep the flame burning that long?

37   *Kafka on Wilhelmstrasse*

Every year the contemporaneousness of *The Castle* increases. Chill and terror are present everywhere in the world, but they are difficult to localize in a special spot in either the East or the West. Fear returns and is strengthened, and it affects our lives so that we look behind us for pursuers, the police, the supreme power.

This time I am reading Kafka on Wilhelmstrasse, in the Hotel Adlon where I live. And I go into Goebbels' former Propaganda Ministry on Thälmannplatz (formerly Wilhelmplatz), which is also Wilhelmstrasse, directly opposite the field where the Reichschancellory stood, and where the East Germans will soon be building a gigantic statue of Ernst Thälmann.

The building which I enter represents faithfully the frightful prison style of the Nazi epoch, the restrained pomp which was reserved for the central offices of the Third Reich. The next building, presently the Guest House of the Government of the DDR, is much more attractive. What I have never been able to understand is why so many of the hideous, gigantic buildings from the time of Hitler are left, and there are so few of the old, attractive buildings.

The American influence in West Germany is unquestionable and natural, but it is more obvious in Frankfurt than in West Berlin. The Russian influence upon East Germany is just as unquestionable, but not so natural.

I hear often: "We could make out with the Russians all right, but not with the East German Communists." This evaluation, of course, stems from the knowledge that the Soviet Union is a world power while Ulbricht is only a vassal of the Russians.

When I made my first visit to the big building, the Amt für Information, which is the East German central office for propaganda, was quartered there.

The control system at that time struck me as particularly ingenious: the necessary pass was made out by the doorman. It was then checked by a guard in the next room. I visited two different offices. A notation was made on my pass of my time of arrival and departure, and it was signed by the appropriate functionaries. I was not allowed to leave alone; a girl accompanied me to the exit.

"Do you have guards in the toilets?" I asked.

At the exit hall I was met by a third guard who checked the notations on my pass, after which I was obliged to leave the well-marked document with the same doorman who had written it out.

The East German Information Office has been moved elsewhere by the time of the Foreign Ministers' meeting in January, 1954. Hundreds of newsmen from East and West use the building as their working headquarters. There are a post office, a switchboard, and a restaurant. In the former vestibule one can buy any quantity of fruit or liquor, items which are in scarce supply in the East Berlin shops. I have my work room on the second floor. On the day before the end of the conference I get a printed name card on my door, with all names correctly spelled.

Three important offices have now moved in. There are the Prime Minister's Press section, the National Council of Democratic Germany, and finally the Society for Cultural Relations Abroad.

The doorman's room is now populated with three guards who are busy writing out passes for their respective offices.

"I am looking for a certain Frau W., who should be employed by the Society for. . . . ," I say.

"*Should* be employed," says the female guard craftily. "Don't you know what she does? What do you want?"

"I want to know if a certain Frau W. works here."

"And then?"

"I want to meet her. That is, if she is here."

After much hesitation she writes out a paper, but I get no further than the vestibule. Frau W. meets me there and convinces me that the visit is altogether unnecessary.

What do I want? I can read official pronouncements in *Neues Deutschland*.

"Didn't I tell you that your visit was unnecessary?" says the doorwoman even more craftily, as I hand her my pass.

Some time later I am struck by the humorous fact that the functionaries in this building, if they work overtime, can read the illuminated newspaper on Potsdamer Platz on the West side. The news glides past under the inscription *Die Freie Berliner Presse meldet* (The Free Berlin Press reports).

One can even read this newspaper from the Hotel Adlon if one has a room facing No Man's Land, the open field in front of Potsdamer Platz.

Of the hotel's 325 rooms there are about 70 left. The hotel, which has experienced so many German rulers, belongs today to the hotel chain of HO. The foyer is decorated with pictures of Pieck and Grotewohl and with political appeals of one kind or another ("Against the Communist Party ban in West Germany." "Long live the Communist Party!"). In front of the entrance there is a large courtyard in which I have sometimes found pieces of tile from the bathrooms of the luxury hotel. Of the former Adlon there is not much left besides the name and a memory.

My bathroom is of marble with Cupids on the walls; the desk is heavy and has mahogany inlays. My bed is wide. I have a view over the empty Wilhelmstrasse. The servants' bells have not functioned since 1945, and the corridors terminate in an empty nothingness, provisionally blocked off by a brick wall.

The Adlon opened its doors for the first time in 1907 and the Kaiser was overjoyed with his first visit. Every room had "a telephone and a standard clock." The tip-top of society lived in these rooms—kings and ministers, singers, and all kinds of rich people. After 1933 the restaurant was taken over pretty much by the Brown Shirts.

In her book of memoirs (1955) Hedda Adlon has described the hotel with unforgettable eloquence:

There was hardly a king or great prince who was not at some time a guest there. The princes of international finance and trade were at home there. Diplomats and statesmen of every language and pigment used the Adlon as their headquarters when they came through Berlin. They came from all countries, the legendary maharajahs and the famous artists, and the Adlon was their meeting place. . . . To have danced at the Adlon, to have dined at the Adlon, to have spent a night at the Adlon—if possible, the nuptial night—these were ardently desired things with which one could later regale one's children and grandchildren at bedtime!

I frequently eat sole and drink beer in the tiny restaurant which has been set up for the hotel guests; but I have no intention of mentioning this to my grandchildren. One of the waiters is in the habit of showing me pictures from the big parties of the past: a sea of gorgeous dresses in the big ballroom.

It seems that there is some kind of night life which still goes on at the Adlon.

One morning about five o'clock I am awakened by loud knocking on one of the neighboring doors. Some indistinct sounds can be heard from inside the room.

"The woman must go, the woman must go," whispers a shrill

voice threateningly. After a time I hear heavy boots on the staircase. The knocks on the door begin again, but this time louder. A policeman is trying to persuade the guest to open the door. After some threats this happens, and I can hear steps and sobs on the stairway.

An automobile starts up. It is a hazy morning. And I go to sleep again.

On days when I have nothing else to do I try to work out a balance-sheet concerning what the East German regime has accomplished, and its present situation. How much has been achieved? Where are they going? What is the significance of this new, revolutionary German state?

I cannot escape these questions, least of all on the winding back stairs of the Adlon.

38   The Poor Brother

Poverty dominates the scene in East Berlin, in Meissen and in Magdeburg. This is completely verifiable—and understandable. It gives an impression of grayness, silence, discontent. While West Germany by luck and generous help got off to an enviable start, East Germany was impoverished by the reparations deliveries, the total sum of which has been estimated by Western economists at considerably more than the 10 billion dollars promised at Yalta and Potsdam. Conspicuous are the many railway lines with only one track—the Russians removed the other one—and the factories not yet in production.

One speaks of the West German miracle as though it were due to wise investments and German industriousness. The German worker east of the Elbe and Werra has also been industrious. In the decade since 1949 East Germany has consolidated its economy in a conspicuous way. It must also be remembered that the Russians carried on a ruthless policy of impoverishment and exploitation in East Germany until about 1955. After that the situation was reversed. According to American calculations the Russian investments since that time have amounted to 400 million dollars.

In 1950 the living standard of the West German worker was twice as high as that of the East German worker. In 1957 this difference had been reduced to something over 20 per cent (according to Western sources). East Germany continues to reduce the discrepancy. Its industry is developing rapidly, and not so many mistakes in planning are made as before 1952. At the same time East Germany has become an increasingly more significant link in the economy of the Eastern bloc, which is now subject to a common planning center. East Germany has been given the responsibility for building up the chemical and heavy machine industries, which means that Ulbricht's state will become indispensable to the Soviet Union. Something of a rivalry has developed, particularly with Czechoslovakia and Poland, who feel that they have been treated unfairly. In many fields East Germany is already in a position to supply serious competition in Western markets, and particularly in the underdeveloped countries. The annual increase of industrial production is 10 per cent, and the turnover in retail trade is increasing by 6 to 8 per cent annually. But with the present high rate of investment the living standard is bound to climb more slowly than might otherwise be possible. East Germany is building jet-driven passenger planes, and researchers in the technical fields have nearly unlimited resources at their command.

The difference between real incomes in East and West is still so great that West Germany remains inviting. The price differences are greatest on specially desired items: refrigerators, TV sets, automobiles, coffee, and clothes. The real difference between the two German currencies has been reduced greatly. I agree with the English journal which wrote: "German Communism, whatever its crimes and its failures in administering the Soviet-occupied zone, still has men and qualities of the sort that the country as a whole most needs."

Any calculation about the economic stability of the East German economy is full of uncertainties. It is a burden to the economy that "parties and mass organizations" have over 70,000 full-time people on their payrolls, many of them young people. Rearmament costs money. The extremely generous social and cultural policy is economically expensive. Enormous sums of money are lost to the state because its government has provoked a mass exodus of refugees to the West. Every young student or doctor, scholar or industrial worker who flees to the West represents a wasted investment. This amounts to millions. The absolute drop in population in East Germany between 1950 and 1958 was *one million* despite a relatively high birth rate. Furthermore, the median age has gone up since a large percentage of the refugees are young people. The age pyramid in the whole of Germany is also abnormal (those in the 35-45 bracket were lost in the war) but it is especially true in East Germany.

I ask myself: will the government recognize its mistakes? Why can the Communist leaders of East Germany not understand that the political intolerance, the constant harrying of so-called enemy, or bourgeois, or revisionist elements can lead only to a spiritual crippling? Why do they continue with a stupid, short-sighted policy which forces many of the state's best people to flee?

The former East German Minister of Culture, the ex-poet

Johannes R. Becher, has noted down the following thought in his published diary:

> I refuse to listen to a bourgeois who asserts that life is not safe here, as if under the rule of the bourgeoisie the safety of human life had been guaranteed. One should ask the more than 70 million victims of the two world wars, the two catastrophes for which the bourgeoisie was responsible within half a century. . . . No, no one's life is safe so long as this kind of rule exists.

Becher evades the central question as to whether the citizens of East Germany have safety or not. Freedom from the kind of fear that bourgeois society is supposed to contain is one of the socialist principles, but I have experienced so much fear and so many mysterious arrests in East Berlin that no one can get me to believe that the opposite is true, that is, that there is safety there.

In the spring of 1958 the East German comic magazine, *Eulenspiegel,* published a cover picture which showed a functionary coming home from work. He was pictured as divided into two parts: half of his body is still outside the door, a copy of *Neues Deutschland* is sticking out of his pocket, he has a socialist badge of honor on his lapel. The other half is already dressed in a snuff-brown smoking jacket and is in a home atmosphere of plush, withdrawal, and repose. This is the divided East German.

The picture is an excellent caricature, but it is not entirely correct. One needs first to make a sharp distinction between the atmosphere of East Berlin and that of East Germany, in "the Zone." In terms of consumer goods the East Berliner is presumably better provided, but the political atmosphere is harsher and marked by a collective neurosis the presence of which I have often noted. In the East German cities and villages one is free from some of the restrictions which bind East Berliners (such as the necessity of showing one's *Ausweis!*). Socialization of agriculture has certainly made progress, the political system is certainly Stalinist, but the heightened living standard and the concentration upon greater productivity have had their effect. To overestimate the East German system is just as dangerous as to underestimate it. These areas of Germany had, in the past, an overwhelming majority of large landholdings. One would err if one thought that a restoration of the old, plus democracy, could suddenly make East Germans happy.

The average East German is not permitted to criticize socialism as a principle, least of all East German socialism. The words of the party song are still pertinent: "The Party, the Party, is always right, and, Comrades, leave it at that: For he who fights for the right is always right against lies and exploitation." He may criticize the effectiveness of labor, the quality of goods, and bureaucracy. The fear of discussing larger principles is striking. A new kind of inner emigration is appearing: there is a duality which leads to conflicts of duty. One grudgingly participates in demonstrations, one grudgingly raises one's hand in assent. Immediately afterward one regrets it bitterly. Family conflicts also occur, as in the time of Hitler. Parents are opposed to the regime, at least doubtful. The children know no other world than that of the Pioneer organizations; FDJ and Jugendweihe are a matter of course. At the same time the young people are the cause for difficulties because they are more sensitive than the older people to the sweet attractions of the West, which are beamed at them steadily by Western radio and television—a daydream from the other side of the border, fascinating in the promise that you today, even now, can achieve what you want. Socialism (particularly the East German) speaks of a tomorrow when happiness will reign. But this has been heard so long that tomorrow can become nauseating.

Even with the poorer brother there are oases of security. A part of Germany has been recreated, social conditions have been changed, and an experiment has been begun the consequences of which no one really knows. An unsuccessful experiment, say many; despotism, violence, threat, say others. But above all one needs to remember that the picture of East Germany is not uniform.

There is a dynamism here that can express itself in another June 17 or in a faster economic development. It is not attractively packaged, this Eastern variant of German life.

39   The New Leader

According to the latest Bonn-mot the Berlin Social Democrats wish to win the forthcoming election for themselves by means of two especially attractive representatives: the female voters will be won over by Mayor Willy Brandt, the male voters by his charming wife.—
Der Spiegel, June, 1958.

Brandt—the man with two party cards in his pocket—has been able to ward off a plebiscite in West Berlin against atomic death only with hangings and stranglings, with threats, appealing to the Ami—Foreign Minister Dulles, who plans to breeze into Berlin in a few days.—East Berlin newspaper, April, 1958.

Herr Brandt has been in Honolulu, and where all I don't know. (Laughter.) Would it not have been simpler if he had stayed in West Berlin and begun to clear out the espionage agents of the Bonn government and the Western occupation troops? (Applause.) The organizers of traffic in human beings, who are trying to lure people from the German Democratic Republic by the most disgusting means, who are recruiting girls for the brothels of Hamburg and

New York, must be cleaned out of West Berlin. (Very true! Applause.) Is it not time that Herr Brandt turned his attention to the bloody Nazi criminal judges who are holding office in West Berlin? (Applause.)—Walter Ulbricht, according to *Neues Deutschland*, March 10, 1959.

These are but a few examples of the ways in which the Eastern authorities attack Brandt, particularly since he has emerged as a symbol of West Berlin's resistance after the Russian ultimatum on Berlin of November, 1958.

One newspaper in West Berlin places him in its horoscope among film stars and other celebrities. Brandt was born under the sign of Sagittarius (Archer), December 18, 1913, and according to this newspaper he has, like all archers, worked hard to achieve that which was not given to him.

As governing mayor of West Berlin he has quarters and offices on the second floor of the city hall in Schöneberg, in the same building in which the American Freedom Bell strikes every day at twelve o'clock as a reminder to Berliners of the blockade and the struggle for freedom.

Brandt's room looks out over a little square, some new buildings, a park, and relatively sparse traffic. The building is situated away from the larger traffic arteries. The city hall in Schöneberg is perpetually provisional—that is, until unity has been achieved.

Brandt has a square, energetic, almost dangerous face. He looks younger than he is, is an excellent speaker, and seems to have all the qualities (among them the ability to handle public and press relations) to mark him as a strong personality, worthy to succeed Reuter.

During a conversation in his work room he confesses that the big city of Berlin did not impress him favorably at first when he lived there illegally in 1936. He did not become a Berliner until after the war.

Herbert Karl Frahm was the name of a young man who was graduated in 1932 from the Johanneum secondary school in Lübeck, where he was born and grew up. As a schoolboy he had worked on the Social Democratic *Lübecker Volksboten,* the editor-in-chief of which, Julius Leber, seems to have exercised a determining influence upon Frahm. But while Leber looked upon Social Democracy as the genuine future party of the people, Frahm had views quite to the contrary. He was radical, and belonged to the independent, leftist Sozialistische Arbeiterpartei (Socialist Workers' Party).

Frahm went into exile in Norway. As a journalist and author he began to use the pseudonym "Willy Brandt," under which he published some ten books in Norwegian and Swedish. In 1946, when he returned to Germany as a Norwegian citizen and as press attaché in the Norwegian military mission, he was an unknown person in his homeland. In Scandinavia he was well known as a journalist and political writer. He had also arrived at a better understanding of the tactics of the reformist workers' movement, with its aim of slower reconstruction of society, than Herbert Karl Frahm, the student, ever had.

His opponents would say, in short, that he had become a right-wing Social Democrat.

Brandt (who had also officially changed his name) decided in 1947 to give up his Norwegian citizenship and stay in Germany. "It is better to be the only democrat in Germany than to be one of many democrats in Norway." Brandt began his meteoric career.

In the autumn of 1949 he was elected to the Federal Parliament, the next year to West Berlin's city parliament, and in the autumn of 1954 he became its president. Exactly three years later he was elected mayor of West Berlin (by 86 votes out of 118). His reelection as mayor after the Berlin elections of December, 1958, was almost unanimous.

In January, 1958, Brandt became chairman of the SPD-Berlin, replacing Franz Neumann, who had been chairman for more than ten years. This was presumably more difficult than to be elected mayor.

Neumann had become the hero of his party in 1946, when he worked energetically against any forced union with the Communists. The relations between Neumann and Reuter were never very good. In this internal struggle Brandt was on the side of Reuter. But, in contrast to Reuter, Brandt perceived that he needed the support of the members and the basic organizations if he hoped to win against Neumann, the party bureaucrat, the tactician, the dogmatic socialist. Brandt advanced slowly within his party in Berlin and he is today its unchallenged leader—despite the fact that his views are by no means always popular. In the SPD of West Germany, which is weak in leaders, he has great prospects of being one of the top men, yes, even the leader. He is the incarnation of a new kind of politician, little bound by class consciousness (with all that that means in the way of advantages and disadvantages), he has a winning personality, and he thinks and acts quickly.

How does he interpret his task for *his* Berlin?

"Development in the Western zones of Germany began as early as 1945, but Berlin has had a chance only since the end of the blockade in 1949. Before that it was just a matter of trying to survive, of taking each day as it came. The question we had to answer in regard to Berlin's partition was: should we bide our time and wait until Germany was reunited? Or should we try to do everything possible in our part of the city?—We were at the zero point. Industrial production was down by 17 per cent as compared with the 1936 level; we had 300,000 unemployed. Today our production is 115 per cent of the 1936 level and unemployment has been reduced to about 90,000."

The unemployment is due in part to her isolated position, but

the main reason is that West Berlin is not the capital and therefore has a large number of unemployed civil servants. They are
white-collar proletarians who cannot be employed in the building trades. This unemployment will continue to be more or less
constant unless several government offices are moved to West
Berlin or it becomes the capital. The Russian threats have had
certain effects upon the economy (which the Senate in West Berlin tries its best to deny). Private savers, as well as industries,
have begun to place their money in West Germany. The rate of
investment has sunk. Industrial production in West Berlin has,
to be sure, continued to rise but a certain amount of unjustified
nervousness has had its effects. If they were to study the matter
more closely both private savers and industries should know that
West Berlin is just as safe (or unsafe) as the Federal Republic.
I cannot get away from the thought that even Berlin politicians
share responsibility for the fact that attention has been concen-
trated so completely upon the Berlin question (European problems have become Berlinized, goes the saying) which, after all,
can be resolved only within the framework of general relaxation
of tensions. Brandt seems to be aware of this danger, as is evident from some of the innumerable interviews and statements
he has given since November, 1958.

"Today we are 85 per cent self-sufficient; the balance must be
collected from various sources."

"Forever?"

"Yes, so long as the partition lasts. But industrial production
is just one aspect of our task. We must build up the city. We are
building today over twenty thousand new housing units annually, but that isn't enough. However, the destruction makes
it possible to build a new Berlin which is light and airy. To see
the new Berlin, you must not go to Kurfürstendamm, but compare the backyard tenements in Wedding, the remnants of the

speculative building of the eighties, with the new structures in the area."

While Brandt is speaking he walks back and forth between the windows and a conference table. He takes a cigarette from the table at regular intervals and lights it. He is a chain smoker but he does not seem nervous. He speaks Norwegian perfectly; he raises his voice just as quickly as he drops it to a whisper. At home, too, he speaks Norwegian; he married in Norway and has two boys.

Brandt's brown-paneled office is well insulated. Despite the rumbling traffic outside, the quietness of this room is unreal. Two secretaries who sit on the other side of the wall prepare Brandt's daily schedule and send away casual visitors. The telephone rings constantly. But in here it is quiet.

"We have a task which concerns not only ourselves," continues Brandt. "Berlin is a place of refuge for people from East Germany. Therefore, in our own way, we can work for reunification and try to normalize the relations to the East."

At this point in the conversation—and this was before November, 1958—I ask Brandt if he thinks there will be another blockade, and his precise answer is: "I do not believe at all that Russian policy is set upon dramatizing the situation in Berlin. That could have negative consequences."

I do not refer to this prophecy in order triumphantly to show how wrong Brandt was, but rather to draw another, related, conclusion. Just like the government of the Federal Republic, which in the final analysis is responsible for foreign policy, Brandt had accommodated himself to the status quo following the airlift in 1949. Not too much thought was given to how dangerous West Berlin's position was, and neither was any alternative policy for negotiations with the Russians evolved. George F. Kennan, to be sure, in his book, *Russia, the Atom, and the West,* did sound a warning against overconfidence with respect to West Berlin, but this warning was overshadowed by other theses in the book.

To my question of what he thought of a reunited Berlin without a reunited Germany Brandt answered with just the same correct arguments he employed later when he rejected the Russian plan for making Berlin a "free city":

"It is impossible. That would mean a third currency, a third Germany in addition to the two which already exist. We don't want any Danzig solution."

About this time he glances at the clock, which I interpret as a discreet sign.

West Berlin is frequently compared to Madrid: when Madrid was lost the battle for Spanish democracy was over. If Berlin is lost it will be a defeat for democracy. Berlin is a testing place of democracy's will to resist. The politicians of West Berlin often sound off with hollow and phony rhetoric. It is to Brandt's credit that he seems aware that slogans have their limits, that the position of West Berlin in the world will be judged by its acts, not by references to its heroism. Brandt's trip around the world, his position as a living advertising bureau for Berlin have given his opponents political ammunition, but he has in an admirable way managed not to get mired in political clichés. He is also aware that there is no possible solution of the Berlin question *without* or *against* the Russians. The fact that, on the other hand, he refuses to indulge in private conversations with Khrushchev is understandable.

Khrushchev at an East German rally

SPD

Geschäftsstelle
der
SPD
Kreis Lichtenberg
des Landesverbandes
Berlin
Berlin NO. 55, Tiekstraße 10

Arbeiter Wohlfahrt
der Stadt Berlin E.V.
Geschäftsstelle Kreis Lichtenberg

40   *As You Like It*

Saturday night in East Berlin, warm spring weather, the smell of grass and flowers in the air. Prime Minister Khrushchev is scheduled to speak at the Frankfurter Tor in the middle of Stalinallee.

I walk there from Alexanderplatz and note that a large number of people are stirring about. This time there is a departure from the usual visiting plan, which was followed when the Russian leader came in 1957: a parade past Marx-Engels-Platz and past the leaders, who were installed on a white reviewing stand. Those who are coming there tonight are doing so out of curiosity. Many are West Berliners. A stage show, with folk dances and gay music, has been going on already for an hour. Searchlights illuminate the entire area around the Frankfurter Tor. Down at the base of a tall building is a modest platform for the awaited guest. Fifty yards away, right in the middle of the crowd, there is another platform on which rows of TV cameras have been set up, with their lenses sighted on the platform. The big camera crane belonging to the East German television system sways overhead.

With some difficulty, I manage to reach the press box, only to discover that the view is poorer from there than from the street, since the cameras cut one off. Groups of newsmen are standing on the narrow platform. Many of them are puffing on cigar stumps. Many of them have been in Leipzig and have come here with Khrushchev. I guess the crowd to be 70,000. Others say 10,000, others 100,000. Everything seems to be very spontaneous, as though people had come here as an objective

Rudolf Müller outside the Social Democratic headquarters
in Lichtenberg, East Berlin

for their evening stroll. There is a fireworks display which lights up the skies. A Canadian TV reporter is recording some commentaries with an effective background of rockets. The musical program has ended.

After Khrushchev arrives, there are hurrahs, and long-winded speeches of welcome. He is referred to as Comrade Nikita Sergeyevitch Khrushchev. On the platform there is a tired leader, exhausted after all the handshaking and schnapps-drinking at the Leipzig Fair. However, he gives the impression of great vitality compared to Walter Ulbricht, who has become petrified in his pose as unsuccessful imitation of Lenin. Grotewohl looked tired from the first day that I saw him. Friedrich Ebert has a mask of corpulence and indolence. In addition to these four a number of other top men of East Germany are on the platform. They hear a short speech, which is translated almost simultaneously (the translator can hardly keep up) and which is obviously delivered without a manuscript. The speech sounds familiar to me, and I look up at the illuminated buildings. There are people on the balconies and in the windows, but high up in one of the windows I see the silhouettes of a couple who are kissing and making love, apparently undisturbed by the noise from the loud-speakers and the crowd of people. I watch the quiet love-making up there so intensely that I hardly follow the content of the speech. Except one sentence, which, to be sure, is well known:

"The Berlin question must be settled in a way that will satisfy the wishes of Berliners themselves."

The meeting ends with one of German socialism's classical battle songs, the beautiful "Brüder, zur Sonne, zur Freiheit." It is already quite late, so instead of crowding into the U-Bahn I walk past Alexanderplatz and East Berlin's city hall to Unter den Linden and take a look at the East German women's styles which are on display at the corner of Friedrichstrasse.

I remember what they say in the West—that those in authority in East Germany have long wanted to tighten their grip on West Berlin. A revealing episode is told about the eight or nine thousand inhabitants of East Germany, that is, those on the edges of Berlin, who have their jobs in West Berlin. They have been threatened with reprisals on many occasions by East German authorities, but an especially drastic action was launched when a group of commuters was called into the East German administration and instructed to sign a declaration that they would stop working in West Berlin. Those who refused had their identity cards taken from them and were threatened with the loss of their housing. But one of these men complained to the Russian commandant, as a consequence of which all the identity cards were returned and the people could continue working in the West.

At any rate, Khrushchev felt called upon to disturb the peace around Berlin in November, 1958. On November 10 he made his sensational speech at the Sports Palace in Moscow; seventeen days later the Soviet ultimatum was delivered in which the Four-Power Pact on Berlin was declared no longer valid, and a promise was made to turn over all authority in Berlin to the East Germans on May 27, 1959. One can rightly interpret this action as one link in the chain of Soviet world strategy, but a comparison with the blockade threat of ten years earlier is inexact in many respects. In the years which have gone by the power position of the Soviet Union has become considerably stronger, and its attitude toward the German problem much tougher. The desirability of German unification has, to be sure, been recognized in declarations emanating from both East and West, but it is psychologically correct to realize that the partition is looked upon as advantageous and useful in wide circles. West Germany has become a cornerstone in the Atlantic community and in West European economic cooperation, while at the same time in

France there has been secret satisfaction over the fact that the West German Republic does not include the whole of Germany. One can find equally pertinent reasons for the partition of Germany in other quarters.

There are many other examples which show with what anxious correctness the parties concerned have maintained the gentlemen's agreement which divides Europe and which has hitherto prevented a bloody collision. The blockade of 1948-49 was a sample of the cold war, which was conducted with such propriety that Russian officers on the airfield at Tempelhof checked to see that the fully loaded planes landed in proper order. On June 17, 1953, a detachment of Russian tanks strayed into West Berlin territory but were turned back politely at one of the intersections by a traffic officer in West Berlin, who pointed out that they were going in the wrong direction. After which the tanks turned around and went back into East Berlin.

The Russian ultimatum led immediately to speculation about the possibility of a new airlift. It was observed that West Berlin had far greater reserve supplies than in 1948, but that night flying could be hindered effectively by jamming radio beams. The psychologically most important point was expressed to me by a West Berliner: "A blockade? In 1948 we didn't have anything and therefore had nothing to lose, either. Now we have cars, television sets, lipstick, and comforts. We don't want to be without them. And supplying us by air would give us only the bare necessities."

Actually, few West Berliners seriously considered the possibility of a new blockade. I must follow on one point the strange legal grounds upon which the Russian note on Berlin is built. Mention is made of "wartime agreements which regulated Germany's occupation and which previously gave them [the Western powers] *the right to stay in Berlin.*" (My italics—J.D.) This thesis, that Berlin had never been given status as a fifth zone of occupation, but was expressly understood to be under the "highest authority" of the Soviet occupation administration, and that the Western powers were only guaranteed a kind of *"Mitbesetzung"* (co-operation) and *"Mitverwaltung"* (co-administration) has been official doctrine in East Germany since the beginning of 1958.

That the Soviet Union looks upon all of Berlin as *properly* belonging to East Germany is evident from the note of November, 1958. Unfortunately, no one in the West has paid attention to the fact that Professor Herbert Kröger, who is regarded as the highest authority on international law in East Germany, had already expressed this same idea and "proved" it in the first issue of *Deutsche Aussenpolitik* in 1958, in an article entitled "Zu einigen Fragen des Staatsrechtlichen Status von Berlin." He supplements his arguments exactly a year later in the same journal. It follows therefrom that the Soviet note hypocritically can depict this proposal to make Berlin into a "free city" as an act of grace, a special favor because the Soviet government "is concerned that the removal of the occupation governments shall not be accompanied by a painful change in the way of life which has been established in West Berlin." As early as the state treaty between the DDR and Soviet Russia in September 20, 1955, writes Professor Kröger, the following took place: (1) In 1945 Berlin belonged to the Russian zone of occupation; (2) The Soviet Union relinquishes its sovereignty in this former zone of occupation to the DDR; (3) This comprises all of Berlin. For those familiar with the texts in question the November note was no surprise. The action was possibly well prepared: Professor Kröger's article of January, 1958, does not seem to have been a mere coincidence.

If the East Berlin authorities were thus able to feel pleased in their hunger for West Berlin, they soon discovered that Russian policy was not just a game about Berlin or Germany. There were more far-reaching goals, and the Berlin ultimatum was only a single play of the cards. Meanwhile, a tremendous number of hypotheses and ideas about Berlin and Germany were broached, and there was hardly a self-respecting Western journalist who did not publish a series of articles on the matter. Secretary Dulles advanced (and then withdrew immediately) the so-called "agent theory," to the effect that the East German military, who would presumably take over regulation of the Western military transportation to Berlin after May 27, 1959, could be considered acting as "agents for the Russians." Others proposed UN guarantees for Berlin, there was talk about a corridor, a free land route to West Berlin, and from the East emerged a new hit number, "Confederation of the two German States." East Berlin began a long-planned scare campaign against West Berlin: a tremendous number of airplane seats to West Germany for the days preceding May 27 were booked anonymously; there were also anonymous phone calls to West Berlin drayage firms with moving orders for well-known West Berliners.

Perhaps most macabre was the practice of sending hearses to the homes of West Berlin officials and politicians to take away the dead, who themselves were frequently at home and denied responsibility for the naturally anonymous orders. The only visible result of the scare campaign (except for certain presumably temporary economic side effects) was that three thousand business people and non-Berliners moved to West Germany with their families. One of my friends, a member of the city's most fashionable tennis club, said that approximately one-sixth of the members changed their place of residence at year end, 1958-59. He did not regret the loss.

On May 27, 1959, John Foster Dulles was buried in Arlington Cemetery in Washington, D.C., and Louis Armstrong put on a concert in Berlin. On the same day the Berlin Hilton opened its

roof garden, "El Panorama." Four hundred Western newsmen
waited vainly in Berlin for something to happen, while on the
other hand the tourist trade was down from the same period in
1958. Russian soldiers politely saluted American soldiers who
were on their way to West Berlin, while the East German Foreign Minister, Bolz, sat alone in Geneva awaiting the return of
his colleagues from Washington.

41   The Parliament

The room in which the city deputies of West Berlin meet is
decorated with the Berlin coat-of-arms, the standing bear. The
only thing shared in common by the two city halls—the Western
one in Schöneberg and the Eastern one on Rathausstrasse—
is the coat-of-arms with the bear. Around the coat-of-arms in
Schöneberg are the gold-red-black bunting of the Republic and
the flags of the states of the Federation. There is a large audience of several hundred persons. At the right of the Speaker,
Willy Brandt is sitting alone on his side of the platform; he
looks as if he would like to yawn.

It is question time.

A consistory inspector belonging to the CDU fraction wonders why the Association of Football Referees in Berlin has been
given permission to hold its annual banquet on the night of
Maundy Thursday although public entertainment is forbidden.
It could be that drunken football referees reeling home from

the party might encounter innocent church people on Good Friday morning. Shouldn't this be prevented?

"Football referees," mildly replies Frau Ella Kay, the Senator for Youth and Sports, "are professional people with regular Sunday work. Maundy Thursday is one of the few evenings in which it is possible for referees to go out on a party. There is no danger that they will meet church folks since the exceptional privilege granted specifies that the festivities are to end at five o'clock. But since the banquet is an exceptional affair, special permission must be granted each year."

"Is it possible that permission will be granted next year also?" asks the disturbed consistory inspector.

"Negotiations between the Senate and the Association of Football Referees have not yet taken place, since Easter, and therefore the banquet, is only recently over. The matter must be handled later," explains Frau Kay, still mildly.

The consistory inspector is silent.

Official debates and votes in the West Berlin parliament are usually formalities, since the government coalition of the two parties, SPD and CDU, obviates parliamentary opposition. Despite their absolute majority the Social Democrats do not seem disposed to drive through their wishes without listening to their coalition partners. This is a departure from the practice in West Germany, where the party cleavage between the CDU and SPD has made such cooperation nearly impossible. West Berlin politicians are in the habit of praising themselves for their ability to demonstrate in practice a will to cooperate. Sometimes they look upon themselves as little white lambs compared to the fighting cocks in West Germany.

"Cooperation is a necessary evil," say many Social Democrats.

"Why necessary?" I ask.

"Because we live in a front and border city," is the answer.

Others say: "Brandt obeys the orders of Adenauer and the CDU more faithfully than Adenauer's own ministers. This coalition is bad."

But a few say: "The CDU in Berlin is more decent than the West German party. Adenauer's influence has not penetrated here. Berlin has a good effect upon the CDU."

"The SPD in Berlin is much more decent than the West German party," say many Christian Democrats. "The empty radicalism of West Germany and the air bubbles of Bonn have not reached Berlin. But one can never know about the future."

"Hate for the Communists is the guiding star in the policies of Berlin Social Democrats," say others. "For that purpose they would even make a pact with the devil."

"A pact with the devil?" I say. "Why?"

"It started in 1945."

The Russians permitted the democratic parties to begin their work immediately. They wanted to lay the groundwork for a political system that they could use. The four parties which began working in Berlin were the Communists, the Social Democrats, the Christian Democrats, and the Liberal Democratic Party (later called Free Democrats, FDP). The tasks of the first Berlin Magistrat (city administration) were so overwhelmingly great that nobody had time to think about differing points of view. The streets were cleared and the water was pumped out of the flooded U-Bahn tunnels. In the midst of destruction Berliners tried to return to a normal life. District mayors of the city were appointed by the Russians in cooperation with German emigrant Communists. The mayors were usually bourgeois or Social Democratic, but the Communists saw to it that key positions remained in their hands.

In the last free elections to the German Reichstag the Communist Party in Berlin had been the strongest party, followed closely by the Nazis and Social Democrats. The working-class parties dominated the city by a two-thirds majority. As late as November, 1932, Berlin was a Red city.

Thirteen years later many Communists in Berlin thought (as everywhere in Europe): Has not the end of Hitler's tyranny strengthened our front? We do not need the cooperation of the Social Democrats; we are strong enough without them. But the election in Austria in November, 1945, came as a shock to the German Communists. In Austria the Social Democrats got 40 per cent of all the votes, the Communists 4 per cent.

Only then did the German Communists begin to talk about a united front. It was a simple matter in the Russian zone and in East Berlin, since Russian control officers supervised all Social Democratic meetings where a fusion of the two working-class parties was discussed. But the party in West Berlin, under the leadership of Franz Neumann, rose up to do battle against the idea of union. An effort was made to get the matter submitted to a party vote, but this could be effected only in West Berlin, where more than 80 per cent of the members voted against a merger, although more than two-thirds said that the two labor parties should work together.

The forced merger of SPD and KPD took place on April 21-22, 1946. The new party was called the Socialist Unity Party of Germany (SED). And on the following day appeared a new party newspaper, *Neues Deutschland*. Otto Grotewohl, Social Democrat, and Wilhelm Pieck, Communist, were selected chairmen of SED. Grotewohl, who had been a minister in Braunschweig as early as 1923, was the only really well-known Social Democrat who supported union. During the days of Weimar he had been in the German Reichstag; he had been arrested by the Nazis and spent the war years inside the country, in the underground after 1944.

It is not wholly incorrect to think that Grotewohl's support of party union was sincere. His speech at the union congress of the parties is especially tragic if one accepts this interpretation. Grotewohl believed sincerely in the slogans which were voiced by the Communists in regard to parity and equality between the Social Democrats and Communists, and which, to begin with, were observed. He was not the only one who was motivated by an illusion. For that reason it is not far-fetched to assume that Grotewohl is today a prisoner in the "Ulbricht system." He is formally prime minister but practically subordinate to the orders of Ulbricht. "Despite all the persecution by the opportunistic leadership of the Social Democratic Party in the Western zones of occupation"—writes the Central Committee of the SED, March 11, 1959, on Grotewohl's 65th birthday—"and despite the intervention of the imperialistic occupying powers, you have struggled unswervingly at the head of the class-conscious Social Democrats for the union of both parties of the German workers."

Simultaneously with the emergence of the Unity party Franz Neumann, supported by the party leader, Schumacher, became the hero of West Berlin Social Democrats by holding the party together in West Berlin. The fusion was artificial, and had been carried through by force. Sometime later the East German CDU was transformed into a satellite party when the elected party leaders, Ernst Lemmer and Jakob Kaiser, were forced to resign. Lemmer, publisher of the newspaper *Kurier* in West Berlin, later became Minister of All-German Affairs in Adenauer's cabinet and was the candidate of his party for mayor of West Berlin in the election of December, 1958. He is a jovial, capable, and winning type of politician.

The election in October, 1946, proved conclusively that Franz Neumann had been right and Otto Grotewohl wrong. The Social Democrats emerged as overwhelmingly the largest party of Berlin, and were of no mind to capitulate. This election of 1946 was the only one up to now to be held in the whole of Berlin.

	SPD	CDU	LDP/FDP	SED
1946				
Votes	1,015,609	462,425	194,722	412,582
Per cent of				
total votes	48.7	22.2	9.3	19.8
Seats	63	29	12	26
1948				
Votes	858,461	258,664	214,145	——
Per cent of				
total votes	64.5	19.4	16.1	——
Seats	76	26	17	11
1950				
Votes	654,025	360,864	337,493	——
Per cent of				
total votes	44.6	24.6	23.1	——
Seats	61	34	32	——
1954				
Votes	684,906	467,117	197,204	41,375
Per cent of				
total votes	44.6	30.4	12.8	2.7
Seats	64	44	19	——
1958				
Votes	850,127	609,097	61,119	31,572
Per cent of				
total votes	52.6	37.7	3.2	1.9
Seats	78	55	——	——

In 1947 the representation from the East sector was left untouched since the partition was looked upon as only temporary. By their votes in these elections the people of West Berlin expressed their opposition to the blockade policies of Russia; and ten years later, on December 7, 1958, they rejected emphatically the renewed Russian demands. While the SED, received only 1.9 per cent of the votes cast, thus getting less than the 5 per cent necessary in order to be represented in the Abgeordnetenhaus (House of Delegates), the third party, FDP, also lost the largest part of its support. Thus West Berlin reinforced the tendency to a two-party system which had already been characteristic in West Germany.

The city parliament in East Berlin is elected in the usual way by a "single list," at the time of the election to the People's Chamber.

The Social Democratic Party is the only one in Berlin which can claim continuity back to the days before Hitler. If it can continue to produce strong leaders of the type of Reuter and Brandt it will certainly dominate the situation in the future. In the election of 1958 the Social Democratic campaign was centered primarily upon Brandt; he became the unifying symbol in whose name the party could bring home victory. It has been pointed out that the majority of the SPD in the whole of Berlin would presumably have been even larger: the party had an absolute majority in 1946 in all eight of the districts which now belong to East Berlin.

42   The Invisible Mayor

I am one guest who can often be seen in the red brick city hall in the heart of East Berlin, across from Marie Church. I have never received any invitation, and as far as I can see I am not very welcome either. But I continue persistently to trot along the echo-filled corridors.

I wish to talk to the mayor of East Berlin, Friedrich Ebert, son of the great Ebert and member of the Central Committee of the SED.

I know from previous experience that the East Berlin administration also functions effectively, and that here too they have big plans for the future, some of which are being realized. The two cities are administered similarly, even though the work in East Berlin is in the name of socialism and that in West Berlin in the name of freedom. The city officials are not different, whether in East or West.

Normally I go to the Press Bureau in the red City Hall. It is almost microscopic when compared to the elephantine set-up which has been established in the City Hall in Schöneberg, where a staff of sixty persons tries to seem as busy as possible. Every West Berlin Senate and district administrative office has, furthermore, its own press bureau with personnel who try to look just as busy.

Instead of complying with my wishes, the press chief at the red City Hall gives me a sheaf of typewritten items of information. In these I read that East Berlin has 177 city councillors (over half of whom are workers and farmers), who serve the cause of real democracy in contrast to the sham democracy in West Berlin.

I repeat my request for an interview with Friedrich Ebert.

No, that is impossible. As a member of the Central Committee he has many duties and seldom visits the City Hall.

I request an interview with Ebert's deputy, Waldemar Schmidt.

No, that is impossible too. As Ebert's deputy he has many duties and seldom visits the City Hall.

I request an interview with Schmidt's deputy. Or with Schmidt's deputy's deputy.

No, that is impossible, too. Schmidt's deputy has many duties since Ebert and Schmidt are away.

After I have exhausted my German vocabulary of deputies and alternates, and to some degree my store of swear words, I stop visiting the red City Hall.

On the other hand, I go past it often and gaze at the tower clock, the only attractive thing in the entire brick barrack.

In the newspapers I read that Ebert is receiving foreign party delegates at the airport in Schönefeld or at the Ostbahnhof. I see him in newsreels at the newsreel theater, DEFA-Zeitkino, at Bahnhof Friedrichstrasse, and I read his speeches in *Neues Deutschland.*

I begin referring to him as the man who disappeared, or the invisible mayor.

43 · *Face of the City*

"For the poor, through thick and thin," she said scornfully.

"Well, is this any worse than supporting your country through thick and thin? One chooses sides once and for all—it can, of course, be the wrong side. Only history can decide that." (Graham Greene: *Confidential Agent*).

I am headed for Britz, and am in a hurry. The tram creeps slowly along in the Saturday traffic. Finally it stops altogether and the passengers begin to twist and shift in their seats. Busses are lined up, police cars with shrieking sirens are headed this way, and there are automobiles on the street as far as I can see. The asphalt is wet with rain.

I step off and try to find a taxi.

I walk past the lines of cars and see that there has been an accident. A crowd is gathering, curious people want to get a look at the injured one (or is anyone injured?).

Here among thousands of Berliners who are waiting for transportation home I begin again to wonder what is meant by the face of a city. Has this city a face which distinguishes it from other large European cities? Berlin lies in the flat landscape of the March of Brandenburg area. I know that it has a distinctive political character. I know that the warm climate makes Paris more colorful than Berlin. I know that in Rome people live on the streets.

Could it be, I think to myself irreverently, that the name Berlin opens up a world of associations dependent only upon personal experiences and accidental feelings? The popular conception is that Berlin is dramatic, and is marked by political tension which might crack at any moment. It is East and West, kidnappings and political murders, a threat of world war.

But daily life in Berlin does its best to dissipate such illusions. Daily life is daily life in Berlin also, with normal experiences and normal work. Even the absurd—I mean the partition—has become something normal.

The solution to the problem is accommodation. The Berliners have accommodated themselves. They cannot earn their daily bread simply by longing for a reunited Germany. They must work and build.

For me, the experience of the city is bound up with politics. This may be pure chance. If I had not climbed some high towers, and if I had not flown over Berlin, I should not have known that the city is flat. If I had not encountered politics on my first visit to Berlin I should not have conceived of the city in the same way.

I have found a free taxi and ride in it to Neukölln. From there I take a tram to Britz. As I ride I think back.

I came to Berlin the first time in 1952. Then I didn't realize at all that I ought to have come in 1922. Many people talked about Weimar, some about the Kaiser. Others spoke about the last days of 1945, about Russian terrorism and about fear of Communism.

I believed that a social experiment had been begun in the eastern part of Germany and in East Berlin which was deserving of support. Was it not possible here to find a way out of the German dilemma, the gap between technical expansion and a deficient human balance, which had led to so many misfortunes?

I came here to seek political reality.

I was disturbed by the lying fashion in which the respective sides depicted their opponents. I heard both complaint and praise in Berlin. I talked with Berliners in Bierstuben and at

Aschinger's. Berlin became a problem of conscience, the perpetual political question of a choice between two poles. It proved impossible for me to make a choice in such concrete terms as many would have wished.

By chance I happened to find a small pub in East Berlin. The building was a scantily-repaired ruin, but in the basement there was a cabaret and dance restaurant, Hajo. It was open until three in the morning, the only pub with late hours in Friedrichstadt. Hajo was always packed. And at that time both East and West Berliners mingled freely in the pubs of East Berlin.

One evening I went into Hajo, paid my entrance fee, and got a seat at a large table. A cabaret program was under way. A man was sketching pictures, which he quickly wiped out and replaced with new ones.

"This is the old Berlin, which is now destroyed," he said without evidence of nostalgia. "Here you see the people and the buildings."

People were listening almost reverently. I could not feel as the others did. For me, Berlin was here and now; I could not conceive of the city without ruins, without that peculiar odor of death, which to me belonged to both the idea and the city of Berlin.

I got to know Siegrid, who was sitting at my table with a theater man. We danced on the little spot of floor, only a few yards wide, where the cabaret numbers were performed. It grew late, she kissed me, and I felt happy. I forgot about the gabled houses on Friedrichsgracht, the Gothic church, the black market and the narcotics salesmen. We drank wine, and I dug into my pockets for more money. She laughed at me, and I felt a sensation of escape and of relief. We went out arm in arm and the theater man was left there with his schnapps.

I have a hard time remembering how she looked.

But we went to Hajo frequently, saw the program five—or was

it ten?—times, and took long walks in the city. She worked at the Charité Clinic and planned to become a doctor. She did not complain much about the East German government. It provided her with her board and room. I would meet her after working hours under the trees near the statue of Robert Koch. Till finally one day she didn't come and didn't answer the telephone.

Afterward I returned frequently to Hajo.·

The political situation had changed. I had begun to waver in my belief that the cause of the poor was being served by the East German regime. Was this not some new oligarchy, a new tyranny which had arisen in the heart of Germany under false pretenses? There is no better cause, I thought—and still think—than to fight against injustice and oppression in the world.

I wanted to know where the front line ran in Berlin. I began to think of the city as a symbol of the front line throughout the world. Finally I began to suspect that the front line did not run parallel to the sector boundary, and that good and evil were distributed otherwise in the big game that was being played.

Now, much later, the entrance to Hajo was barricaded when I went past. I felt a pang in my heart. The name Hajo was still dimly legible over the doorway, but there was nothing to indicate that this was once a place where one could dance and be happy.

I noticed recently that Hajo had moved to West Berlin. Its sign has become considerably larger. It is located in the same building on Nollendorfplatz where Piscator played Toller's *Hoppla, wir leben!* Hajo is now neither a cabaret nor an intimate restaurant, but a jazz hall which has a Tea Dance for Teenagers on Sunday afternoons.

The woman in the coat room tells me that the owner decided to move to the West after an incident in his East Berlin pub involving an American soldier. He began to feel the ground growing hot under his feet.

But I have no desire to sit down. The old feeling just won't come back.

One day as I ride past I notice that there is blasting across from Hajo's. The tower of the destroyed American church is still standing. I watch as the street is cleared, and wait for the explosion.

The tower crumbles and there is nothing left but a heap of bricks. Hajo's sign is undamaged.

But now the story gets a new twist which seems almost unavoidable in Berlin. My story of Hajo has been somewhat sentimental, and I have remarked that the fate of this pub is tied to politics. This is right, and to a greater extent than I had thought. I have since learned that Hajo in the East was a popular gathering place for agents and spies, and that the same is true of Hajo in the West. East Germans now come frequently to Hajo, including such prominent persons as the radio commentator, Karl Eduard von Schnitzler, the cynical and intelligent star commentator on the East German radio. American military personnel have orders to stay away from Hajo, which is really unnecessary, because every little careless word that they utter is probably picked up also at Resi or in some other dance locale.

Then later I think I see a specter out of the past when I sit in the balcony in the Fritz-Karsen-Schule in Britz and listen to the speeches on party day. My journalistic colleague sits and reads *Intime Revue,* and doesn't listen.

"We must not change the foundations of our Berlin policy," says Willy Brandt. He is defending his opposition to a proposal that a plebiscite be held in West Berlin on atomic rearmament. He sometimes raises, sometimes lowers his voice. He speaks with evident anger.

What he means by "the foundations of our Berlin policy" he has clarified earlier: it is the coalition with the CDU, and the sharp line drawn against "the charlatans and poisoners on the other side of the Brandenburg Gate." It is a matter of not being *either red in the Eastern sense of the word, or black*. The Social Democrats do not want to negotiate with, or cooperate with, the enemies of personal and political freedom. In his wrath Brandt even threatens to resign as mayor.

It is an impassioned debate. The party is split on this question. Senator Lipschitz repeats what I have often heard before: that it was the fear of an atomic war which restrained the Russians from taking over West Berlin in 1948. This means, in other words, that the atom bombs would have saved the city. Isn't this also demagogy?

In the final vote between the two party factions Brandt wins a bare victory. "The foundations of our Berlin policy" have been saved, the coalition with CDU will continue, and the newspapers in East Berlin can again angrily charge that Adenauer's lackey, Brandt, has won another victory—even though it was close.

When I leave Britz it is late in the evening. The parks are empty. The violent antagonisms and the heated debates seem to recede like an empty shadow.

I wander along empty streets until I see finally a beam of light and movement somewhere in the distance. I head that way, since where I go is of little consequence.

44   *The Permitted Party*

The Social Democrat, Kurt Neubauer, member of the Federal Parliament in Bonn, lives on one of the streets which intersect Stalinallee. He is one of the twenty-two members elected by the West Berlin City Council to serve in the Federal Parliament. He is a young and progressive man.

Kurt Neubauer began his political career in the district of Friedrichshain in East Berlin, where he is addressed properly as "Parliamentary Deputy," and where he enjoys all the privileges normally accorded to East German politicians. He lives within the confines of a hostile and ill-disposed state, in a country which the Federal Parliament chooses not to recognize. Neubauer is thus an absurdity.

"But I'm not the only one of my kind," he says. "One of my colleagues also lives in East Berlin. And my good friend here, Rudi Müller, is a member of the City Council in West Berlin despite the fact that he lives in Lichtenberg in the East. There are seven such council members, all of them Social Democrats.

"That's nothing unusual. That's Berlin," says Müller, a man of some fifty years who enjoys repeating impudent Berlin witticisms and loves to joke with everybody he meets. Müller is a tribune of the people, a worker; Neubauer is an intellectual. Their friendship does not stem only from the fact that they live in East Berlin and are politicians in the West. During the days of Hitler Müller was engaged in illegal work with Neubauer's present father-in-law. He was sent to the correctional institute at Luckau, was freed, and later served with a forced labor company. He was sent to Africa but his campaign in the desert was ended after ten days when he was taken prisoner by the Americans and sent to a camp on the Mississippi.

"I was born and grew up in Lichtenberg," says Müller. "I am chairman of the party branch in Lichtenberg and I don't want to leave my friends in the lurch. They have it hard enough anyway. We are the only Western and democratic party that is permitted to work in East Berlin. We have our own branches and party offices in every East Berlin district. Our organization was smashed and our members disappeared in 1946 when the SED was founded. But we have managed to build the thing up again."

Müller lives in a back courtyard on Herzbergstrasse in Lichtenberg. From his small, dark apartment one cannot see the "colony cottages" and gardens on the other side of the street. Next door there is a large factory, Elektrokohle.

In Müller's living room there is a round table, some cupboards, a well-filled bookcase, and a radio. Müller's old mother sits in an armchair and makes pointed comments on life and politics. Müller and I sit at the round table while his wife serves some food. As in the homes of workers and peasants everywhere in the world it is a shame not to help oneself freely. Müller's mother sees to it that I eat three plates of soup and two plates of meat stew. When that is over I feel swollen like a balloon.

"And now we'll drink some HO-coffee," says Müller when we have finished eating. "Good and nourishing."

I taste the coffee. "This isn't HO-coffee," I say.

"I know it, but I wanted to see if you could tell the difference."

He shows me a plant newspaper from one of the larger enterprises in Lichtenberg. An agitated little story deals with a certain Chittrich, a worker at the plant.

Chittrich is a Social Democrat, and it seems that he makes no secret of the fact. He was often called before the leaders of the SED, to the FDGB, or to some other enlightened organization to discuss his distorted views on the work of reconstruction in

the German Democratic Republic. These edifying sessions did
not make him any better, says the paper. One day he told an
official of the SED: "Kiss my bottom and go to hell!"

The newspaper is rightly incensed over Chittrich's crude and
uncomradely behavior.

"It is absolutely true that Chittrich said that to the SED man,"
says Müller. "But he became very popular after the event. And
the Party popes have left him alone."

The doorbell rings as we are talking. Müller has invited in
a number of his party comrades in Lichtenberg. In order not
to arouse unnecessary attention they arrive one at a time.

"One can't be too careful here in the Eastern sector," says
Müller. He opens a bottle of brandy and pours a drink. We
empty our glasses quickly. In the dimly-lit room we seem like
shadows.

The new arrivals begin to talk. Herbert, who speaks first,
works at the same large factory as his friend Hanns, where they
make transformers and other electrical equipment. They are
skilled workers and earn 650 Eastmarks per month, sometimes
more.

"I didn't want to stay in Berlin after the war, but my mother
was here and I lived with her. I would much have preferred to
go to one of the Western zones. I became a Social Democrat in
1945 because I noticed that you couldn't work together with the
Communists. They are enemies of that freedom which we associate with socialism. I have not had occasion to change my
mind. Last year my uncle was sentenced to a term of twenty-
five years because he had a Western newspaper in his home. In
school they have tried to get my boy to join the Young Pioneers.
He came home and asked what he should do. I told him to say
that our family is Social Democratic and doesn't want to have
anything to do with the Young Pioneers.

"The other day my boy told me that a girl in his school had

been asked by the teacher to give the name of Berlin's mayor. 'Willy Brandt,' she answered immediately. Then the teacher got mad and asked her if she listened to RIAS (a radio station in West Berlin). She ought to know that the mayor of democratic Berlin was Fritz Ebert. 'We listen to RIAS,' answered the girl. And all the others in the class shouted and yelled: 'We listen to RIAS, too.'

"But nothing happened because you can't toss out a whole class."

"Why don't you escape, then," I ask. "If this is happening everywhere."

"We live here and we have our jobs here. It's not easy to leave one's home. Recently they haven't bothered us so much, even though we are Social Democrats. But there are many who are fleeing from our factory."

"They say that there are East Berlin handicraftsmen who have done well in recent years," I say, "and who have deposited their extra income in banks in West Berlin. Do you know anything about that?"

"Yes, we do," says Müller. "But the new measures against East German handicraftsmen are designed to lower their income level."

"I can't afford a savings account," says Hanns.

He empties his glass and begins to talk.

"I am also a party member, but only since 1952. I am called up to the SED officials in our factory quite often, and must listen to political lectures. They talk about unity of action. Sometimes these discussions last three hours and the business pays full salary despite the fact that I have only sat in an office and talked politics. Do you think we can have 'brotherly co-operation' with those who imprison our comrades and repress the least beginnings of political freedom? We can hold meetings only in our party headquarters, and we are forced to go to

Marx-Engels-Platz whenever the SED arranges demonstrations.

"Even though we are Social Democrats," he continues, "they try to get us to join *their* organization. The choice is free: FDGB or FDJ or SED, or Society for Sports and Technology or Society for German-Soviet Friendship, or what have you. Or the People's Army. There are recruiters who come around with enticing offers of 320 marks a month plus free quarters, But why do they send recruiters to an enterprise that needs all of its employees? Stupidity!"

"Are you married?"

"Yes. When we became engaged my fiancée told me that she was a member of the SED. Then I told her: either you are going to get married to your party or to me. But if you stay in the party you can go to hell.

"And so we got married. For years we tried to get new housing. I have been living in a small, damp room with my wife and two sick children. I have filled out a whole pile of forms, told my life's story, and got promises and more promises. Finally I got so mad I sent a letter to *Berliner Zeitung*. The newspaper called the housing commission and threatened to publish everything. I got a place in a week. I have two rooms with a kitchen and bath for which I pay sixty marks in rent. I am not unhappy about my forty-five square yards." (It might be pointed out here that necessities of life, such as housing and food, are extremely cheap in East Berlin, an economic fact which makes it possible to live just as well—or badly—for 400 Eastmarks in East Berlin as for 400 Westmarks in West Berlin.)

Herbert and Hanns, two of many workers in East Berlin, belong to the small, organized opposition, which continues to carry on the rather hopeless fight under difficult circumstances. They know the odds, but they do not intend to give up. They are not frightened by threats from the SED.

When I am standing with them out on Herzbergstrasse, I

notice that Hanns is a war invalid. We walk for a bit and he has a hard time keeping up with the rest of us. Like Herbert, he knows that a free election in the whole of Berlin would result in victory for their party. They are waiting for that day, but meanwhile continue to build transformers for the East German state.

45 The Graves of Lichtenberg

"I have eighteen new apple trees on my lot," say Rudi Müller proudly. We are walking on Herzbergstrasse. On one side of the street there is a row of dark houses, and on the other side are the "colony" gardens where the workers of Lichtenberg spend their Sundays now that it is spring. Müller cultivates one of these small, fenced-off parcels of ground.

We go by some new gardens, student housing, some half-finished sections of a new ball-bearing factory. We are on our way to the party headquarters in Lichtenberg.

"We were forced out of our earlier location in 1950. But luckily we got a new and better one. It is right next to the S-Bahn, and we are the only SPD office in East Berlin that has a neon sign. At night it lights up the track and the trains so that the passengers can see that we haven't given up the fight in East Berlin.

"The Lichtenberg office is famous—both Gaitskell and Richard Crossman, as well as Willy Brandt, have visited it. This branch of the party has something over 1,000 members, but we accept only absolutely dependable Social Democrats. We got enough of SED infiltration earlier."

The office is located in the corner of an apartment house which has a small lawn in front of the entrance. (I suggest that they throw some garden parties.) This office has been so distasteful to the East regime that the SED, has, among other things, hung fiery red transparencies and political appeals in front of the neon light and the sign so that no one could see that the Social Democrats had a party office there. These banners, however, could not survive forever. The texts threatened reprisals against the betrayers of Social Democracy.

The party headquarters was once a pub. It had to close its doors because of black market operations. There is a meeting room large enough for 200 persons, an office room, and a number of smaller rooms. On the wall behind the speaker's rostrum there is a portrait of Schumacher as well as photographs of comrades in Lichtenberg who have spent time in East German jails because of the grave offense of being Social Democrats. All of them have since been released, but three of them spent eight years in prison.

"You must understand that there is no sense in our holding a meeting here in East Berlin in opposition to atomic rearmament in West Germany," says Müller, "even if we are its opponents. Then the SED would start talking immediately about unity of action. Our primary concern is good internal harmony. We don't have any public meetings. We are careful and don't keep any important papers here, even our list of members. Harmony within the party is most important."

We leave the party headquarters at sundown and go down the street toward the churchyard in Friedrichsfelde. On the way we go past some stone-cutting establishments, which are always to be found near cemeteries. I am told that the stone cutters, like the florists within the walls of the cemetery, are still private entrepreneurs.

The so-called Gedenkstätte der Sozialisten (Memorial Place for Socialists) is in Friedrichsfelde. Here, inside a low circular wall, Socialists and Communists lie side by side. Despite the lawns and trees and the forest of gravestones the area in front of this burial place has the atmosphere of a place for demonstrations. Near the steps to the Socialist graves there is a speaker's platform, with built-in recesses for microphones. It is here that the East German bigwigs constantly, but constantly, pour out their eulogies.

Müller, who grew up with the laboring class and with the workers' movement in Berlin, and who is a resident of one of the proletarian sections of Lichtenberg, speaks with sadness of the old days. He is a brave man who does not want to depart one iota from his point of view. He is also a sad man, because he regrets the tremendous gap between Social Democrats and Communists. He cannot understand that such men as Otto Grotewohl, with friendly words and great hopes, agreed to the merger which eventually meant losing everything.

Opposites are united only in death. At the Gedenkstätte der Sozialisten one can find the gravestones of the Social Democratic Reich Chancellor, Herman Müller, of Liebknecht, Luxemburg, Thälmann, Franz Mehring, the dead in the Spanish Civil War, casualties of the revolutionary struggle, and many others. Not all of them are buried here, but the name plates serve as reminders of their common struggle—once more a political move by the government in the East!—which may not have been a common struggle at all.

Places where one preserves and commemorates the dead are depressing, and that is true of this round enclosure, where names follow names and wreaths follow wreaths. It is not death that conjures up depression. But it seems barbaric, heathenish

—these stone wastes in the big cities, these richly or poorly decorated graves, which extend over such large areas.

Here in the cemetery it makes no difference if the dead person was a worker or a bourgeois. He is dead, and there is nothing that can be done about it. But the Gedenkstätte der Sozialisten is repugnant primarily because of the speaker's platform. As though names and stones and flowers were not enough, one must also carry on agitation and propaganda.

Another reaction is also possible: the realization of how many worthy German men and women have died from terror and persecution. The realization of the tragedy which Hitler's Reich inflicted upon Germany, which Germany inflicted upon herself! The sins of the German workers' movement are many, but they cannot be compared to those of the German bourgeoisie.

The feeling comes over me suddenly that I have been in Berlin too long. One accommodates oneself so easily. One takes for granted the ruins, the partition, the trains, the silence and the sounds, the high roadbeds of the S-Bahn, the poverty and the riches, and everything implied by the word "German." I try to encourage myself to be curious, not to take anything for granted.

But on the train back to West Berlin I fall asleep. The last I remember is warmth and cigar smoke, voices and evening lights. I am anonymous among other anonymities.

46   Private Entrepreneurs

There is conflicting information about the status of private enterprise in East Berlin, apparently because it is built upon second-hand information, scare reports in West Berlin newspapers, or the one-sided praise and one-sided satisfaction that one gets in East Berlin newspapers. At the one extreme is the insistence that private enterprise is doomed and its liquidation only a matter of time; at the other extreme is the claim that private entrepreneurs are making so much money that they exchange much of their profit into Westmarks and have deposits in the banks there. The latter may be true in some exceptional cases. At the same time it is true that private enterprise still plays a certain role in the East German economy, and however much the East German government might like to see it rooted out, it must be conceded that the SED-men are to some extent realists and act in terms of the requirements of the moment.

I have become acquainted with a few private businessmen in East Berlin, but since the laws of the republic in respect to persons who "slander the regime" or practice "boycottism" are very severe, I must give my description a somewhat fictitious character.

F. is a master carpenter with eight employees and he is located on the edge of Berlin near the border to East Germany. His place is on a shady lane near one of the so-called Parks of Culture. He has a rather large lot on which he parks his old truck. F. inherited the business from his father, and even now one can see an old, faded sign by the side of the road on which his father's name is printed in Gothic letters. It must date from before the war.

The house was only slightly damaged during the war and certain minimal repairs have been made on it. F. cannot afford more than the most necessary expenditures—at least that is what he himself says. I am sitting across from him in a small office that has a view out over the bare trees and the old truck in the courtyard. His staff of employees consists of some faithful veterans who worked for his father and some young apprentices. He has a wife and children to support, and his brother, who works for him, lives in the same crowded house. It is autumn.

F.'s chief worries are the following.

The direct and indirect taxes are extremely high. His freedom of action is limited in every respect. Maximum wages are fixed for his workers, and they are considerably less than the maximum wages in state enterprises or in the so-called Produktions-genossenschaft des Handwerks (handicraft productive association). As a consequence he has a considerable turnover among his apprentices. They leave him and go to better paid jobs with VEB (Volkseigene Betriebe, people's-owned enterprises).

Since inspection by the government bureaucracy is so painstaking he must himself spend most of his day filling out papers and making calculations. If he makes a mistake he runs the risk of being sold out. And he refuses to accept that eventuality.

His primary specialty is doors and windows. He has orders which will keep him going for a long time, and the sales price is fixed by the Specifications Section of the Ministry of Construction, which has published a thick book for guidance in determining the price. Some 38,000 types of windows are listed in this book. At this point in his account F. becomes so irritated that he throws the book on the table: "Madness!"

F. is sometimes invited to avail himself of state financial support, which in practice would mean socialization. Efforts are also made to get him to join the above-mentioned handicraft collective, but he pays no attention to these siren strains. He takes the same negative attitude toward the young people who call from FDJ and ask him to sign some petition.

Possibly F. has a tendency to exaggerate his own difficulties to some degree, but he certainly has no surplus to deposit in the West. The only luxury he has allowed himself is a TV set. In his home he has numerous Western goods and papers, but this can be explained in large part by the fact that he has relatives in the other Berlin. Under present circumstances F. sees no purpose in moving over to the West, where it could be just as hard for a carpenter. He seems capable of shrugging off the political pressures around him, and in some respects seems to be living outside the community. The factor that is most decisive in keeping him here is the lack of capital. His wealth consists of the lot, the building, the furniture, and the machines. To move them would be impossible. It is possible that he will stay here even if the state takes over his business, but the experience of other people in a similar situation has been that they pack up a few things and take the first S-Bahn train to Marienfelde, where they report to the refugee reception center.

As I said before, F. does not have to worry about a market for his goods and the price level is constant. A private baker in the neighborhood has a somewhat different story to tell. He too lives and works in his own house, and the first room one enters is his sales shop. He sells everything that he bakes in this shop. He is in competition with both state and cooperative bakers, but seems to be doing very well. I would not be surprised if he had a large income. But then he is already over seventy years of age, and in the past he has sold to many other outlets.

We are sitting eating some baked goods and drinking brandy. As he sits in his rocker he peers out of half-closed eyes. He impresses me as being astute, and really rather satisfied, because things are going well for him. There is an old barn in the court-yard where he keeps his pigs and his hens. They have just slaughtered an animal, and in the kitchen I almost stumble over a large bucket of freshly steaming blood. It is evening; the shop is closed and the baker has finished his daytime sleep. He will work during the night just as he has done for fifty years. He is a widower but his sons are there to help him and when he passes on (which he believes will be very soon) they will undoubtedly take over the business. He seems so alive and strong that I try to refute his prophecy about an early death. But he just laughs.

Finally, a visit to two brothers who have a commercial flower garden. They are just about to close the gate when I arrive. Just like the baker, they have little to do with, or competition from, the state or cooperatives. They sell their products (like the baker for fixed maximum prices) to private flower shops, and despite the fact that East Berliners employed by the state or the Party are warned not to deal with private businesses, police officers and Party bigwigs often come to him and buy flowers. This is not necessarily because of the quality, but per-haps because of a deep-seated feeling (held even by Com-munists) that private shops sell better products.

The whole system discourages the brothers from trying new experiments. The prices on various kinds of flowers are the same the year around. The price of roses is the same in July as at Christmas. This is conformity carried to the absurd. No nurseryman wants to cultivate rare plants and flowers under such circumstances.

The brothers read Western newspapers, but since they can-not get permission to travel to the West they take fuller ad-vantage than I had thought possible of organized tours to East-ern countries. One brother has been in Czechoslovakia and Hungary, and the other is planning a trip to Bulgaria. Oh yes, if one has money one can travel to the Crimea or to China, but the two brothers don't have quite the means for that. They cannot really be called opponents of the regime; they are indifferent, and they too seem to have developed a kind of immunity to political propaganda.

Private businessmen are naturally a disappearing little group in the vast population of East Berlin, and, as in the cases I have told about, it is usually a matter of a family business which is operated without outside help.

The private tradesmen with whom I have spoken do not suffer from a fear neurosis. They judge their situation realistically and coldly. They will carry on so long as they can. How long nobody knows.

47   The Republic of Kreuzberg

With its face to the east, the district of Kreuzberg in West Berlin borders upon three East Berlin districts. Its mayor is a Social Democrat, Willy Kressmann, a man of fifty years with dark, bushy eyebrows. His headstrong policies have earned him the displeasure of the highest circles in West Berlin. He is called "Texas-Willi," a nickname given him by the Communists when he returned from a visit to the United States dressed in a big Texan hat. Kressmann is popular with his constituents, indeed the most popular district mayor in the whole of Berlin. To ride around Kreuzberg with him is suggestive of the visit of a king among his people: he is hailed by most of them, and he returns the salutation.

In 1955 Kressmann invited the three mayors of the neighboring East Berlin districts to a discussion of common problems such as bridges and road-building. He got an immediate reprimand from the Senate, who felt that it was not the business of a district mayor to involve himself in Eastern contacts. Kressmann answered more or less openly that he thought this was rubbish, and that he intended to repeat his invitation in the future.

Kressmann is primarily a practical man who is concerned about establishing human contacts with the East. He is not afraid to travel to East Berlin, and he has no fear of the authorities in the East.

"The SED is much too weak for us to worry about them. When I returned from my emigration and worked in the city administration I had no trouble working with the Russians. But the German Communists. . . ."

His friends (and sometimes he himself) refer to him as the mayor of the Republic of Kreuzberg. And he prefers this freedom to any high post in the Senate of West Berlin. He doesn't mince any words, and this, combined with his enormous popularity, has led to dissension and jealousy on the part of some of his party comrades. Unfair tactics have been used against him: when in a statement Kressmann referred to East Germany as a *fact*, this was twisted into *factor*, which is very different.

By nature and temperament Kressmann is a middle-of-the-road man, not unlike a Laborite in Great Britain. But he is of the opinion that West Berlin should not just coldly refuse to deal with the East; it should actively concern itself with what is happening beyond the Brandenburg Gate. When he permitted an exhibition of Polish posters to be set up in the city hall this was something unheard of in West Berlin—culture of a people's democracy in the city of freedom. The anger which it aroused showed that the atmosphere in the West, too, can easily be inflamed. On the other hand, no one has opposed his activating a building program on the western side of the sector boundary. As a consequence those on the eastern side of the line, too, have been forced to start rebuilding. During a tour along the eastern edge of Kreuzberg (the street on which we travel is actually on the east side) I can observe how familiar Kressmann is with the minutest detail of his district.

Every year Kressmann arranges big festivals at the sector line for the children of East Berlin. He labels them, "We Are All One." A well-oiled advertising apparatus distributes pictures of Kressmann in the role of friend of the children. And he is that. In addition he is a member of football associations, bowling clubs, and choral societies. He can put in an appearance as a swimmer, or whatever else might strike his fancy.

As I am waiting in the outer office of Kressmann's headquarters a man is there looking for housing. He is an invalid, goes on crutches, and complains of his fate. Kreuzberg is, except for the former center of the city (now in East Berlin) the worst damaged section of Berlin. Most of the buildings remaining from the prewar period do not meet the needs of our time. Kreuzberg, which is the smallest district in Berlin, has the densest population.

An old woman employee comes into the room with a pot of coffee and gets a friendly slap on the seat by the male employees. Then the door opens and an alert, disheveled woman of fifty comes dashing in.

"Greetings from Copenhagen," she says gaily, and sits down at the table. "I have been in Denmark on a holiday."

"Did you see the King?" says a thin-haired civil servant who is turning over the papers in some folders.

"Yes, indeed, it was on Princess Margarethe's birthday. We

saw the whole thing on TV. And the ice cream torte was as big as a house. And she was so sweet, and the King so handsome. There is something special about kings. There's something special about Denmark. And in the restaurants and pubs there were menus as long as this, menus three yards long. Yes, really! You don't believe it? And the food was cheap. And good!"

"Did you do anything except eat?" says the man laconically.

"Certainly, I traveled around in Denmark. I went to Elsinore—Hamlet's town, you know—and to Odense. That's Hans Christian Andersen's birthplace. We looked at everything."

"And you had a good time?"

"Very good, but it was too cold. There was ice when we got to Elsinore. So next time I'm going to Italy."

The girls sigh and empty their coffee cups. Everyone seems to have fallen into a trance. No one does anything. They just stare emptily into space.

Then Kressmann comes in.

He occupies a large flower-decked room which exudes light and peace.

"I understand that you receive threatening letters because you participate in the campaign against atomic rearmament."

"I don't pay any attention to the cold warriors." He shows me a bundle of letters, and then adds: "When I returned from England after the war I hoped that Germany had learned from her mistakes. Here in West Berlin there is no good soil for Nazi infiltration, but we must be on our guard, nevertheless, and not try to be self-righteous just because our opponents in the East are bad.

"What concerns me is my own district."

This is true. Kreuzberg concerns Kressmann. This densely populated section of the city was the one most destroyed on the West side, and 20 per cent of the ruins are still there. But

Kressmann hopes that within ten years, if he gets the time and the money, everything will be completely restored.

In his free and impulsive way Kressmann is considerably more dangerous to the Eastern authorities than other politicians in Berlin, who are perhaps too engrossed in conducting Big Diplomacy. Thousands of unknown persons sent him flowers when he got married in 1959—and he had them sent to the hospitals. Up to 20,000 East Berliners see daily movies in a special performance near the sector boundary. Kressmann is liable to be any place where something is happening.

In his district I see the older pensioners as well as the most recent ones. The helicopter airport for Berlin is going to be built in Kreuzberg. Elderly ladies sit on the park benches around the hill, which has given Kreuzberg its name, and munch on sandwiches. They can look out over the trees, the Schultheise Brewery, and a sea of houses.

48   The Church and Communism

Dr. Otto Dibelius, the (Protestant) Bishop of Berlin and Brandenburg (East Germany), usually preaches in the Marienkirche in East Berlin. In his external appearance Dibelius is strikingly like Walter Ulbricht. Both of them have well-groomed goatees.

Their personalities are just as different as their meetings are infrequent. Ulbricht gets his biggest public at the Marx-Engels-Platz, very near the Marienkirche.

West Berlin looks upon Dibelius as a hero, Ulbricht as a swine. It is just the opposite in East Berlin. There I can read about Dibelius' anti-Semitic utterances during the days of Hitler. In West Berlin the opinion is that Dibelius must be judged by his actions, not according to anything he might have said in the past. The fact is that Dibelius was not always one of Hitler's opponents. But how many of the present East German party functionaries were?

In West Berlin Ulbricht is criticized and called a puppet. In East Berlin he is praised for his resolute fight against imperialism and oppression. In short, the two are alike only in their mutual hate and their similar beards.

Dibelius conducts high mass in the Marienkirche on Easter Sunday. The church is filled to overflowing an hour before the start of the service. Long rows of automobiles from West Berlin are parked along the neighboring streets. Dibelius is the incarnation of open opposition to Ulbricht's regime. That is why he is popular. Hundreds of people are unable to find a place in the church. They wait patiently and are seated in a side chapel.

Dibelius speaks in a firm voice, and without sentimentality. It is deathly quiet in the church auditorium. His text is from the twenty-eighth chapter of the Gospel of Matthew: "He is not here, for He is risen, as He said."

But Dibelius does not speak at first on this text. He reads from *Neues Deutschland*: some days before the paper had explained that peaceful coexistence between the church and Communism was impossible.

Dibelius gives an answer to this statement, unmindful that this is a high mass and that a resurrection is ostensibly being celebrated:

"This is like a blow in the face for those who still think that the two sides can be linked to one another. To us it is bitter that our people, still so divided, should have this chasm reopened. As Christians we can only answer: an ideology should never make fellowship in the Lord Jesus Christ impossible. In any case we hold both of our hands outstretched, even if those on the other side slam the door in our faces."

Then Dibelius goes over to the other subject. He is surprised that today's German youth are asking, "What is the purpose of my life?"

In earlier days our young people did not ask about the meaning of life, says Dibelius. Instead they acted. Does he consider earlier German young people so purposeful, brave, idealistic, and strong that their certainty and spiritual immobility were to be preferred to asking the simple question about the meaning of life?

Dibelius offers the safety of the Sermon on the Mount and of the parables as an alternative to uncertainty, to questions. The way through God becomes the way of liberation.

Above the sorrow of the Easter sun glows the light of liberation. It is a Christian teaching of propitiation, with gentle forgiveness, and a Hollywood happy ending. Wickedness and crime fulfill a function in the great system of sin and forgiveness.

The Christians wish us to be reconciled to death. Is such a reconciliation possible, and is it necessary?

The collection plates are passed after the high mass. They are quickly filled.

I walk to the middle of the church, and go past the graves of the great, which have nothing to say to me. Count and Field Marshal Sparr died in 1668, and is now immured in the wall of the church. Otherwise, it is a naked church, only slightly affected by nineteenth-century tastes, just as ascetic as Protestantism is dry and cold.

On my way back to West Berlin to my usual eating-place I

reflect over the gradual worsening of relations between the Protestant church and the East German state. Dibelius is not entirely without fault that it is so.

The Evangelical German Church (EKD) is the only all-German institution which is still in existence. The Church assumes stubbornly that Germany is one and undivided, even though the political cleavage is wider than ever.

In March, 1957, as chairman of EKD's highest council, Bishop Dibelius concluded an agreement with the Federal government providing that chaplains should minister to the Federal Army. This agreement inspired the East German government and the State Secretariat for Church Affairs (created in the spring of 1957) to attack EKD. Dibelius' agreement, they asserted, meant that even the East German church was now involved in the spiritual care of soldiers in the Federal Army. Did this not mean, reasoned the East German dialecticians, that the Evangelical Church was thus giving its blessing to atomic rearmament?

In Evangelical circles there were at once pangs of conscience, and also defences of the agreement along the line: "Better an agreement than no chaplains at all." The All-German Evangelical Synod, which met in Berlin in April, 1958, was of the opinion that the agreement with the Federal government in regard to the military care of souls should be reconsidered. A warning was directed to both German governments to refrain from atomic rearmament. The majority of the delegates to the Synod were of the same opinion as the East German professor of theology, Professor Vogel: "To make man, whom God so loved as the Gospel tells us—to make him, even in one's thoughts—the object of methods of mass annihilation is a sin. It is worse than crime and madness. It is of greater consequence than any human goal, yes, greater than the saving of the whole of the so-called

Christian West. Does not something simple follow therefrom; to wit: Hands off?"

In his hardness and irreconcilability Bishop Dibelius is presumably not representative of the opinion of the Evangelical Church. However, by representing himself publicly as the spokesman for the opposition in East Germany, he has been given a partially unearned halo as a hero. It is the East German government's own fault that its spitefulness makes heroes out of those who are perhaps not of heroic mold.

The church becomes a fighting church, and is carried back to an earlier period of history when its members fought on the side of the oppressed.

The Evangelical Synod pointed out in its resolution that confirmation and the atheistic *Jugendweihe* are incompatible. All indications are that the Eastern area with its dedication of young people is trying hard to win the battle for the soul of youth.

49   The Battle for Youth

The dawn was slowly appearing over Berlin. I was standing on the station platform at Ostkreuz, shivering in the cold lazy morning breeze. Faces seemed gray in the silence of Sunday morning. The tracks in the distance were swallowed up in a light fog which was slowly dispersing. There were figures in

gray and black; a station attendant in a black overcoat. A dog was barking incessantly.

I lit a cigarette and looked over at the bench where Käthe was sitting and chatting with her friend.

I had been sitting in an overcrowded dancing pub in East Berlin reading the Sunday editions of the West Berlin newspapers. It was there that I met Käthe and her girl friend. They had been celebrating the friend's birthday and wanted to continue the festivities. They looked disapprovingly at my newspapers, but this didn't prevent me from dancing with Käthe. She is a lively, slender girl of twenty years. And she likes to talk about books.

We continued the birthday celebration until four o'clock in the morning and then took the first S-Bahn train to Ostkreuz. Now I am standing here and waiting for the first train to Biesdorf, despite the fact that Käthe has asked me to go home.

It is full daylight by the time we get to Biesdorf. The birds are singing. The fog has lifted and I have stopped shivering. I take the girls by the arm and start down the long main street past the pub, Zur Alten Post, where some thirsty hikers are vainly awaiting a glass of beer. It is as quiet as in the country; there are few automobiles and few people.

"That's where the Russians live," says Käthe. She points to the right beyond the buildings and the woods. Karlshorst is the nearest neighbor to Biesdorf. Both of them are in Lichtenberg.

It is a long way to Käthe's home, a small villa set in fields and woods. This is a Berlin which is a stranger to the bustle of the inner city. It is quiet on the clay byroads.

Käthe is pleased with her celebration, her day, her work, and she is now humming a song the words of which I do not recognize. In her free time she reads books or goes to the movies. At times she cooks for her brothers and her parents.

It is about one of these brothers that I want to write. He is shortly going to be present at the *Jugendweihe*.

"This is a big event in his life," says Käthe emphatically, and does not smile. Her friend nods.

The first youth dedications were held in Berlin in March, 1955. The number of youngsters who are taking instruction has climbed rapidly. It has more variety, and it is more fun, than religious confirmation. Pressure is exerted on the young people in the schools. Anyone who allows himself to be confirmed is considered hardly fit to be a worthy citizen in the workers' and peasants' republic.

"We can remain silent no longer," says an East German pastor," when people are branded as undependable citizens or second-class individuals just because they are Christians."

The *Jugendweihe* is a secular copy of confirmation, but it is not an East German invention. It has old socialist roots. The instruction takes place under the direction of the Central Office for the Dedication of Youth. Every effort is made to make the program as attractive as possible for the youngsters. They visit factories and theaters, they go out into the country and live in tents, they visit the National People's Army and make the acquaintance of national and socialist tanks and cannons. The relationship of the individual to the workers' and peasants' state is discussed in the courses.

The dedication itself is just as solemn as confirmation. Here also a promise of loyalty is involved. But the church and its doctrines have been replaced by the German Democratic Republic and its political concepts.

Instead of changing young people and giving them a real alternative to the church's articles of faith the Republic is satisfied with substituting the word *State* for *Church*. This, then, is training not for responsibility and freedom (at least in the

Western sense) but for collective submission. A seventeen-year-old is caught up in a unity which he does not feel.

But for Käthe and her brother, who have known no other time than that of Hitler (as children), of the Russian occupation, and of the present-day East Germany, the *Jugendweihe* is an important turning-point in life. Henceforth, they are adults.

I ask Käthe if she thinks that all of them will be true to their pledges. She does not answer. The young people take the following oath:

Are you prepared, as true sons and daughters of our workers' and peasants' state, to work and fight for a happy life for all German people? If so, answer:
Yes, we solemnly promise!
Are you prepared to dedicate your whole strength, with ours, to the great and noble cause of socialism? If so, answer:
Yes, we solemnly promise!
Are you prepared to support friendship among peoples, and, with the Soviet people and with all peace-loving peoples of the world, to secure and defend the peace? If so, answer:
Yes, we solemnly promise!
We have heard your solemn promise. You have set for yourselves a high and noble goal. You have enrolled yourselves among the millions of people who are working and fighting for peace and socialism.
We receive you solemnly into partnership with the older activists of our German Democratic Republic and promise you support, protection, and help.
With combined strength—Forward!

I am present when Käthe's brother, together with his friends, takes the oath in the Theater of Friendship in Berlin. Käthe holds my hand and presses it hard. She seems tense with excitement. After her brother has sworn the oath she relaxes.

A Party orator speaks of promises and duties, promises about the future and duty in respect to the present. The youngsters are well-dressed and their faces are serious. They have just completed some exciting weeks.

Yet I am nauseated. I don't like confirmations or churches. Earthly churches are no less repulsive.

But the *Jugendweihe* will become popular with young people; it is already. The church has presumably seen the deadly danger which threatens. Neither under the Kaiser nor under Hitler was the power of the church endangered, even though many churchmen openly opposed Nazism. The new danger will come after a long period of tremendous advantages, which the church has perhaps not appreciated sufficiently.

I am just as convinced as the Evangelical Church that the *Jugendweihe* and confirmation are absolutely irreconcilable. But churchmen are not the right propagandists against this form of promises, since they themselves have practiced it for hundreds of years. It is the heathen, the doubters, who must protest against the *Jugendweihe*, not because its creed is so different from that of the church, but because they are so closely related.

Käthe herself, young and sensitive, has earlier sworn the oath. She belongs to a new kind of Eastern citizenry, for whom Berlin is East Berlin. She likes to swim in Müggelsee, and doesn't think for a moment of fleeing. She is dangerously indifferent, and accepts what is given her.

It is hard for me to associate with Käthe and her brother. I do go to the movies with them, and I admire Virna Lisi in *Die Frau des Tages,* and we discuss trivialities. But in most respects they are as hard to pry open as clams. Have they learned the worst of all human characteristics—political suspicion? Have they arrived at that point which *Neues Deutschland* refers to as "socialist consciousness"?

50   Why Points of View

It has been said that today's youth, the youth who live in an age of
industrial mass society, belong to a generation of skeptics, without
sentiment, a program, or watchwords; that they are withdrawn,
do not seem to wish to get involved (cautious, but successful); that
they have a sense for the personal and the concrete; that within
their own callings they are seeking social security, accommodate
themselves, feel themselves as young adults, and are quiet and
unrevolutionary (what is lacking seems to be an overriding passion);
that they show a kind of consumer's attitude (consumption of
schools, leisure, the state, church, etc.), whereby they achieve a
great deal; that they are relatively open to religions . . . etc. Since you
belong to this generation, what do you think of these judgments?
Are they correct, or must the diagnosis run differently?—From a
questionnaire for West German young people.

Many of the 5,000 persons in the Sports Palace are from East
Berlin, but their clothes are not distinguishable from those of
all the others. They show their identity cards at the cashier's
window to pay in Eastmarks. This is one of the advantages
whereby the West Berlin Senate believes it is supporting the
brothers and sisters of the East. They can use their Eastern
currency to see certain Western performances, get into the
movies and see wild westerns at a cheap price, and climb up
into West Berlin's public monuments, such as the Siegessäule.

This is called propaganda for Western culture.

Tonight, Johnnie Ray is on the program at the Sports Palace.

The Sports Palace played a frequent role in the lives of
Goebbels and Hitler. The Nazis held their big meetings there
both before and after the seizure of power. It is not to be as-

sumed that the entertainment which I have now come to witness has anything to do with Nazism. But the young people who are waiting outside were born during the last years of the Hitler era, and they have forgotten. This forgetfulness is not their fault, but that of their teachers.

I have arrived early and I find my cheap seat high up, just under the roof, about as far from the stage as it is possible to get. I can see how the seats are shaking from the rhythmic stamping: *John-nie, John-nie!*

Some teenagers—one wearing glasses—are sitting just to my right. They seem isolated from the rest of the audience; they are not participating in the stamping, but are quietly smoking and watching the crowd.

The management has tried to give a kind of cultural touch to the program by having a prize-winning Iranian clarinetist perform. He is standing far from the microphone, and less than half of the audience can hear his music. The Oriental melodies which he is playing, undoubtedly with skill and sensitivity, are drowned out by the stamping and loud conversation. He moves about the stage self-consciously as 5,000 critical glances are cast in his direction.

After the intermission the master of ceremonies warns the audience to be quiet and set a good example. Johnnie Ray runs out on the stage. As he enters he gives the appearance of a modest young man, but the nearer he comes to the microphone, the more his manner approaches the ideal image of him in the minds of young people. Because of the shrieking and the stamping his songs are lost to all of us sitting on the upper seats, perhaps to all the others also. A couple in leather jackets seize the occasion to slump down on their seats in a passionate embrace.

Ray is just the visible excuse for the noise. He could just as well be replaced by a marionette, or a jumping-jack—he is constantly jumping—who is presenting a program with a purely incidental relationship to music. They say that his admirers shriek. But he himself shrieks.

At the conclusion of his numbers he is transformed into a normal being. He stands on the stage, quiet and reserved. He has been instrumental in releasing impulses and relieving boredom. This represents the total of his well-paid contribution. Hundreds of amateur photographers are pressing around the platform; others storm forward but are stopped by the police.

Only my immediate neighbors to the right seem capable of restraining themselves.

Panic breaks loose when Ray's performance is over. The crowd storms up to the stage and tries to pursue him, but he wisely withdraws. A number of police officers rush up and try to clear the pit where the orchestra is helplessly imprisoned.

Someone begins to toss chairs, and others join in the fun, and the policemen begin to wield their sticks. The young men not only fight with the police: they fight with each other. This does not do much good, because the officers drag off the worst of the offenders. The uproar ends as quickly as it started, and the crowd of 5,000 moves respectfully toward the exits. A few groups begin fights outside of the Sports Palace, but they end quickly.

This picture of the 5,000 is not particularly Berlinish, perhaps not even particularly German, but authorities in Berlin assure me—with touching unanimity—that the restlessness which one finds in Berlin is the same on both sides of the boundary. Rowdies and trouble-makers do not discriminate between East and West.

But I do not delude myself that the shrieks of the 5,000 in the Sports Palace are lacking in Berlin characteristics. There is something about the atmosphere of this island that distinguishes it from other German cities, and leaves its mark also on the rebellious young people. In the East they are weary of the

pressures, weary of the necessity of being concerned with politics. And in the West they are weary of roads that terminate in
roadblocks or check-points and which lead nowhere.

Why should one have a special feeling for Berlin? It is a
place to which one has come and where one is forced to continue living. But there seems to be no emotional mechanism
that can call forth love at the mere mention of the word Berlin.

51   The Story of Lipsi

East Berlin authorities have made serious efforts to provide for
the leisure time of young people. Swimming pools, pioneer
houses, and club headquarters have been built. Various sports
have been heavily propagandized, and efforts have been made
to develop world champions. In cycling, track, swimming, and
winter sports, at least, they have had considerable success.
Young people represent the hope of the East German state,
since hope has been abandoned that the whole of the older generation will manage to evolve "socialist consciousness."

But if you ask the young people of East Berlin if they are
going out dancing they will say: "No, we don't go there. They
only play 60-40."

60-40 is not a parlor game. It is an order; that is, that dance
orchestras in pubs and other places must play at least 60 per
cent Eastern music and not more than 40 per cent Western. The

usual explanation for this rule in East Berlin is that the state has in the past been forced to pay out millions of marks in royalties to hit composers in the West. This has been too expensive. Furthermore, it is maintained that Western music is escapist (which it is, frequently) and decadent. Some orchestras have managed to find a loophole in the rules: they play Western music on Saturdays and Sundays and then revert to Eastern music for the normally empty halls during the rest of the week.

In the East German musical film, *Meine Frau macht Musik,* which was tremendously popular in the whole republic, there is a hit song which runs as follows: "Kiss me, kiss me Angelina / kiss me, kiss me evermore / kiss me, kiss me oh Bambina / no one kisses just like you!" Apparently in responsible circles this was not considered to be exactly what one might expect in a socialist country, and writers were enjoined to concern themselves with this cultural matter. This injunction brought no improvement. On the other hand, a ray of light appeared when a Leipzig dance teacher, René Dubianski, came out with "Lipsi" (after Lipsia, which is Leipzig's old name), a dance tune in 6/4 time. East German newspapers, from *Neues Deutschland* to the smallest provincial organ, were mobilized behind a campaign for Lipsi.

In March, 1959, the weekly magazine, *Sonntag,* a semi-official organ of the East German Ministry of Culture, advertised a competition for dance and entertainment music. I was present at the evening discussion at the Club der Kulturschaffenden on Otto-Nuschke-Strasse, where the contest was first announced. The chairman for the evening was Professor Gerhard Eisler, brother of the composer, Hanns Eisler, and brother of the ex-Communist, Ruth Fischer. There were some two hundred people and a dance orchestra present in the light and imposing salon. Various dances were presented, and it was said that while

Demonstration of the Lipsi in Haus der Kulturschaffenden

Willy Kressmann, Mayor of the Kreuzberg District

Western music formed 99 per cent of the dance repertoires as late as 1952, this had sunk to 35 per cent by 1958.

"It isn't a matter of what one plays or dances," says one of the older discussants, "but rather how one does it. In Moscow they dance politely and decently, but in Berlin (in both East and West) they dance in a decadent and erotic embrace."

"Love, just love, that's the theme of all hits," said someone else unhappily. But then Professor Eisler protested, gave a rapturous description of his experiences with Negro music in the United States, and added that most people get involved at least somewhat with love. And this can't be helped.

There was also a complaint that popular composers and lyricists make altogether too much money, but this was met by the argument that one cannot pay too much for a good hit tune.

"The object of commercial music in the West," it was said, "is to convert humans into animals. Ours is to sublimate this tendency and achieve a pure and natural joy in life."

From a composer: "Most of the hit tunes, whether from the East or the West, are sadly deficient in musical ideas."

Finally, Lipsi was demonstrated by some selected dancing partners. "It seems to need a terrible amount of floor space," said a man in the crowd. "And our dance restaurants have very small dance floors."

The most important part of the program was the announcement of a competition for lyrics. A few months later the magazine Sonntag had received 6,297 entries, and twenty-one lyricists were given prizes amounting to a total of 9,750 Eastmarks. The texts were then submitted to composers of popular tunes in a new competition, and in the autumn of 1959 the new socialist hit tunes were introduced with considerable fanfare.

One of the prize winners, Dieter Lietz, has written a number entitled "Lipsi," which is obviously designed to be sung to that dance tune. In this song he has skillfully taken cognizance of the popularity of American jazz among East German young people and merged it with some rather crude propaganda on behalf of the East German state: *

> Mr. Brown aus USA
> war bei uns zur Messe da.
> "Alles, was ich seh',"
> sprach er, "ist okay,
> doch was mich am meisten packt,
> das ist dieser Lipsi-Takt'."
> Als er dann zu Hause war,
> rief seine ganze Kinderschar:
> "Hast du uns was mitgebracht?"
> Da hat er nur gelacht:
>
> *Refrain:*
> "Daddy bringt was feines mit,
> Daddy bringt den Lipsischritt,
> Lipsi ist der neuste Tanz,
> Daddy zeigt's euch, Daddy kann's."
> Kinder riefen: "Einfach toll!
> Dieser Tanz ist wonderfull!"
> Und sie tanzten Lipsi
> Made in Germany.

The effort of the East German government to win popularity— almost at any price—is evident. But there is reluctant recognition that Western infiltration cannot be stopped. Reluctantly they have begun to manufacture hula-hoops, while trying to be on guard and protect what is regarded as national and socialist.

---

* Mr. Brown from the U. S. A. was here for the Fair. "Everything I see," he said, "is O. K. But what I like best is the Lipsi-beat!" When he got home he called together all his children. "Have you brought something with you for us?" He only laughed.

Refrain: "Daddy is bringing something fine with him. Daddy is bringing the Lipsi step. Lipsi is the new step. Daddy will show it. Daddy knows how to do it." The children cried: "Simply crazy! This dance is wonderful!" And they dance Lipsi, made in Germany.

One night in Melodie, an East Berlin pub in the Friedrich-stadtpalast, I happen to overhear a conversation between a middle-aged man, who is drinking champagne out of a tall glass, and a girl who has a sugared cocktail sitting in front of her.

"What is the name of the piece the orchestra is playing?" asks the man.

"I don't know. It is some American number. We students hardly learn to speak a single English word."

"But you know Russian?"

"What would we do with Russian?"

"In the future. . . ."

"Oh, the hell with the future."

"It's better to learn Russian now than later."

"What do you mean by *later*?"

"Little gal, let's talk about something else. Let's have a Western cigarette." He takes out a package of filter cigarettes which he has bought in West Berlin, offers one to the girl, to me (standing next to him), and to the bartender, who slips his quickly into a drawer and bows politely.

And we fall into conversation.

Carina has just bought herself a dress in West Berlin, and a bit earlier a pair of shoes. If there were no West Berlin the man would not be able to buy Western cigarettes and Carina would not get the dresses she wants. The necessity of making purchases in the West costs Carina four of her Eastmarks for one Westmark. This is a burden from which she suffers and draws pleasure. She has no intention of fleeing. She is studying cartography, likes East Berlin's dance halls and West Berlin's shops. But she doesn't like Russian, or Lipsi, and doesn't like to be pressured.

"It is possible that I shall find a husband in the West. After all, the majority of Germans are already there."

52   Three Young People

Heinz is twenty-four years of age and is studying rocket technology at the Technical University in West Berlin. He had a choice between Berlin and Braunschweig, the two German cities where the subject can be studied. Because he is so slender I suspect that he may, as a child, have been undernourished, and it is quite possible. He does not live too well even now. His great idol is Wernher von Braun; his great dream is to go to the States and continue his studies under the master. But it is likely that by the time he has completed his studies in Berlin the Germans will be making their own rockets and he will be needed at home.

He describes his daily life:

"I have a small scholarship which is enough to cover my rent and food, but no more. And during the school terms I don't have time to earn anything extra, although I do work between semesters. Once a week I go to a movie or to a dance with my friends. Once in a while we indulge ourselves and go to the Sunday afternoon dance at either the Palais am Funkturm or some other place. Usually we get acquainted with some models. . . ."

It is hard for me to imagine Heinz in the company of models. But maybe he has developed a worldly flair from his studies of rocket theory. He has not been in East Berlin for a year, and I have the impression that his day is pretty much filled with studying, listening, eating, going to and from the university, and preparing for the next examination.

Now he is sitting on a bar stool with his friends and is drinking beer and Dornkaat aus Kornsaat.

K. is a taxi driver. He drives a big Mercedes which is not his, earns a monthly salary of 450 marks, but supplements that by tips. He is slender, but when he talks about himself there is a determined expression on his face.

"No, I don't plan to get married until I have my own taxi. No thanks, I don't smoke, although I'll join my friends for a little drink once in a while. No, I don't want to move from Berlin because this is my home. I have never thought of leaving. Yes, I look at the future this way: I'll earn enough to buy my own taxi and become a private operator. I'll get my own apartment in a new building, perhaps I'll get married if I find a girl that I like. No, I wouldn't want a lot of children—maybe two, at most three. But it gets to be too expensive."

He is not unhappy in Berlin, nor is he particularly happy. On Sundays during the summer he drives out to Wannsee, just like a million other West Berliners. He has no particular thoughts about Berlin, about East or West, and it is immaterial to him whether Germany remains divided or not.

The present is his Bible and his security. His only dream about the future is to become a private operator. He is incapable of thinking beyond that.

Undoubtedly one would think that K. lives a life which is too ascetic and impoverished. If he seems to lack imagination it is not his fault, but the world's. He does not wish to live differently from the way he is now doing. He seems so sober, so composed, in everything that I cannot imagine him as any kind of agitator.

His sobriety borders upon submission and opportunism, but it is not really that. He belongs to a new German generation, although perhaps more smoothed and laundered, neither bourgeois nor proletarian, just a citizen. He seems to pose less of a problem than his contemporaries in East Berlin, where the government forces people to get involved in politics.

Politics is something that K. does not understand. Man is a political animal, it is said. This must be a monumental lie. If he is asked anything that is not involved with his own future, with his car and apartment, K. refuses to answer. There are newspapers that concern themselves with such matters. Why bother about opinions so long as we have food and shelter?

Brigitte, too, is sober, serious and purposeful. She is twenty-three years of age and still not married. Her face is rather square and stony, but she moves with the assurance of a model. She has a one-room apartment on Hohenzollerndamm, makes the meals for her landlady, but works in a hotel. She has an attractive, deep voice.

"I started to study voice at the Hochschule für Musik, but, like many of my friends, I had to support myself. I worked for a company that sold flowers to pubs. I rode in my boss's Volkswagen, dressed in my best outfit, hopped out when the car stopped, went in to the pubs, and showed off. I got 10 per cent of everything I took in, and the income wasn't bad. Frequently we didn't finish until 6 o'clock in the morning. It wasn't easy then to get to school by 9 o'clock and act as though one had slept well."

We are sitting in the little night bar, Atlantic, on Kurfürstendamm. A two-man band is playing softly, some prostitutes are conversing just as quietly at a table. They haven't much to be happy about. The place is almost empty. We are perched on the bar stools.

A family is sitting just behind us, father, mother, and daughter. They seem somewhat out of place in this environment, but are bravely downing their Moselle wine.

To the right of me there is a tall, blond man who knows only a few words of German. He is garrulous, and sits and drinks alternately beer and Coca Cola.

"Look at these Germans," he says to me and looks at the family. "They seem satisfied and happy. You know, they've gone through a lot. They are energetic. There's nothing wrong with them. And what fighters! My pals tell me that there aren't any better in the world."

"Yes," I answer in English, "fighters."

"The bravest in the world. It's hard for them to accept defeat, but it wasn't for lack of bravery, you know."

"No, that's certain."

"The Germans are among the bravest and best people in the world." He takes a hearty slug, and continues: "Unfortunately I don't speak German. Do you speak English?" he says as he turns to Brigitte.

She speaks English.

"You are popular in Berlin," I say. "Very popular, and right-fully so."

"That's nothing to discuss," he says, and nearly blushes. "Look at these Germans," he repeats. "I like the Atlantic because you can order beer without having to buy wine or whiskey. It's a fine place."

Then I listen to Brigitte. She has sold flowers at the Atlantic many times.

"But finally I gave it up. I quit selling flowers because I couldn't study during the daytime. And I quit studying voice because I didn't want to be just an average singer. I have a good voice, but I knew that perhaps five people in the whole world become really good, really famous. And in order to do that you have to sacrifice both family and children. I didn't want to do that, so I took a job at a hotel."

"But you didn't have a family when you quit. Couldn't you have waited?"

"I don't know. Now I've got Karl."

"Who's he?"

"He's my man, almost. But we have never met. Karl lives in Canada. He advertised for a pen pal and I answered.

"So I am practically married," says Brigitte seriously as we walk along Bundesallee.

"But you can't be married if you haven't seen him?"

"You see, I like his appearance in the pictures which he has sent, and he likes me. If we still like each other when we meet, we will just get married. Karl wants to move to Berlin and get a job here as a baker. He is flying in tomorrow."

A few days later Brigitte informs me that Karl fulfilled her expectations. He is just as charming as in the pictures. He has rented a car in Berlin. When Brigitte gets off work they drive around the town. Karl has not been in Berlin before.

It will be almost a year before he can move over and marry her. But Brigitte is satisfied. She has a future, and she need never, never work at the hotel again. Karl has promised her that.

53   *Justice*

It is depressing and dark in the court, as it is always in the presence of the law and the bar of justice. Outside, the birds are singing.

This is in East Berlin.

The three who are being tried are minors. I am the only outsider in the courtroom. The others present are: the mothers of the accused, the general prosecutor, the judge, assistants to the judge, secretaries, experts, and witnesses.

The three boys who are sitting on the bench got hold of a girl on New Year's night, held her, kissed her, and squeezed her breasts. She resisted, but couldn't get away before some older persons came along. The three boys did not try to run, but walked around until they were apprehended by the police. They have all been sentenced by a court before. One of them stole a bicycle at one time. One of the others, the oldest, is not considered to be entirely responsible. He worked in the fire department but was dismissed because of drunkenness. He is wearing tight-fitting black velvet trousers. The third boy has been involved in fights.

The boys seem unconcerned about the outcome. They seem bored with the whole proceedings and want to hear their sentences.

The girl whom the boys assaulted is a twenty-year old employee in a bookbinding firm, round and short and self-confident. I have the feeling that it wouldn't be too hard to seduce her without violence.

"No, I didn't notice that they smelled of liquor. He—that one over there—squeezed the hardest."

The next witness is the real villain. He is a boy with slick hair and an amazingly cocksure attitude. He has on an elegantly-tailored jacket, and stands like a model in front of the judge. He is dressed as though going to a party.

He had met the three boys outside a movie house in Adlershof. Someone had suggested that they buy some liquor, since it was New Year's night. They pooled their resources, went to the nearest HO-restaurant, and bought three small bottles of brandy.

"Who bought the bottles, showed his *Ausweis,* and paid the money?"

"I bought the bottles, but we all paid for them."

"You should have known that the defendants were not old enough to be allowed to drink."

"I had no way of knowing how old they were."

The elegant bearing is now not quite so elegant. He is beginning to slouch. They all went to his house (his mother was out). They soon emptied all the bottles, cleaned up the mess, and then went out again. But when the three others assaulted the girl this witness was some distance away.

"Why?"

"I stood there. Is that a crime?"

When the testimony is over the judge, a gray-haired woman in her forties, delivers a warning speech. Two of the mothers hold their hands in front of their faces, the third one weeps openly. Their sons are better clothed than they are themselves.

"You have not improved your habits despite the fact that you have been punished before. Why don't you utilize all the free facilities for sports and recreation that are available to all citizens instead of hanging around on the streets? At least in our part of Germany we must try to guarantee the security of the individual. There are parks in West Berlin where girls do not dare go alone at night. . . . You have got to take responsibility—for our republic and for your own lives. . . ."

All of this takes place on Littenstrasse, East Berlin, in the Justice Building. It is a large building with many hallways. There is a book shop in the vestibule. A watchman sits by the entrance.

Things look just about the same on Turmstrasse, Moabit, West Berlin's Criminal Court. But in the vestibule there is no book shop, only strolling police constables and cigarette-smoking witnesses.

What, then, is the difference?

"We turn over criminals who are being sought by the East police only if we know that their punishment there will not be

greater than under our own laws. Persons who are guilty of
political crimes according to East German laws we do not turn
over."

The above is what I have learned in West Berlin. It is said,
further, that special agreements have been made with law authorities in the East respecting certain criminals. And the other
party has hitherto always held to its agreements. Furthermore,
no refugee from the East can assume that he will evade his
punishment if, for example, he has embezzled money on the
other side. But in such cases he is permitted to sweat out his
punishment in the West.

"Our cooperation with the police authorities of West Berlin is
better now than it was earlier. We are connected by teletype
and we maintain a joint search, each in his own territory.
Fathers of illegitimate children leave the girl in one sector and
flee to the other. We turn them over. The partition of the city
has created special problems, but we are trying to resolve
them."

The above is what I have learned in East Berlin.

These civil servants, in the midst of their dusty files, do not
want to put hindrances in the way of cooperation. But there are
stronger forces at work, and they are more concerned about
political prestige than about the solution of concrete problems.
Some of them have a hard time understanding that a minimum
of cooperation is necessary, even though the other side is represented by "villains and criminals."

There are enough difficulties the way things are. The East
side holds the view, like Soviet law, that the theft of private
property is a lesser offense than the theft of public property.
The difference in sentences is extreme.

A young, red-haired man with a briefcase is standing outside
of the courtroom in Moabit. He is a psychologist and legal ad-
visor in cases involving young people.

"All of these cases are so much alike that one grows tired of them. The same offenses: borrowing of cars, small thefts, fights, sexual offenses. The same causes: bad home environments, crowded living quarters, parents away from home, the father dead, etc."

"There is nothing that is peculiar to Berlin?"

"Only that they run to the other side and are arrested there."

We go in. There is a recess and the judge is standing before a class of school children who are lined up in the spectators' seats. He is speaking about the functions of German law.

The two defendants have served sentences for offenses similar to those of the three youths in East Berlin. Only they had been more thorough and more violent. This time they were in because they had been responsible for a fire at the place where they worked.

The two young men are dressed like those in the East, except that they are older and more self-confident.

The symbol of justice is hanging outside the room, encircled by serpents. Or is it serpent-like paragraphs?

The window is open. Here, too, the birds are singing.

I take a taxi from Turmstrasse.

"It's nice weather today," says the driver.

"I don't feel well," I reply.

"I can sympathize with you, there are a lot of things wrong here in West Berlin."

"What do you mean?"

"I don't like the atmosphere of this cold war."

"I don't either. But that isn't what makes me feel ill."

The driver remarks that he is happy because he is soon going on a vacation. He has two cars, a Mercedes 220 which he uses for business, and an Isabella, which is his private car.

"It's a great car. Next week I'm driving to Italy."

This is something that his colleagues in East Berlin can't do.

In the afternoon I walk along the streets of Moabit, which are suddenly filled by a mass of workers from the factories. The huge buildings empty themselves of thousands of persons who hurry to catch a bus or some other conveyance. Some have their own cars, others have motorcycles.

A half hour later everything is deserted, the great spaces of the factories are abandoned by people—here, just as in Siemens-stadt, in Westhafen, and in the whole of industrial West Berlin, its economic heart, its unwashed, barren face.

And so night comes over Berlin. Box of pills in hand, I wander into a small, warm pub. All of the guests seem to be playing skat. Somebody curses his luck. Somebody curses his poverty. Some-one is eating Bratwurst.

It is perhaps the fault (or merit) of the bad light that I no longer know whether I am in the West or the East, that I have forgotten which kind of justice prevails in the West and which in the East. It is probably because of my bloodshot eyes that it seems to me that the Bierstube in which I am sitting could well be in almost any part of the city.

54   Departure

The train gathered speed, the streets and buildings in the western part of the city slipped past—those solid, ugly streets, those massive, ugly buildings in the Victorian German style, which yet, with all the pleasant green of the streets, the window boxes bright with red geraniums, the air of order, of substance, and of comfort, had always seemed as familiar and as pleasant to George as the quiet streets and the houses of a little town. Already they were sweeping through Charlottenburg. They passed the station without halting, and on the platform George saw, with the old and poignant feeling of regret and loss, the people waiting for the Stadtbahn trains. Upon its elevated track the great train swept on smoothly toward the west, gathering momentum steadily. They passed the Funkturm. Almost before he knew it they were rushing through the outskirts of the city towards the open country. They passed an aviation field. He saw the hangars and a flock of shining planes. And as he looked, a great silver-bodied plane moved out, sped along the runway, lifted its tail, broke slowly from the earth, and vanished.

And now the city was left behind. Those familiar faces, forms, and voices of just six minutes past now seemed as remote as dreams, imprisoned there as in another world—a world of massive brick and stone and pavements, a world hived of four million lives, of hope and fear and hatred, of anguish and despair, of love, of cruelty and devotion, that was called Berlin.

Once when I arrived in Berlin it was cold, with a hint of frost in the air, sudden snowfalls that covered the streets and the roofs with a mantle of white, but soon turned into brown, dirty water and slowly ran down into the sewers. The people were dressed in the past winter's furs and coats. They stared bitterly at the sky, and then bent again into the freezing wind.

This is northern Europe's inhospitable cold, I thought then, and wished that I were in a beach café on the Riviera. Passively I followed the stream of people, gray faces, women in tight shawls, who were going home with their begging boxes, leading a child by the hand.

But now I feel, as I go along the bank of the Spree, a warmer current of air, the cry of birds on the wing, a clear sky, and warmth underfoot. Some bulbs are sprouting through the grass. From a distance they look like weeds, or loose candy wrappers. The hedges, which have been dark, like bundles of sticks, are beginning to turn green and living.

There is a premonition of full summer, but there is no breaking up of ice, since there is no ice or snow. There is a premonition of growth and of leafy parks, the fragrance of blossoming lindens and bird-cherries in Berlin's heat.

I have an urge just to live and to breathe, not to act, not to participate. This is a false hope, an illusion of "life which is free as the birds'." But to dream a while is a pleasant escape, if one longs for the good life, sensory pleasures, and rest, while another part of one's self wishes to act and to participate.

I came to find out the answer to a question which Berlin poses, but I have forgotten what the question was about, or what the answer should have been. I walk along the edge of the stream and kick pebbles into the water. An old man is sitting there, dangling his legs over the water. His fishing rod is motionless, and gives no sign of a bite. The smoke from his cigar rises nearly straight up in even spirals, which eventually disappear into the blue heavens.

A little further away some houseboats are lying at anchor. One of them has a TV antenna on the roof, and flowers in the windows. No barges are approaching, nothing is happening. I listen to the distant noises of the S-Bahn trains and the automobiles somewhere in the Tiergarten. Above me is the same sky that covers all mankind, around me are the millions of the big city, whose ceaseless movement sweeps toward me in a challenge to act.

Author's Note on Sources

A book on Berlin? Really! There are 5,000 books on Berlin. I have often heard that comment and I need only add that there are undoubtedly ten times that number of books on Berlin. And a book about Berlin can hardly avoid speaking of Germany, and indirectly of Europe.

This edition of *Report from Berlin* is a thoroughly revised version of the original Swedish edition and the Finnish translation (both published in 1958). I have tried not only to take note of the political events of 1959 but also, on the basis of three visits to Berlin during 1959, to check the factual data in my account. However, I do not claim to have written a work of scholarship. It is a description of a city as seen in the mind's eye of one observer.

I should like to comment on some of my sources:

Page xvii. Quotations are from Georg Brandes: *Berlin som tysk rigshovedstad* (P.G. Philipsens Forlag, Copenhagen, 1885); Heinrich Mann: *Essays,* Volume II (Aufbau Verlag, Berlin, 1956); Katherine Anne Porter: *The Leaning Tower* (Harcourt, Brace and Company, New York, 1934).

Page 4 and later. The Swedish author is Vilhelm Ekelund: *Tyska intryck* (Albert Bonniers Förlag, Stockholm, 1913).

Page 4. Quotation is from Friedrich Stampfer, March 15, 1957, cited in Willy Brandt: *Von Bonn nach Berlin* ("Eine Dokumentation zur Hauptstadtfrage," Berlin, 1957), from which I have also taken certain points of view in a later discussion of Berlin as a capital.

Page 14. The impact of "Lili Marlene" on the Western Allies during World War II is described in John Steinbeck: *Once There Was a War* (Viking Press, New York, 1958).

Page 17. Quotation is from George Grosz: *A Little Yes and a Big No: The Autobiography of George Grosz* (Dial Press, New York, 1946).

Page 18. Quotation is from the East German commemorative publication, *Heinrich Zille zu seinem hundertsten Geburtstag* (Henschel-Verlag, Berlin, 1958). The literature on Zille is enormous. I will mention Otto Nagel's biography (Henschel-Verlag, Berlin, 1955), several books published by Hans Ostwald, and an immense number of new reprints of his drawings. A classical German silent film, *Mutter Krausens Fahrt ins Glück,* is based upon a Zille motif.

Page 25. Quotation is from Christopher Isherwood: *Good-Bye to Berlin* (Random House, New York, 1939). This book, as well as *The Last of*

Mr. Norris (William Morrow and Company, New York, 1935), is still unsurpassed of its kind, but can be compared to what Richard Crossman and Stephen Spender have written on the same theme.

Page 30. Quotation is from George Grosz: *A Little Yes and a Big No*, cited above.

Page 54. Quotation is from Margaret Boveri: *Der Verrat im xx. Jahrhundert* (3 volumes, Rowohlt-Verlag, Hamburg, 1956-   ).

Page 77. Galbrecht appears in a novel, *The Man with One Arm*, in Irwin Shaw: *Mixed Company* (Random House, New York, 1950).

Page 80. Gerhard Reitlinger: *The Final Solution* (London, 1953). On the opposition movement against Hitler, which included Jews to the extent possible, see the documentary collection of Günther Weisenborn: *Der lautlose Aufstand* (Rowohlt-Verlag, Hamburg, 1954, second edition) and Annedore Leber: *Das Gewissen steht auf* and *Das Gewissen entscheidet* (Mosaik Verlag, Berlin/Frankfurt, 1956-1958). Emanuel Litvinoff, in *The Lost Europeans* (New York, 1958), discusses the problems of Jews in Berlin very penetratingly.

Page 82. Quotation is from Christopher Isherwood: *Good-Bye to Berlin*, cited above.

Page 94. Some of the cabaret references mentioned here can be found in Ulrich, Herbst, and Thierry: *Die Stachelschweine* (Blanvalet, Berlin, 1956).

Page 98. This and the following quotation (page 99) are from Georg Kotowski: *Der Kampf um Berlins Universität* (Berlin, 1954).

Page 100. Quotation is from Dieter Meichsner: *Die Studenten von Berlin* (Berlin, 1954).

Page 115 and following. The quotations from Brecht's play are taken from Bertolt Brecht: *Stücke I-XII* (Suhrkamp Verlag, Berlin/Frankfurt, 1953-   ). The foremost Anglo-Saxon treatments of Brecht are John Willett: *The Theatre of Bertolt Brecht* (Methuen & Company, London, 1959), and Martin Esslin: *Brecht—A Choice of Evils* (Eyre & Spottiswoode, London, 1959). Of the more recent German works, that of Volker Klotz: *Bertolt Brecht—Versuch über das Werk* (Gentner-Verlag, Darmstadt, 1958) is interesting, and that of Willy Haas: *Bert Brecht* (Rembrandt-Verlag, Berlin, 1959) very bad. The East German cultural magazine, *Sinn und Form*, has published two valuable pamphlets, *Sonderheft Bertolt Brecht*.

Page 116. Mathes' speech, except for the last part, has been printed in *Neues Deutschland*.

Page 118. Quotation is from Arthur Koestler: *The Sleepwalkers* (Hutchinson, London, 1959).

Page 121. Quotation is from Doris Lessing: *A Habit of Loving* (MacGibbon & Kee, London, 1957).

Page 128. The collected critical writings of Herbert Ihering have been coming out since 1958 under the title: *Von Reinhardt bis Brecht, Vier Jahrzehnte Theater und Film* (Volume I: 1909-1923), published by Aufbau-Verlag in East Berlin. Kerr's *Die Welt im Drama* is available as an abstract (Kiepenheuer & Witsch, Cologne-Berlin, 1954).

Page 131. Quotation is from Volker Klotz: *Bertolt Brecht—Versuch über das Werk,* cited above.

Page 135. Anna Seghers' books are published by Aufbau-Verlag. Her best known novel, *The Seventh Cross,* was filmed in Hollywood during the war by Fred Zinnemann.

Page 138. Victor Klemperer: *LTI, Notizbuch eines Philologen* (Max Niemayer Verlag, Halle/Saale, 3rd edition, 1957). See also Sternberger, Storz, Süskind: *Aus dem Wörterbuch des Unmenschen* (Claasen Verlag, Hamburg, 1957).

Page 142 and later. Facts about Kleist and the quotation are from Curt Honoff: *Heinrich von Kleist in Selbstzeugnissen und Bilddokumenten* (Rowohlt, Hamburg, 1958). His newspaper is now in a different edition: *Berliner Abendblätter, herausgegeben von Heinrich von Kleist* (offprint by the J.G. Cotta'schen Buchhandlung, Stuttgart, 1958). The prematurely ripened literary geniuses of the early nineteenth century all ended their lives tragically, except for Kleist, Büchner, and Lenz.

Page 146. Data on the Ullstein empire can be found in Herman Ullstein: *The Rise and Fall of the House of Ullstein* (Simon and Schuster, New York, 1943).

Page 153. Quotations are from Arthur Koestler: *Arrow in the Blue* (Collins with Hamish Hamilton, Ltd., London, 1952).

Page 160. Sanssouci is treated in Willy Kurth: *Sanssouci* (Henschel-Verlag, Berlin, 1956). On the Potsdam decisions see Richard Thilenius' excellent guide, *Die Teilung Deutschlands* (Rowohlt, Hamburg, 1957), and for general European perspective, Wenzel Jaksch: *Europas Weg nach Potsdam* (Deutsch-Verlags-Anstalt, Stuttgart, 1958). In this connection I want to mention Golo Mann's big work, *Deutsche Geschichte des 19. und 20. Jahrhunderts* (S. Fischer Verlag, Frankfurt, 1958); his efforts to synthesize have been very helpful to me.

Page 168. Quotation is from Richard Thilenius: *Die Teilung Deutschlands,* cited above.

Page 170. *Ibid.*

Page 171. Quotation is from Rainer Maria Rilke: *The Notebook of Malte Laurids Brigge,* translated by John Linton (Hogarth Press, London, 1930).

Page 172. Quotation is from Willy Haas: *Die Literarische Welt* (Paul List Verlag, Munich, 1957).

Page 174. The Swedish writer mentioned is Bertil Malmberg: *Tyska intryck* (Albert Bonniers Förlag, Stockholm, 1936).

Page 175. One of the most outstanding postwar German intellectuals on the East side was Professor Alfred Kantorowicz, who subsequently defected, and who deals with this period in *Deutsches Tagenbuch* (Kindler Verlag, Munich, 1959).

Page 177 and later. Reuter's quotation from Willy Brandt and Richard Lowenthal: *Ernst Reuter—Ein Leben für die Freiheit* (Kindler Verlag, Munich, 1957).

Page 178. Quotation is from Margaret Boveri: *Der Verrat im xx. Jahrhundert*, cited above.

Page 181. Quotation is from Lucius Clay: *Decision in Germany* (Doubleday, Garden City, 1950). The blockade is the subject of W. Philipps Davidson: *The Berlin Blockade* (Princeton, 1958).

Page 186. Quotation is from Richard Thilenius: *Die Teilung Deutschlands*, cited above.

Page 191. Quotation is from Wolfgang Leonhard: *Die Revolution entlässt ihre Kinder* (Kiepenheuer and Witsch, Cologne/Berlin, 1955).

Page 193. The statistical yearbook has come out since 1956.

Page 203. Quotation is from *The New Statesman and Nation*, May 6, 1957.

Page 204. Quotation is from Johannes R. Becher: *Auf andere Art so grosse Hoffnung* (Aufbau-Verlag, Berlin, 1955). Becher became in time a very bad poet, but while Minister of Culture he had a liberalizing influence, especially if he is compared to his successor, Alexander Abusch, who was a stern adherent of Stalinism.

Page 208. Quotation is from Willy Brandt: *My Road to Berlin*, as told by Leo Lania (Doubleday, Garden City, 1960). Willy Brandt published a number of books in Norway and later in Sweden; for example, *Förbrytare och andra tyskar* (Albert Bonniers Förlag, Stockholm, 1946).

Page 224. An addition of the percentages does not equal 100, since various small groups have been left out.

Page 228: Quotation is from Graham Greene: *Confidential Agent* (Viking Press, New York, 1952).

Page 277: Quotation is from Thomas Wolfe: *You Can't Go Home Again* (Harper & Brothers, New York, 1940).

Two newer, quite interesting, books about Berlin are John Mander: *Berlin: The Eagle and the Bear* (Barrie and Rockliff, London, 1959) and Walter Kiaulehn's more anecdotal *Berlin, Schicksal einer Weltstadt* (Beck, Munich, 1958). And with that I get over to cultural history, which is endless, since no German author of significance has neglected to write something about the city. This is evident in Mario Krammer's cultural history, *Berlin im Wandel der Jahrhunderte* (Berlin, 1956). Newer Berlin anthologies are *Berlin*, edited by J. J. Hasslin (Munich, 1955); *Berliner Cocktail*, edited by Rolf Italiaander and Willy Haas (Hamburg/Vienna,

1957); and *Berlin—Lob und Kritik,* edited by Walther G. Oschilewski (Berlin, 1951). Cultural history is also prominent in the better East Berlin journals such as *Berliner Heimat* and *Der Bär von Berlin* (annual calendar put out by the Verein für die Geschichte Berlins). But I have also taken material from almanacs, statistical handbooks, picture books, maps, novels, poems, travel books, daily newspapers, etc. Also from the magazine *Spiegel.*

The chief Western publishers of Berliniana are Arani-Verlag and Blanvalet in Berlin; the chief Eastern ones are Henschel-Verlag (its specialty is art and art history) and Verlag Das Neue Berlin. It is not my intention to take up the great quantity of literature dealing with special questions, but I should like to record my gratitude to a number of journals of varying usefulness. Erich Kuby's hotly debated book on Germany, *Das ist des Deutschen Vaterland* (Stuttgart, 1957) has an interesting approach to the problem. Pliever's *Berlin* does not compare with Heinz Rein's *Finale Berlin* (Berlin, 1948), which was published in the East. The history of Berlin as a theater city is best described by Gerhard Wahnrau. The first volume is entitled *Berlin—Stadt der Theater,* and covers the years 1322-1889.